The Slow Cooker
COLLECTION

Transcontinental Books
1100 René-Lévesque Boulevard West
24th floor
Montreal, Que. H3B 4X9
Tel.: (514) 340-3587
Toll-free: 1-866-800-2500
www.canadianliving.com

Bibliothèque et Archives nationales du Québec and Library and Archives
Canada cataloguing in publication

Baird, Elizabeth, 1939-
The Canadian living slow cooker collection
Includes index.
ISBN 978-0-9809924-5-8
1. Electric cookery, Slow. I. Canadian Living Test Kitchen. II. Canadian Living.
III. Title.

TX827.B34 2009   641.5'884   C2009-941637-9
Project editor: Christina Anson Mine
Copy editor: Miriam Osborne
Indexer: Gillian Watts
Art direction and design: Michael Erb
Production coordinator: Erin Poetschke

Printed in Canada
© Transcontinental Books, 2009
Legal deposit – 3rd quarter 2009
National Library of Quebec
National Library of Canada
2nd print: October 2009
ISBN 978-0-9809924-5-8

We acknowledge the financial support of our publishing activity by the
Government of Canada through the BPDIP program of the Department of
Canadian Heritage, as well as by the Government of Quebec through the
SODEC program Aide à la promotion.

For information on special rates for corporate libraries and wholesale purchases,
please call 1-866-800-2500.

Canadian Living

The *Slow Cooker*

COLLECTION

By Elizabeth Baird and The Canadian Living Test Kitchen

Transcontinental Books

Have you ever noticed how

solutions bubble up to the surface when there are challenges? Take the time crunch most families face, for example.

Nowadays, parents are expected to be miracle workers. Get the family off to work and school, work a full day, catch up on chores, commute and support an amazing array of family activities, from buying birthday presents to putting in a garden to chauffeuring kids to guitar lessons to coaching hockey. (Phew!) And on top of this more-than-two-full-time-jobs schedule, you're expected to whip up meals because – and this is a very big because – sitting and eating together is the most important part of the day for the family.

One solution to this get-supper-on-the-table-now challenge: a simple ceramic pot nestled in a metal housing containing heating coils. Thank you, slow cooker. It's not a new appliance – my parents brought one home from Florida in the 1970s and my mother's baked beans were never better – but its genius was rediscovered a decade ago and it's enjoying a renaissance.

Slow cookers are incredibly handy. They come in large sizes for entertaining, small for empty nesters and mini for dishes such as dips. They braise food beautifully, turning out classic stews, pot roasts, chilis, curries and ribs. How convenient for Canadians, who appreciate a comforting dish in a climate that's chilly more often than we care to admit.

Slow cookers can do much more than just the expected soups and stews. They're also great for hot drinks, scalloped

potatoes, lasagna, side dishes, dressing, chocolate sauce and
yummy puddings and fruit desserts. They do everything from
the proverbial soup to nuts.

If a slow cooker were looking for a job, its resume would
tout the following qualifications:

> A boon for the budgeter; especially talented
  at tenderizing inexpensive, less tender cuts of meat
  and poultry
> Excellent with long-cooked vegetarian items, such as
  chickpeas, lentils and beans
> Works well with lighter, healthier dishes, whole grains
  and vegetables
> Flexible, with settings to suit your day (no oven or stove top
  timing to go wrong)
> Reliably puts dinner on the table without a lot of last-minute
  cooking – an advantage when entertaining family and friends
> Easy to clean, with only one pot to wash up after dinner
> Always well prepared, greeting you at the door with
  the welcoming aroma of a home-cooked meal

Given the talents of the slow cooker, all you need to succeed is
a collection of recipes that deliver taste, good value and
convenience. This collection contains all that and more.

Happy cooking with *Canadian Living* and your favourite
slow cooker,

Elizabeth Baird

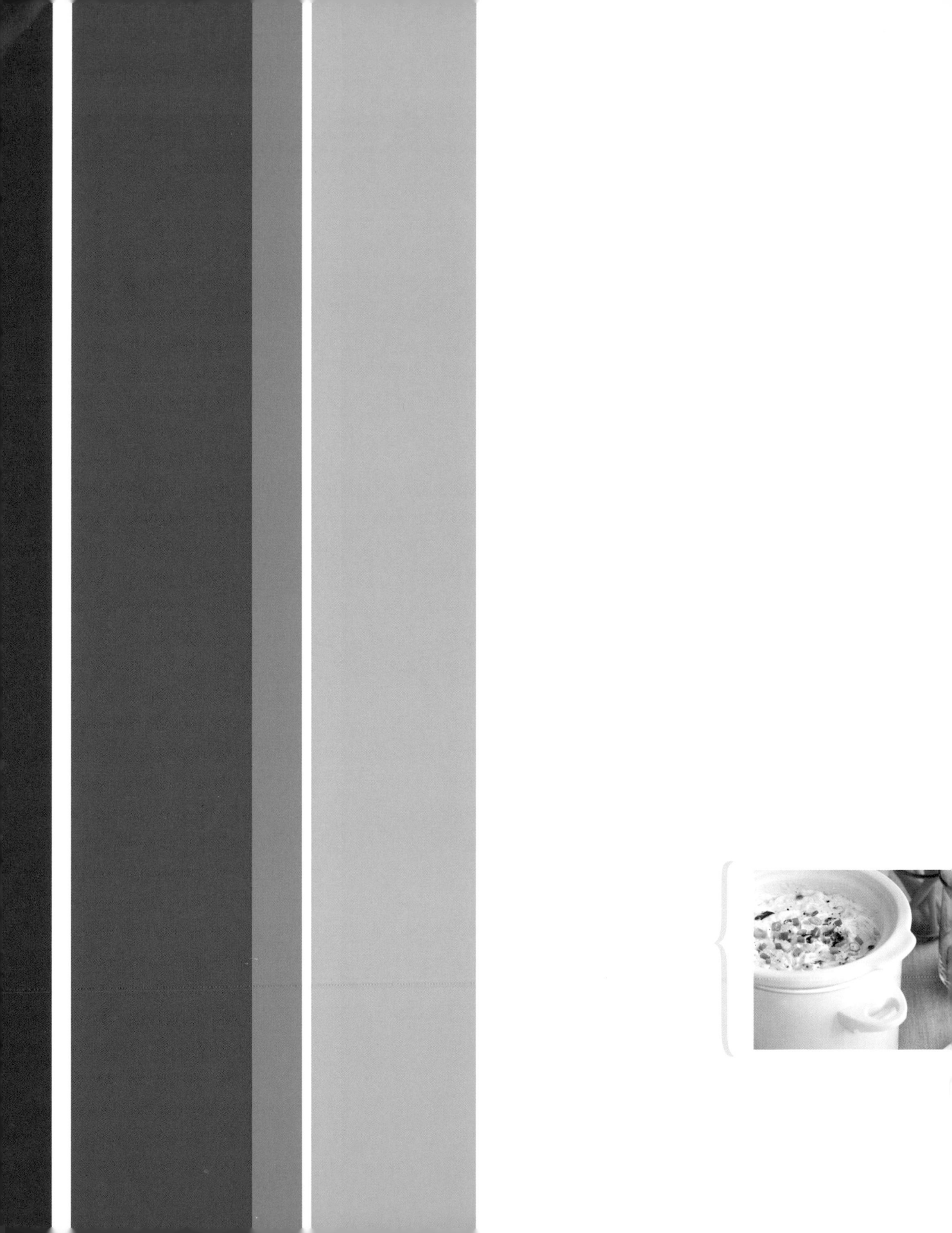

Slow Cooker

Know-How

Slow Cooker Advantages

Saving time, fuss and effort are our favourite reasons for using a slow cooker. But there are plenty of other pluses to firing up this convenient appliance.

> It can be a backup stove, handy when the burners and oven are already crowded.

> For potlucks, just slip the stoneware insert into an insulated carrier and surprise your hosts with warm Creamy Mushroom Meatballs (page 199) or Chicken & Sausage Gumbo (page 112).

> The slow cooker makes wonderful stocks and cooks dry legumes, such as beans, chickpeas and lentils, to perfection while you do other things.

> A slow cooker full of food is an excellent way to help out neighbours, family and friends when there's a new baby or in times of sickness or need.

> Always popular, larger slow cookers make about 8 servings, meaning a small household has amazing leftovers for meals later in the week – or month. They're also perfect for entertaining, especially at family gatherings.

The Best Cuts of
Meat & Poultry

The cuts that deliver top succulence in the slow cooker are less expensive, often from the tougher shoulder area. Slow cooking breaks down the collagen in the muscle's connective tissues, leaving the cooked meat moist and tender. No matter the cut, The Canadian Living Test Kitchen recommends trimming off excess and visible fat.

For specific slow cooker beef cuts, see page 146. For lamb, see page 106. For chicken, see page 118. For pork, see page 172.

Slow Cooking Times

In our recipes, you'll find a large range in cooking times, such as "cook for about 6 to 8 hours." Slow cookers vary a lot, from manufacturer to manufacturer and even slow cooker to slow cooker. Newer models are more efficient and cook more quickly than old ones.

Check for doneness halfway through and again at the shorter suggested time. You can overcook a dish in the slow cooker just as you can on the stove top or in the oven, so it pays to check early.

Browning:
The Secret to Superior Flavour

There's a myth that all you need to do is fill the slow cooker, turn the dial and leave it to work its magic. While this may do for some dishes, we find that there's more flavour when some of the ingredients are browned first.

Here's why: When savoury items, such as meat, poultry, onions, garlic, mushrooms or vegetables, hit hot dry heat, a meeting of protein and carbohydrate called the Maillard reaction takes place. This is the source of the tasty brown bits on the bottom of the browning skillet or Dutch oven.

When you deglaze the pan by adding liquid and scraping up those bits from the bottom, you capture that extra flavour. The bits dissolve into the cooking liquid or sauce, giving the dish a richer taste. Browning also renders out some of the fat in meat or poultry so you can drain it off.

Browning Tips

❯ Dredge meat or poultry in flour if you can. This adds flavour and helps the pieces brown quickly and intensely. Use leftover flour later on to thicken the cooking liquid into gravy.

❯ Brown cubes of meat or poultry for stews in batches – no more than 8 oz (250 g) at a time. Adding too many pieces at once causes them to steam, not brown. Make sure to add more oil if necessary and reheat the pan and oil between batches.

❯ Drain off the fat after browning meat or poultry. There is usually enough left in the pan to fry the onions, garlic, celery, herbs, etc. Later, you can reduce the dish's fat content further by skimming the sauce before thickening. A third window opens if you make the dish ahead and chill it. Fat rises, hardens and is easy to lift off and discard.

Low or High?

Most of the savoury recipes in this collection are cooked on low to suit your busy schedule and have dinner ready when you get home – not in the middle of the afternoon. High heat tends to make meat and poultry stringy, so low is a better choice anyway.

If you want to speed up a dish, start the slow cooker on high and switch to low after 1 hour or halfway through cooking. For some desserts, high is the only choice. This is always indicated in the recipe.

Shape: Oval and rectangular inserts allow more flexibility than round ones, especially with large cuts of meat. You don't want your beautifully browned pot roast to get stuck!

Insert: Some slow cooker inserts are suitable for browning, but a standard one paired with a good skillet or Dutch oven for browning allows for ultimate versatility.

Lid: Make sure it fits tightly. (A little jiggle is acceptable.) Clear glass lids make it easy to peek without letting heat escape. Just tap the surface to clear condensation and check how your food is coming along.

Handles: They should be easy to grip with oven mitts. The hot stoneware insert is already heavy, and when it holds a yummy stew, it gets even heavier.

Anatomy of a Slow Cooker

Capacity: Choose a size that suits your household and/or entertaining needs. Count on 4 to 8 servings from a 4½- to 6-quart (4.5 to 6 L) slow cooker. You'll have enough for family-size meals or meals with leftovers. We tested most of our recipes in this range of sizes. For desserts, appetizers, sauces and vegetables, smaller slow cookers are fine. Can't decide which size is best? Try a slow cooker with various-size inserts. If you love slow cooking, consider having two: a smaller one for family meals and a larger one for entertaining.

Programming: A lot of slow cookers now come with programmable and automatic timers. Most have a warm setting, either manual or automatic, which is a lifesaver for those days when you're delayed. Choose the features that meet your needs.

Take Care of Your Slow Cooker

❯ Avoid sudden changes in temperature when handling the insert. For serving, leave it in its metal housing, or remove and set on a trivet, protective mat or thick folded towel. Wait for the insert to cool down to room temperature before washing.

❯ Do not freeze or refrigerate food in the insert.

❯ Rather than scrape off residue or use an abrasive scrubber to remove cooked-on food, fill the insert with warm sudsy water and let soak. Use a nonabrasive brush or pad to clean the surface.

❯ Never put the metal housing in water or fill it with water. Wipe after each use to remove any spills.

Six *Essential Tips*

1. No peeking. Lifting the lid to peek or stir adds 15 to 20 minutes to the cooking time. Peeking is allowed when checking for doneness, turning a large ingredient or adding thickening at the end of cooking.

2. Watch the amount of liquids. When you assemble ingredients in a slow cooker, the liquid may not cover the solids, but it will increase during cooking as foods release their juices and steam, which has no way to escape, builds up. Leave at least 2 inches (5 cm) between the top of the food and the rim so the food can come to a simmer.

3. As a general rule, the slow cooker should be no less than half full and no more than two-thirds to three-quarters full.

4. Always defrost meat and poultry thoroughly before placing in slow cooker. Frozen vegetables can be added near the end of cooking and heated until piping hot.

5. When lifting the lid, avoid tipping it so the condensation on the underside spills into the food. And always keep your face away from the hot steam. Many new slow cookers come with a hinged lid that stays in place while you stir or serve.

6. To refrigerate or freeze a dish ahead, transfer the contents of the slow cooker to shallow container(s). Let cool, uncovered, for 30 minutes. Then let cool completely, still uncovered, in the refrigerator. Cover, and according to the recipe, either refrigerate or freeze. Let frozen food thaw in the refrigerator before reheating.

Canadian Living *Ingredients*

Unless indicated otherwise:
- Eggs are large, at room temperature if baking
- Pepper is freshly ground
- Salt is regular table salt
- Butter is salted
- Fruits and vegetables are medium-size; washed; peeled; and cored, seeded or hulled if appropriate
- Dried herbs are crumbled, not powdered
- Vegetable oil can be canola or other oil. Canola can replace olive oil if desired.
- Milk and yogurt are 2%
- Spices are ground or grated
- Lemon juice is freshly squeezed
- If a choice of ingredients is offered in a recipe, the first is preferred. The second is a reasonable alternative, but the taste may be slightly different

Food Safety Considerations

❯ Never brown meat the night before and refrigerate overnight. Browning just cooks the outside, and harmful bacteria grow very quickly on partially cooked meat and poultry. Prep you can do ahead: cutting and sautéing just vegetables and measuring out seasonings, sauces and liquids. You can trim and cut meat; just refrigerate it separately from all other ingredients.

❯ You can fully cook ground meat or poultry ahead. Brown it in a skillet, making sure it's crumbly and no longer pink, then refrigerate or freeze it. Frozen cooked ground meat is handy to keep on hand for multiple recipes.

❯ Never reheat in the slow cooker. The food won't reach a safe temperature quickly enough to eliminate harmful bacteria. Always reheat on the stove top, in the oven or in the microwave. If you really want to present a dish in the slow cooker, say on a buffet table, fill the insert with hot water to warm it (don't heat the insert empty), then drain and fill with food that's been safely reheated. Set the dial to warm.

How to Convert Your Favourite Recipes to the Slow Cooker

Everyone has a cherished family pot roast, stew, chili or curry recipe that's designed for the stove top. But wouldn't making it in the slow cooker be more convenient? Definitely. Here's how.

> The first step is still browning the meat or poultry. Then cook the onion, garlic and seasonings, such as spices, curry paste and tomato paste. A high-sided Dutch oven is ideal for pot roasts; a large skillet for stews. However, there is less spattering with a Dutch oven and you may just want to use this in any case.

> You may need to cut things smaller and/or rearrange the order they go into the slow cooker. Because root vegetables take longer to cook in a slow cooker, cut them into pieces no larger that 1 inch (2.5 cm). Add them first, underneath meat or poultry. Garlic can burn if placed on the bottom of the insert; mix it with other ingredients or place on top.

> Choose the low setting for most recipes. High heat tends to toughen meat and poultry, making them stringy. As a rule, beef, lamb and pork dishes cook for 6 to 8 hours; chicken and vegetarian dishes, for 4 to 6 hours. Since slow cookers vary greatly, start checking for doneness halfway through and at the shorter suggested time.

> Adjust the liquid. Unlike cooking on the stove or in the oven, there's no place for liquid to evaporate in a slow cooker. You'll need to reduce the liquid by about 50 per cent for most recipes. If you find you still have too much liquid at the end of cooking, skim off fat and strain the liquid into a large shallow saucepan. Boil hard until it reaches the desired consistency and flavour. If you have too little liquid, on the other hand, heat water, broth or another liquid compatible with the recipe and stir into sauce.

> If you're not using thickening agents, such as flour and cornstarch, to dredge the meat or poultry, mix them with liquid (usually cold water) and whisk into the gravy or sauce near the end of cooking.

> Long cooking fades the flavour of herbs and spices, especially fresh herbs. One solution: add an extra sprinkle just as the dish finishes cooking to spark up the flavour.

> Sweet green peppers can turn bitter with long cooking, so add them near the end of cooking.

> To prevent dairy products from separating, always add them near the end of cooking. Try creamy, lower-fat evaporated milk instead of cream or milk. It boosts calcium and is a healthful, delicious substitute.

Read Before You Start

No matter the appliance, no matter the dish, always read the recipe all the way through. Prep and measure out ingredients before you start cooking – you're less likely to forget one or mix up a measurement. And, of course, don't forget hand washing. Suds for as long as it takes you to sing "Happy Birthday."

Food Storage: The Right Temperature

To do its job properly, a refrigerator should be between 32 and 41°F (0 and 5°C) and a freezer should be below 0°F (–18°C).

Appetizers, Snacks & Drinks

1½-quart (1.5 L) slow cooker

Makes 3 cups (750 mL)

Sun-Dried Tomato & Artichoke Dip

This is a perennial party pleaser, one that's easy to make with pantry staples. Serve with a variety of crackers, pita chips and vegetables.

1	can (14 oz/398 mL) artichoke hearts	1
1	pkg (8 oz/250 g) cream cheese, cubed and softened	1
½ cup	each sour cream and mayonnaise	125 mL
¼ cup	grated Parmesan cheese	50 mL
¼ cup	chopped drained oil-packed sun-dried tomatoes	50 mL
1	clove garlic, minced	1
¼ tsp	pepper	1 mL
2 tbsp	chopped green onion	30 mL

❧ Drain artichoke hearts; pat dry and chop. Add to slow cooker along with cream cheese, sour cream, mayonnaise, Parmesan cheese, sun-dried tomatoes, garlic and pepper; stir to combine.

❧ Cover and cook on low, stirring twice, until blended and hot, about 2 hours. Sprinkle with green onion.

PER 2 TBSP (30 mL): about 89 cal, 2 g pro, 8 g total fat (4 g sat. fat), 2 g carb, 1 g fibre, 16 mg chol, 88 mg sodium. % RDI: 3% calcium, 2% iron, 5% vit A, 3% vit C, 4% folate.

Curried Nuts & Bolts

Who would have thought that you could make nuts and bolts (also known as party mix) in a slow cooker? You can, very well indeed – and you can easily vary the cereal and nuts according to what's on hand.

1½- to 2-quart (1.5 to 2 L)
slow cooker

Makes 9 cups
(2.25 L)

2 cups	small pretzels	500 mL	1 cup	unsalted peanuts	250 mL
2 cups	multigrain cereal circles	500 mL	⅓ cup	butter	75 mL
2 cups	cereal squares	500 mL	2 tbsp	mild curry paste	30 mL
2 cups	small cheese crackers	500 mL	1 tsp	Worcestershire sauce	5 mL
			¼ tsp	each garlic powder and onion powder	1 mL

❧ In slow cooker, combine pretzels, cereal circles, cereal squares, cheese crackers and peanuts.

❧ In small saucepan or microwaveable bowl, melt together butter, curry paste, Worcestershire sauce, garlic powder and onion powder; whisk to combine. Pour over pretzel mixture and toss to coat.

❧ Cover and cook on low, stirring twice, until crisp, about 3 hours. Spread on rimmed baking sheets and let cool. (Make-ahead: Store in airtight container for up to 2 days.)

PER ½ CUP (125 ML): about 170 cal, 4 g pro, 10 g total fat (3 g sat. fat), 17 g carb, 2 g fibre, 10 mg chol, 287 mg sodium. % RDI: 3% calcium, 14% iron, 3% vit A, 16% folate.

Glazed Nut Clusters

Use mixed nuts or all of one kind. Wait until the nuts have cooled before breaking them up into attractive clusters.

| ½ cup | liquid honey | 125 mL | ½ tsp | coarse sea salt or kosher salt | 2 mL |
| 1 tsp | cinnamon | 5 mL | 4 cups | unsalted mixed nuts | 1 L |

1½- to 2-quart (1.5 to 2 L) slow cooker

Makes 4 cups (1 L)

◥ In large glass measuring cup, microwave together honey, cinnamon and salt on high until bubbling, about 1 minute. Whisk to combine.

◥ Place nuts in slow cooker. Scrape honey mixture over nuts and toss to coat.

◥ Cover and cook on high, stirring every 30 minutes, until hot, fragrant and glazed, about 2 hours. Spread on parchment paper–lined or well-greased rimmed baking sheet and let cool. Break up into bite-size clusters. (Make-ahead: Store layered between waxed paper in airtight container for up to 2 days.)

PER ¼ CUP (50 mL): about 251 cal, 6 g pro, 20 g total fat (3 g sat. fat), 16 g carb, 3 g fibre, 0 mg chol, 53 mg sodium. % RDI: 4% calcium, 9% iron, 14% folate.

Tamari Almonds

Tamari is naturally fermented Japanese soy sauce often found in health food stores. Slow cooking infuses its fermented, salty flavours into these nuts.

| 4 cups | unblanched almonds | 1 L | ¼ tsp | coarse sea salt or kosher salt | 1 mL |
| 3 tbsp | tamari or soy sauce | 45 mL | | | |

1½- to 2-quart (1.5 to 2 L) slow cooker

Makes 4 cups (1 L)

◥ Spread almonds on rimmed baking sheet. Toast in 350°F (180°C) oven until fragrant, about 8 minutes.

◥ In slow cooker, combine almonds and tamari. Cover and cook on high, stirring every 30 minutes, until nuts are dark brown, 2 hours. Stir in salt.

◥ Spread on rimmed baking sheet and let cool. (Make-ahead: Store in airtight container for up to 2 days.)

PER ¼ CUP (50 mL): about 207 cal, 8 g pro, 18 g total fat (1 g sat. fat), 7 g carb, 4 g fibre, 0 mg chol, 212 mg sodium. % RDI: 8% calcium, 11% iron, 5% folate.

SUBSTITUTION
To make Salt and Pepper Walnuts, substitute walnut halves for almonds and replace tamari and salt with 2 tbsp (30 mL) vegetable oil, 1 tsp (5 mL) coarse sea salt or kosher salt and 1 tsp (5 mL) coarsely ground pepper. Cook as directed.

Swiss Cheese Fondue

The slow cooker is a great appliance for keeping fondue warm during dinner or a party – no messy, flammable fuel. Set the fondue out with cubed baguette for traditionalist dippers, plus blanched broccoli and cauliflower florets, cooked shrimp and steamed baby potatoes.

4-quart (4 L)
slow cooker

Makes about
20 appetizer
servings

1	clove garlic, halved	1
1¾ cups	dry white wine	425 mL
2 cups	shredded Emmental cheese (8 oz/250 g)	500 mL
2 cups	shredded Gruyère cheese (8 oz/250 g)	500 mL
¼ cup	all-purpose flour	50 mL
Pinch	each pepper and grated nutmeg	Pinch

❧ Rub inside of slow cooker with cut sides of garlic; discard garlic. Turn slow cooker to high; cover and heat until insert is hot, about 5 minutes.

❧ Meanwhile, in saucepan, bring wine to boil. In large bowl, toss together Emmental, Gruyère and flour; set aside.

❧ Pour wine into slow cooker. Add cheese mixture by handfuls, stirring thoroughly after each addition.

❧ Cover and cook on high until cheese is melted, about 30 to 45 minutes. Stir in pepper and nutmeg.

PER SERVING: about 98 cal, 7 g pro, 7 g total fat (4 g sat. fat), 2 g carb, trace fibre, 22 mg chol, 60 mg sodium. % RDI: 18% calcium, 1% iron, 6% vit A, 2% folate.

TEST KITCHEN TIPS

It is essential to bring the wine to a boil on the stove before pouring it into the slow cooker. The heat gets the fondue going faster and, most importantly, evaporates the alcohol, which mellows out the flavour. That way, everyone can enjoy the pleasant taste of the cheese rather than being overpowered by the alcohol.

For a party, supplement your fondue forks with medium-length bamboo skewers.

White Bean & Garlic Spread

1½-quart (1.5 L)
slow cooker

Makes 1⅔ cups
(400 mL)

Easy to assemble, this colourful spread is tasty on pita chips and a selection of firm vegetables, such as carrot, cucumber, jicama and celery.

1	head Roasted Garlic (recipe, page 236)	1	1 tsp	white wine vinegar	5 mL
1	can (19 oz/540 mL) white kidney beans, drained and rinsed	1	¼ tsp	salt	1 mL
			¼ tsp	hot pepper sauce	1 mL
2 tbsp	extra-virgin olive oil	30 mL	¼ cup	each diced pitted black olives and roasted red pepper	50 mL

TEST KITCHEN TIPS

Add this spread to an antipasto tray with grape tomatoes, speck (smoked prosciutto) or salami, and feta cheese.

Choose wrinkly oil-cured olives over smooth, briny Kalamatas — they accent the mellow roasted garlic flavour.

⤸ Squeeze garlic into food processor. Add beans, oil, vinegar, salt and hot pepper sauce; pulse until fairly smooth. Scrape into slow cooker.

⤸ Cover and cook on low, stirring once, until steaming hot, about 2½ to 3 hours.

⤸ Stir in olives and roasted red pepper. Let stand for 10 minutes on warm.

PER 2 TBSP (30 mL): about 57 cal, 2 g pro, 3 g total fat (trace sat. fat), 7 g carb, 2 g fibre, 0 mg chol, 166 mg sodium. % RDI: 2% calcium, 4% iron, 1% vit A, 12% vit C, 5% folate.

Cheddar Black Bean Spread

1½-quart (1.5 L)
slow cooker

Makes 2¾ cups
(675 mL)

A small crock of this hot spread, with a knife and an assortment of crisp crackers, crunchy vegetable slices or tortilla chips, will get any party going.

1	can (19 oz/540 mL) black beans, drained and rinsed	1	¼ cup	mild or hot salsa	50 mL
			Dash	hot pepper sauce	Dash
3 cups	shredded old Cheddar cheese	750 mL	¼ cup	finely chopped fresh coriander	50 mL

SUBSTITUTION

For both recipes on this page, you can substitute 2 cups (500 mL) cooked beans (recipe, page 213) for the canned.

⤸ In food processor, whirl beans until almost smooth. Scrape into slow cooker. Stir in cheese, salsa and hot pepper sauce.

⤸ Cover and cook on low, stirring once, until steaming hot and cheese is melted, about 2½ to 3 hours. Stir in half of the coriander; sprinkle remainder over top.

PER 2 TBSP (30 mL): about 81 cal, 5 g pro, 5 g total fat (3 g sat. fat), 4 g carb, 1 g fibre, 16 mg chol, 178 mg sodium. % RDI: 11% calcium, 3% iron, 4% vit A, 2% vit C, 6% folate.

Red Cranberry Mulled Wine

Grocery stores offer both red and white cranberry cocktail. The red is made with fully ripe red cranberries, while the white comes from cranberries that are harvested with barely pink cheeks. You can use either for this simple drink – the red is festive and the white adds a pleasant tartness but no colour.

4- to 6-quart (4 to 6 L)
slow cooker

Makes 8 servings

4	cardamom pods	4	1	bottle (750 mL) red wine	1
1	stick (3 inches/8 cm) cinnamon	1	2 tbsp	granulated sugar (approx)	30 mL
6	whole allspice or cloves	6	1	each lemon and orange, thinly sliced	1
4 cups	red cranberry cocktail	1 L			

➶ Using side of large knife, gently press cardamom pods just until pods crack. Crush cinnamon into pieces. In 6-inch (15 cm) square cheesecloth, tie cardamom, cinnamon and allspice to form bag.

➶ In slow cooker, stir together cranberry cocktail, wine and sugar. Add spice bag and half each of the lemon and orange slices.

➶ Cover and cook on low until steaming hot, about 4 hours. Discard cooked lemon and orange slices. Stir in more sugar, if desired. Add remaining fresh lemon and orange slices.

PER SERVING: about 96 cal, trace pro, trace total fat (0 g sat. fat), 24 g carb, trace fibre, 0 mg chol, 7 mg sodium. % RDI: 1% calcium, 4% iron, 43% vit C, 2% folate.

TEST KITCHEN TIP
The first addition of citrus fruits is for flavour, the second for looks. Note that citrus left too long in mulled wine tends to add a bitter edge to the drink.

VARIATION

White Cranberry Mulled Wine: Replace red wine with white wine, such as Riesling, and red cranberry cocktail with white cranberry cocktail.

Glühwein

4- to 6-quart (4 to 6 L) slow cooker

Makes 8 servings

TEST KITCHEN TIP
Scrub the oranges in warm soapy water and rinse well before studding with cloves.

This German sweet spiced mulled wine comes from executive chef Ron Subden of the Oshawa Golf and Curling Club in Ontario, where it is a holiday buffet staple.

16	whole cloves	16	1 cup	granulated sugar (approx)	250 mL
2	small oranges	2	2	cinnamon sticks, broken	2
6 cups	red wine, such as Shiraz or Cabernet Sauvignon	1.5 L			

❧ Stick sharp ends of cloves into oranges; place in slow cooker. Add wine, sugar and cinnamon sticks. Stir until sugar is dissolved.

❧ Cover and cook on low until steaming hot, about 4 hours.

❧ Discard oranges and cinnamon sticks. Add more sugar, if desired.

PER SERVING: about 111 cal, trace pro, 0 g total fat (0 g sat. fat), 28 g carb, 0 g fibre, 0 mg chol, 9 mg sodium. % RDI: 1% calcium, 6% iron, 2% folate.

Mulled Cranberry Tea

4- to 6-quart (4 to 6 L) slow cooker

Makes 8 servings

A warm drink welcomes guests on a cold fall or winter day. The tea is deliberately unsweetened so guests can add their own honey or sugar. Just set it out beside the slow cooker. A long cinnamon stick makes the perfect swizzle stick.

4	cinnamon sticks, broken	4	2	strips (each 3 x 1 inch/ 8 x 2.5 cm) orange rind	2
2	whole star anise	2	4 cups	red cranberry cocktail	1 L
6	whole cloves	6	4 cups	hot brewed tea	1 L

❧ In 6-inch (15 cm) square cheesecloth, tie cinnamon, star anise, cloves and orange rind to form bag; place in slow cooker.

❧ Pour in cranberry cocktail. Cover and cook on low until steaming hot, about 3½ hours.

❧ Discard spice bag. Stir in tea. Keep warm.

PER SERVING: about 37 cal, 0 g pro, 0 g total fat (0 g sat. fat), 9 g carb, 0 g fibre, 0 mg chol, 3 mg sodium. % RDI: 37% vit C, 1% folate.

Mulled Cranberry Tea

Pomegranate Apple Warm-Up

This inviting pomegranate apple combo is a healthful welcome-to-our-home drink.

4- to 6-quart (4 to 6 L)
slow cooker

Makes 12 servings

1	cinnamon stick, broken	1	6 cups	apple juice	1.5 L
5	each whole cloves and allspice	5	3 cups	100% pomegranate juice	750 mL
2	slices gingerroot	2	¼ cup	liquid honey	50 mL

~ In 6-inch (15 cm) square cheesecloth, tie cinnamon, cloves, allspice and ginger to form bag; place in slow cooker.

~ Add apple juice, pomegranate juice and honey; stir well.

~ Cover and cook on low until steaming hot, about 4 hours. Remove spice bag.

PER SERVING: about 120 cal, trace pro, trace total fat (0 g sat. fat), 30 g carb, trace fibre, 0 mg chol, 10 mg sodium. % RDI: 1% calcium, 4% iron, 62% vit C.

Steamy Tomato Sipper

For après ski or skating parties, or to welcome guests for brunch, here's a drink with spicy warmth. Set the slow cooker and already-garnished mugs out for guests to help themselves. A bottle of vodka also tucked beside the slow cooker gives guests the opportunity to add alcohol if they like.

4- to 5-quart (4 to 5 L)
slow cooker

Makes 8 servings

6 cups	tomato juice or vegetable cocktail	1.5 L		1 tsp	prepared horseradish	5 mL
				¼ tsp	hot pepper sauce	1 mL
2 tbsp	lemon juice	30 mL		GARNISH:		
1 tbsp	packed brown sugar (optional)	15 mL		8	thin slices lemon, seeded	8
1	stalk celery, with leaves	1		8	celery sticks with leaves	8
1 tbsp	Worcestershire sauce	15 mL				

❧ In slow cooker, stir together tomato juice, lemon juice, and brown sugar (if using). Cut celery stalk into quarters; add to juice.

❧ Cover and cook on low until steaming hot, about 4 hours. Discard celery.

❧ Stir in Worcestershire sauce, horseradish and hot pepper sauce.

❧ GARNISH: Pour into mugs. Garnish with lemon slice and celery stick.

PER SERVING: about 38 cal, 2 g pro, trace total fat (0 g sat. fat), 10 g carb, 2 g fibre, 0 mg chol, 695 mg sodium. % RDI: 3% calcium, 9% iron, 11% vit A, 28% vit C, 18% folate.

TEST KITCHEN TIP
For heat fiends, offer a bottle of hot pepper sauce to spice things up.

Rich & Creamy Hot Chocolate

This is definitely not from a mix, and it's not your campfire cocoa. For an even more luxurious drink, top with a dollop of whipped cream and grated chocolate.

4- to 5-quart (4 to 5 L)
slow cooker

Makes 8 servings

12 oz	semisweet chocolate, finely chopped	375 g		7 cups	milk	1.75 L
				1 tsp	vanilla	5 mL

🍂 Place chocolate and milk in slow cooker.

🍂 Cover and cook on low until steaming hot, about 4 hours. Using immersion blender or whisk, blend until frothy. Stir in vanilla.

PER SERVING: about 327 cal, 9 g pro, 15 g total fat (9 g sat. fat), 38 g carb, 3 g fibre, 18 mg chol, 89 mg sodium. % RDI: 24% calcium, 9% iron, 10% vit A, 8% folate.

Soups & Chowders

Vegetable Beef & Rice Soup

Don't hesitate to top each hearty bowlful with a sprinkle of shredded Cheddar or Gouda, or grated Parmesan cheese, and chopped fresh parsley.

4- to 6-quart (4 to 6 L) slow cooker

Makes 8 to 10 servings

8 oz	lean ground beef	250 g
2	large carrots, diced	2
1	large onion, chopped	1
2	stalks celery, diced	2
Half	sweet red pepper, diced	Half
2	cloves garlic, minced	2
1 tsp	crumbled dried rosemary	5 mL
½ tsp	each salt and pepper	2 mL
6 cups	beef broth	1.5 L
⅔ cup	parboiled whole-grain rice	150 mL
1 cup	frozen peas	250 mL
1 tbsp	lemon juice	15 mL

In large skillet, sauté beef over medium-high heat, breaking up with fork until crumbly and no longer pink, about 8 minutes. With slotted spoon, transfer beef to slow cooker.

Drain fat from skillet. Fry carrots, onion, celery, red pepper, garlic, rosemary, salt and pepper over medium heat, stirring occasionally, until onion is softened, about 6 minutes. Scrape into slow cooker.

Add ½ cup (125 mL) of the broth to skillet; bring to boil, scraping up brown bits from bottom of skillet. Scrape into slow cooker along with remaining broth, 2 cups (500 mL) water and rice. Stir to combine.

Cover and cook on low until vegetables are tender, about 5 hours. (Make-ahead: Let cool for 30 minutes. Refrigerate, uncovered, in airtight containers until cold. Cover and refrigerate for up to 3 days.)

Stir in peas and lemon juice. Cover and cook on high until steaming hot, about 15 minutes.

PER EACH OF 10 SERVINGS: about 129 cal, 8 g pro, 4 g total fat (1 g sat. fat), 16 g carb, 2 g fibre, 13 mg chol, 629 mg sodium. % RDI: 3% calcium, 9% iron, 49% vit A, 22% vit C, 9% folate.

Mushroom Barley Soup

Cremini mushrooms and cubes of browned beef give this thick soup a rich colour and the kind of flavour that fully satisfies.

5- to 6-quart (5 to 6 L)
slow cooker

Makes 8 servings

1 lb	stewing beef cubes	500 g	6 cups	sliced cremini or white mushrooms (1 lb/500 g)	1.5 L	
½ tsp	each salt and pepper	2 mL	6 cups	chicken broth	1.5 L	
½ tsp	dried thyme	2 mL	½ cup	pot or pearl barley	125 mL	
2 tbsp	vegetable oil	30 mL	1 tbsp	tomato paste	15 mL	
1 cup	diced onions	250 mL	1	bay leaf	1	
1 cup	diced celery	250 mL				
1 cup	diced carrots	250 mL				

❧ Trim fat from beef; if necessary, cut into 1-inch (2.5 cm) cubes. Sprinkle beef with salt, pepper and thyme.

❧ In large skillet, heat 1 tbsp (15 mL) of the oil over medium-high heat; brown beef, in 2 batches, each about 5 minutes. Transfer to slow cooker.

❧ Drain fat from skillet; add remaining oil. Fry onions, celery and carrots over medium heat, stirring occasionally, until onions are softened, about 5 minutes.

❧ Add mushrooms to skillet; fry, stirring often, until mushroom liquid begins to evaporate, about 5 minutes. Scrape mixture into slow cooker.

❧ Add 1 cup (250 mL) of the broth to skillet; bring to boil, scraping up brown bits from bottom of skillet. Scrape into slow cooker along with remaining broth, 2 cups (500 mL) water, barley, tomato paste and bay leaf. Stir to combine.

❧ Cover and cook on low until barley is tender, about 6 to 8 hours. Discard bay leaf. (Make-ahead: Let cool for 30 minutes. Refrigerate, uncovered, in airtight containers until cold. Cover and refrigerate for up to 3 days or freeze for up to 1 month.)

PER SERVING: about 224 cal, 19 g pro, 9 g total fat (2 g sat. fat), 17 g carb, 3 g fibre, 28 mg chol, 789 mg sodium. % RDI: 4% calcium, 19% iron, 35% vit A, 5% vit C, 12% folate.

4- to 5-quart (4 to 5 L)
slow cooker

Makes 8 servings

Sausage, Potato & Swiss Chard Soup

While spinach can stand in for the Swiss chard, why not try it here and incorporate this handsome vegetable into your repertoire of soups and side dishes? If you do go for spinach, add it to the steaming-hot soup just long enough to wilt its leaves, about 1 minute.

1 lb	Italian sausage	500 g	1 tsp	dried Italian herb seasoning	5 mL
1 tbsp	extra-virgin olive oil	15 mL	½ tsp	pepper	2 mL
1 cup	sodium-reduced chicken broth	250 mL	¼ tsp	hot pepper flakes	1 mL
1	onion, diced	1	2 cups	packed coarsely chopped Swiss chard	500 mL
2	cloves garlic, minced	2	½ cup	coarsely grated Parmesan cheese	125 mL
3 cups	cubed peeled potatoes (3 large)	750 mL			

◞ Cut sausage into 1-inch (2.5 cm) pieces. In large skillet, heat oil over medium-high heat; brown sausage. With slotted spoon, transfer to slow cooker.

◞ Drain fat from skillet. Add broth; bring to boil, scraping up brown bits from bottom of skillet. Scrape into slow cooker along with 3 cups (750 mL) water, onion, garlic, potatoes, Italian herb seasoning, pepper and hot pepper flakes. Stir to combine.

◞ Cover and cook on low until potatoes are tender but not mushy, about 4 to 6 hours. (Make-ahead: Let cool for 30 minutes. Refrigerate, uncovered, in airtight containers until cold. Cover and refrigerate for up to 3 days.)

◞ Stir in Swiss chard; cover and cook on high until wilted, about 10 minutes. Serve with Parmesan cheese.

PER SERVING: about 203 cal, 12 g pro, 12 g total fat (4 g sat. fat), 13 g carb, 1 g fibre, 29 mg chol, 508 mg sodium. % RDI: 6% calcium, 8% iron, 3% vit A, 10% vit C, 4% folate.

Pizza Soup

Brimming with everyone's favourite pizza ingredients, this soup makes a perfect lunch at home or packed for school or work.

4- to 5-quart (4 to 5 L)
slow cooker

Makes 4 servings

1 tbsp	vegetable oil	15 mL	1 cup	diced ham, smoked turkey or hard pepperoni	250 mL
1	onion, chopped	1	1	can (28 oz/796 mL) diced tomatoes	1
2	cloves garlic, minced	2			
2 cups	sliced mushrooms	500 mL	¼ cup	tomato paste	50 mL
1 tsp	dried oregano	5 mL	1	small sweet green pepper, diced (optional)	1
¼ tsp	each salt and pepper	1 mL			
2 cups	chicken or vegetable broth	500 mL			

In large skillet, heat oil over medium-high heat; sauté onion, garlic, mushrooms, oregano, salt and pepper until no liquid remains. Add half of the broth; bring to boil, scraping up brown bits from bottom of skillet. Scrape into slow cooker along with remaining broth, ham, tomatoes and tomato paste. Stir to combine.

Cover and cook on low for 4 hours. Stir in green pepper (if using); cover and cook on high until green pepper is tender, about 20 minutes. (Make-ahead: Let cool for 30 minutes. Refrigerate, uncovered, in airtight containers until cold. Cover and refrigerate for up to 3 days or freeze for up to 1 month.)

PER SERVING: about 180 cal, 15 g pro, 7 g total fat (1 g sat. fat), 18 g carb, 4 g fibre, 19 mg chol, 1,306 mg sodium. % RDI: 8% calcium, 21% iron, 15% vit A, 63% vit C, 13% folate.

Black Bean & Chorizo Soup

Beans are highly nutritious and economical, and they make the very best sustaining and satisfying soups. Flavour accents, such as the chorizo, and toppings of light sour cream, fresh coriander and shredded Monterey Jack cheese transform this simple soup into a feast.

4½- to 6-quart (4.5 to 6 L) slow cooker

Makes 6 servings

12 oz	fresh chorizo sausage, sliced	375 g		2	cans (each 19 oz/540 mL) black beans, drained and rinsed (or 4 cups/1 L cooked beans; recipe, page 213)	2
1	onion, chopped	1		2 tbsp	tomato paste	30 mL
4	cloves garlic, minced	4		1	sweet red pepper, diced	1
2	carrots, diced	2		1½ cups	frozen corn kernels	375 mL
1 tbsp	chili powder	15 mL				
1 tsp	fennel seeds, crushed	5 mL				
¼ tsp	pepper	1 mL				
5 cups	sodium-reduced chicken broth	1.25 L				

SUBSTITUTION
Instead of chorizo, you can substitute hot or mild Italian sausages and 1 tsp (5 mL) sweet paprika.

❧ In large skillet, sauté sausage over medium-high heat until browned, about 5 minutes; drain fat from skillet.

❧ Add onion, garlic, carrots, chili powder, fennel seeds and pepper to skillet; fry over medium heat until vegetables are softened, about 5 minutes. Scrape into slow cooker.

❧ Add 1 cup (250 mL) of the broth to skillet; bring to boil, scraping up brown bits from bottom of skillet. Scrape into slow cooker along with remaining broth, black beans and tomato paste. Stir to combine.

❧ Cover and cook on low until slightly thickened, about 6 hours.

❧ Add red pepper and corn; cover and cook on high until hot, about 15 minutes. (Make-ahead: Let cool for 30 minutes. Refrigerate, uncovered, in airtight containers until cold. Cover and refrigerate for up to 3 days.)

PER SERVING: about 468 cal, 27 g pro, 23 g total fat (8 g sat. fat), 41 g carb, 13 g fibre, 51 mg chol, 1,714 mg sodium. % RDI: 7% calcium, 29% iron, 74% vit A, 73% vit C, 46% folate.

Soupe aux Pois

This hearty pea soup is adapted from a recipe shared almost a decade ago by Claire Lajeunesse-Lewko of Prince Albert, Sask. It's still the Test Kitchen's favourite pea soup. Leftovers keep well in the refrigerator or freezer; however, when reheating, thin with a little water.

4½- to 6-quart (4.5 to 6 L) slow cooker

Makes 6 to 8 servings

2 cups	dried yellow split peas	500 mL
1	ham bone	1
1	large onion, chopped	1
3	stalks celery, chopped	3
2	carrots, chopped	2
1	clove garlic, minced	1

1	bay leaf	1
½ tsp	pepper	2 mL
GARNISH:		
1	small red onion, finely chopped or sliced	1
½ cup	white vinegar	125 mL

↪ In large bowl, soak peas in 6 cups (1.5 L) cold water for 12 hours or for up to 24 hours. Drain and rinse. Place in slow cooker.

↪ Add 6 cups (1.5 L) water, ham bone, onion, celery, carrots, garlic, bay leaf and pepper. Stir to combine.

↪ Cover and cook on low until vegetables are tender, about 6 hours. Discard ham bone and bay leaf. (Make-ahead: Let cool for 30 minutes. Refrigerate, uncovered, in airtight containers until cold. Cover and refrigerate for up to 3 days or freeze for up to 1 month.)

↪ GARNISH: Mix onion with vinegar. Ladle soup into bowls; garnish with spoonfuls of onion mixture.

PER EACH OF 8 SERVINGS: about 236 cal, 18 g pro, 2 g total fat (1 g sat. fat), 38 g carb, 6 g fibre, 13 mg chol, 333 mg sodium. % RDI: 4% calcium, 18% iron, 46% vit A, 7% vit C, 49% folate.

SUBSTITUTION

If you don't have a ham bone, substitute 8 oz (250 g) salt pork or uncooked bacon, chopped, or even a smoked turkey thigh. If you use the turkey, remove the meat from the bone, dice neatly and return meat only to the soup.

Red Bean & Bacon Soup

Inexpensive pantry-friendly ingredients make this soup a weeknight supper lifesaver.

4½- to 6-quart (4.5 to 6 L) slow cooker

Makes 6 servings

6	slices bacon, chopped	6
1	onion, chopped	1
4	cloves garlic, minced	4
2	carrots, diced	2
2	stalks celery, diced	2
2 tsp	dried thyme	10 mL
1 tsp	pepper	5 mL
½ tsp	salt	2 mL
4 cups	sodium-reduced chicken broth	1 L

1	can (28 oz/796 mL) diced tomatoes	1
1	can (19 oz/540 mL) red kidney beans, drained and rinsed (or 2 cups/500 mL cooked beans; recipe, page 213)	1
½ cup	parboiled long-grain rice	125 mL
¼ cup	tomato paste	50 mL

In large skillet, fry bacon over medium-high heat until crisp, about 5 minutes.

Drain fat from skillet. Fry onion, garlic, carrots, celery, thyme, pepper and salt over medium heat until vegetables are softened, about 5 minutes. Scrape into slow cooker.

Add 1 cup (250 mL) of the broth to skillet; bring to boil, scraping up brown bits from bottom of skillet. Scrape into slow cooker along with remaining broth, tomatoes, beans, rice and tomato paste. Stir to combine.

Cover and cook on low until vegetables and rice are tender, about 4 to 6 hours. (Make-ahead: Let cool for 30 minutes. Refrigerate, uncovered, in airtight containers until cold. Cover and refrigerate for up to 3 days or freeze for up to 1 month.)

PER SERVING: about 240 cal, 12 g pro, 5 g total fat (2 g sat. fat), 38 g carb, 8 g fibre, 9 mg chol, 1,173 mg sodium. % RDI: 10% calcium, 24% iron, 46% vit A, 40% vit C, 25% folate.

Sausage Minestrone

Minestrone, the quintessential rustic vegetable-and-bean soup, is enhanced by the addition of spicy Italian sausages. Leftovers make fabulous lunches.

4½- to 6-quart (4.5 to 6 L) slow cooker

Makes 8 to 10 servings

4	hot or mild Italian sausages (about 1 lb/ 500 g)	4
1 tsp	vegetable oil	5 mL
2	each onions, carrots and stalks celery, chopped	2
4	cloves garlic, minced	4
1½ tsp	dried oregano	7 mL
1½ tsp	salt	7 mL
2	cans (each 19 oz/540 mL) red or white kidney beans, drained and rinsed (or 4 cups/1 L cooked beans; recipe, page 213)	2
1	can (28 oz/796 mL) tomatoes, mashed	1
¼ tsp	pepper	1 mL
1	bay leaf	1
2	small zucchini, chopped	2
¼ cup	chopped fresh parsley	50 mL
Half	small cauliflower, chopped	Half
1 cup	small short pasta (tubetti or macaroni)	250 mL
	Grated Parmesan cheese	

❧ Cut sausages into small bite-size pieces. In large skillet, heat oil over medium-high heat; fry sausages, stirring occasionally, until browned, about 10 minutes. Transfer to slow cooker.

❧ Drain fat from skillet. Fry onions, carrots, celery, garlic, oregano and salt over medium heat, stirring occasionally, until onions are softened, about 5 minutes. Scrape into slow cooker.

❧ Add 1 cup (250 mL) water to skillet; bring to boil, scraping up brown bits from bottom of skillet. Scrape into slow cooker along with beans, 5 cups (1.25 L) water, tomatoes, pepper and bay leaf. Stir to combine.

❧ Cover and cook on low until vegetables are tender, about 6 hours. Add zucchini and parsley. Cover and cook on high until zucchini is tender, about 20 minutes. (Make-ahead: Let cool for 30 minutes. Refrigerate, uncovered, in airtight containers until cold. Cover and refrigerate for up to 3 days or freeze for up to 1 month.)

❧ Meanwhile, in saucepan of boiling salted water, cook cauliflower and pasta until cauliflower is tender and pasta is tender but firm, 6 minutes. Drain and stir into slow cooker. Discard bay leaf. Serve with cheese.

PER EACH OF 10 SERVINGS: about 262 cal, 16 g pro, 8 g total fat (2 g sat. fat), 34 g carb, 10 g fibre, 19 mg chol, 1,031 mg sodium. % RDI: 7% calcium, 19% iron, 43% vit A, 45% vit C, 37% folate.

TEST KITCHEN TIP
Pasta or rice cooked for a long time in the slow cooker can turn out gummy and overcooked. The solution: Cook them separately and add at the end of the specified cooking time or after freezing and reheating, as in this recipe.

Pozole

Fans of Mexican food will be familiar with this broth-based soup made with meat and hominy, the distinctively flavoured white corn also used in corn tortillas. Our version takes less time than the traditional but keeps the authentic taste, thanks to the convenience of canned hominy and prepared salsa verde. A garnish platter is part of the pozole experience – everyone can add his or her own final touches. It's great for a party.

4½- to 6-quart (4.5 to 6 L) slow cooker

Makes 8 to 10 servings

3 lb	chicken thighs	1.5 kg
1 tbsp	vegetable oil	15 mL
1	onion, chopped	1
4	cloves garlic, sliced	4
4 tsp	chili powder	20 mL
¼ tsp	each salt and pepper	1 mL
1	bay leaf	1
2 cups	sodium-reduced chicken broth	500 mL
½ cup	pepitas	125 mL
1	jar (430 mL) salsa verde	1
4 tsp	dried oregano, Mexican if available	20 mL

2	cans (each 15 oz/425 g) white hominy, drained and rinsed	2

TORTILLA STRIPS:

4	small flour tortillas	4
1 tbsp	vegetable oil	15 mL

GARNISH PLATTER:

Diced avocado tossed with lime juice

Shredded iceberg lettuce

Diced radishes

Thinly sliced green onions

Chopped fresh coriander

Lime wedges

Sour cream

TEST KITCHEN TIP
You'll usually need to ripen an avocado for three or four days once you get it home. Just set it on the counter out of direct sunlight. To speed things up, wrap the avocado in a paper bag with an apple. The natural ethylene gas emitted by the apple will help it ripen faster.

❧ Place chicken thighs in slow cooker.

❧ In large skillet, heat oil over medium heat; fry onion, garlic, chili powder, salt, pepper and bay leaf until onion is softened, about 4 minutes. Scrape into slow cooker. Add broth to skillet; bring to boil, scraping up brown bits from bottom of skillet. Scrape into slow cooker along with 4 cups (1 L) water. Stir to combine.

❧ Cover and cook on low, periodically skimming off any foam, until chicken is very tender, about 4 to 5 hours.

❧ TORTILLA STRIPS: Meanwhile, brush tortillas on both sides with oil; stack and cut in half. Stack again and slice crosswise into thin strips. Separate strips and arrange on rimmed baking sheet. Bake in 350°F (180°C) oven until crisp and golden, about 10 minutes. Let cool. (Make-ahead: Store in airtight container for up to 3 days.)

›

↩ Meanwhile, in small skillet, toast pepitas over medium heat, stirring occasionally, until puffed and seeds pop, about 6 minutes. Let cool. In blender, purée together pepitas, salsa and oregano until smooth.

↩ Transfer chicken to plate; let cool enough to handle. Stir salsa mixture and hominy into slow cooker. Cover and cook on high until hot, about 15 minutes.

↩ Meanwhile, remove meat from skin and bones; shred and return to soup. (Make-ahead: Let cool for 30 minutes. Refrigerate, uncovered, in airtight containers until cold. Cover and refrigerate for up to 3 days.)

↩ Cover and heat through. Ladle into bowls. Serve with garnish platter items and tortilla strips.

PER EACH OF 10 SERVINGS: about 340 cal, 21 g pro, 20 g total fat (5 g sat. fat), 19 g carb, 2 g fibre, 70 mg chol, 648 mg sodium. % RDI: 4% calcium, 22% iron, 5% vit A, 2% vit C, 50% folate.

Mexican Ingredients to Know and Love

This recipe calls for a few ingredients you might never have used before. Trust us, they're worth seeking out.

> Green salsa, or **salsa verde,** is made from tomatillos, a kind of green tomato covered with a parchment-like husk, and has a smoother consistency than most tomato-based salsas. Purchased salsa verde is usually quite mild.

> **Pepitas** are hulled green pumpkin seeds available in bulk food outlets and supermarkets. They're eaten as a snack and often added to sauces and soups.

> **White hominy,** like this soup, is known as *pozole* in Spanish. These white corn kernels are cooked in limewater (calcium hydroxide), which strips off the hull and germ and gives them their distinctive "tortilla" taste. Hominy can be a little harder to find. Try Mexican or Latin American grocery stores, though some major supermarkets do carry cans of it alongside other Mexican foods.

> **Mexican oregano** is a different plant than the typical Mediterranean oregano we often see in Canada. It's more closely related to lemon verbena than oregano, and its sweeter, stronger flavour is perfect in chilis and spicy dishes. Look for it in Mexican and Latin American grocery stores.

Chicken Noodle Soup

This soup is chock-full of healthy vegetables and is always comforting.

4½- to 6-quart (4.5 to 6 L) slow cooker

Makes 6 to 8 servings

1 tbsp	vegetable oil	15 mL		1	bay leaf	1
1	onion, chopped	1		8 cups	Homemade Chicken Broth (recipe, page 71) or sodium-reduced chicken broth	2 L
2	each small carrots and stalks celery, sliced	2		2	chicken breasts	2
¾ cup	sliced mushrooms	175 mL		¾ cup	chopped green beans	175 mL
1	clove garlic, chopped	1		1 cup	egg noodles	250 mL
½ tsp	each salt and pepper	2 mL		2 tbsp	chopped fresh parsley	30 mL
¼ tsp	dried thyme	1 mL				

In large skillet, heat oil over medium-high heat; sauté onion, carrots, celery, mushrooms, garlic, salt, pepper, thyme and bay leaf until vegetables are softened, about 8 minutes. Scrape into slow cooker.

Add 1 cup (250 mL) of the broth to skillet; bring to boil, scraping up brown bits from bottom of skillet. Scrape into slow cooker along with chicken and remaining broth. Stir to combine.

Cover and cook on low until juices run clear when chicken is pierced, about 3 to 4 hours. Skim off any fat and foam. Remove chicken and let cool enough to handle; remove meat from skin and bones. Dice; return to soup.

Add beans. Cover; cook on high until tender, 10 minutes. Discard bay leaf. (Make-ahead: Let cool for 30 minutes. Refrigerate in airtight containers until cold. Cover and refrigerate for up to 3 days or freeze for up to 1 month.)

Meanwhile, in saucepan of boiling salted water, cook noodles until tender but firm. Drain and add to soup along with parsley.

PER EACH OF 8 SERVINGS: about 147 cal, 13 g pro, 6 g total fat (1 g sat. fat), 8 g carb, 1 g fibre, 29 mg chol, 209 mg sodium. % RDI: 3% calcium, 8% iron, 27% vit A, 5% vit C, 8% folate.

VARIATION

Turkey Noodle Soup: Omit green beans. Substitute 5 cups (1.25 L) Turkey Broth (recipe, page 70) for chicken broth. Follow first two paragraphs, omitting chicken. Cover and cook until vegetables are tender, about 4 hours. Discard bay leaf. Stir in 2 cups (500 mL) cubed cooked turkey and ¼ cup (50 mL) frozen peas. Cover and cook on high for 10 minutes. Increase egg noodles to 1½ cups (375 mL); cook in boiling salted water until tender but firm, about 6 minutes. Drain; add to soup along with parsley.

Turkey Meatball Soup

Check your frozen food supplies – if you have shelled edamame, consider using them instead of the frozen peas. If you've never used them, add a bag of these vibrant green, tender soybeans to your next shopping list.

4½- to 6-quart (4.5 to 6 L)
slow cooker

Makes 6 servings

3 cups	sodium-reduced chicken broth	750 mL	½ cup	frozen peas	125 mL
2	green onions, sliced	2	**TURKEY MEATBALLS:**		
2	stalks celery, sliced	2	1	egg	1
1	carrot, sliced	1	¼ cup	grated onion	50 mL
½ tsp	dried thyme	2 mL	¼ cup	grated Parmesan cheese	50 mL
¼ tsp	each salt and pepper	1 mL	2 tbsp	minced fresh parsley	30 mL
1	sweet red pepper, diced	1	¼ tsp	each salt and pepper	1 mL
1 cup	vermicelli egg noodles	250 mL	1 lb	lean ground turkey or veal	500 g

TEST KITCHEN TIP
To prevent the meat from sticking to your hands when forming meatballs, dip your hands periodically into a bowl of water.

⤸ **TURKEY MEATBALLS:** In bowl, beat egg. Add onion, cheese, parsley, salt and pepper; stir to combine. Mix in turkey. Shape by 1 tbsp (15 mL) into balls. Bake on greased rimmed baking sheet in 400°F (200°C) oven until firm, about 15 minutes.

⤸ Place meatballs in slow cooker. Add broth, 3 cups (750 mL) water, white parts of green onions, celery, carrot, thyme, salt and pepper. Stir to combine.

⤸ Cover and cook on low until vegetables are tender, about 4 to 5 hours.

⤸ Add red pepper, egg noodles and peas. Cover and cook on high until steaming hot and noodles are tender, about 15 minutes. (Make-ahead: Let cool for 30 minutes. Refrigerate, uncovered, in airtight containers until cold. Cover and refrigerate for up to 3 days.) Sprinkle with green parts of green onions.

PER SERVING: about 198 cal, 19 g pro, 9 g total fat (3 g sat. fat), 10 g carb, 2 g fibre, 100 mg chol, 560 mg sodium. % RDI: 8% calcium, 13% iron, 34% vit A, 62% vit C, 12% folate.

Seafood Chowder

The tenderest part of a leek is its white and light green parts, which are also the sandiest bits. Here's an easy way to clean leeks: chop or slice and place them in a sieve, then immerse in a bowl of cold water. Swish well to dislodge sand, then lift sieve out and drain well. Repeat if necessary.

4½- to 6-quart (4.5 to 6 L) slow cooker

Makes 8 servings

3 tbsp	butter	45 mL	½ tsp	each dried thyme and pepper	2 mL
1	large onion, diced	1	Pinch	each grated nutmeg and cayenne pepper	Pinch
1	large leek (white and light green parts only), chopped	1	1 lb	large raw shrimp, peeled and deveined	500 g
3	each carrots and stalks celery, diced	3	1 lb	catfish or tilapia, cubed	500 g
3	potatoes, peeled and diced	3	1 cup	18% cream	250 mL
1	bay leaf	1	¼ cup	minced fresh parsley	50 mL

In large skillet, melt butter over medium heat; fry onion and leek until softened and onion is golden at edges, about 10 minutes. Scrape into slow cooker along with carrots, celery, potatoes, bay leaf, thyme, pepper, nutmeg, cayenne and 6 cups (1.5 L) water. Stir to combine.

Cover and cook on low until vegetables are tender, about 4 to 6 hours. Discard bay leaf.

Stir in shrimp and catfish; cover and cook on high until shrimp are pink and catfish is firm and opaque, about 15 minutes.

Heat cream until steaming; gently stir into chowder. Sprinkle with parsley.

PER SERVING: about 290 cal, 24 g pro, 12 g total fat (7 g sat. fat), 21 g carb, 2 g fibre, 142 mg chol, 214 mg sodium. % RDI: 9% calcium, 16% iron, 67% vit A, 18% vit C, 14% folate.

TEST KITCHEN TIP
This chowder is chock-full of vegetables and seafood with a creamy broth. If you like a thicker broth, stir 3 tbsp (45 mL) all-purpose flour into the onion and leek mixture just before scraping it into the slow cooker.

Thai Squash Soup with Shrimp

When lemongrass is unavailable, substitute a strip of lemon peel, adding it without bruising.

4½- to 6-quart (4.5 to 6 L)
slow cooker

Makes 4 servings

1	stalk lemongrass	1	6	thin slices gingerroot	6
4 cups	cubed peeled butternut squash (half medium)	1 L	1½ tsp	fish sauce (or ½ tsp/ 2 mL salt)	7 mL
1	can (400 mL) coconut milk	1	¼ tsp	packed brown sugar	1 mL
2 cups	sodium-reduced chicken broth	500 mL	1 lb	large raw shrimp, peeled and deveined	500 g
1 tbsp	Thai red curry paste	15 mL	2 tbsp	thinly sliced fresh mint or basil	30 mL

◞ Hit lemongrass with top of knife blade along stalk to bruise; cut into 1-inch (2.5 cm) lengths.

◞ In slow cooker, combine lemongrass, squash, coconut milk, chicken broth, curry paste, ginger, fish sauce and brown sugar.

◞ Cover and cook on low until squash is very tender, about 4 to 6 hours. Discard ginger and lemongrass. Mash squash until soup is smooth. (Make-ahead: Let cool for 30 minutes. Refrigerate, uncovered, in airtight containers until cold. Cover and refrigerate for up to 3 days.)

◞ Stir in shrimp; cover and cook on high until shrimp are pink, about 15 minutes. Stir in mint.

PER SERVING: about 370 cal, 23 g pro, 24 g total fat (18 g sat. fat), 21 g carb, 4 g fibre, 129 mg chol, 719 mg sodium. % RDI: 12% calcium, 45% iron, 178% vit A, 43% vit C, 23% folate.

TEST KITCHEN TIP
The red curry paste makes the soup very hot. Reduce the amount, starting at ½ tsp (2 mL), for people with tamer palates.

Onion Soup with Gruyère Croûtes

5- to 6-quart (5 to 6 L)
slow cooker

Makes 8 servings

There are two parts to this recipe – caramelizing the onions, then simmering the soup – so you can split the recipe over two days if that suits your schedule. The extended cooking time brings out an incredible mellow onion flavour, which contrasts nicely with the crunchy cheese toasts.

3 tbsp	extra-virgin olive oil	45 mL	3	large cloves garlic, sliced	3
1 tbsp	butter	15 mL	1 tbsp	chopped fresh thyme (or 1 tsp/5 mL dried)	15 mL
12 cups	sliced onions (3 lb/ 1.5 kg, 6 large)	3 L	1	bay leaf	1
4 cups	sodium-reduced beef or vegetable broth	1 L	¼ tsp	each salt and pepper	1 mL
¼ cup	dry white wine (or 1 tbsp/15 mL cider vinegar)	50 mL		Gruyère Croûtes (recipe, below)	
				Chopped fresh thyme or parsley	

TEST KITCHEN TIP
Slices from a large onion tend to be long and pesky to get from bowl to bouche without dribbling on your shirt. Eliminate the problem by cutting onions from top to bottom, laying the halves flat and cutting once more into quarters lengthwise. Now slice thinly crosswise.

❧ In slow cooker, cover and heat oil and butter on low until butter is melted. Add onions; toss well to coat. Cover and cook on high, stirring twice, until onions are golden brown, about 6 hours.

❧ Stir in broth, wine, garlic, thyme, bay leaf, salt, pepper and 2 cups (500 mL) water.

❧ Cover and cook on low until slightly thickened and rich brown in colour, about 3 to 4 hours. Discard bay leaf. (Make-ahead: Let cool for 30 minutes. Refrigerate, uncovered, in airtight containers until cold. Cover and refrigerate for up to 3 days or freeze for up to 1 month.)

❧ Ladle soup into bowls. Float Gruyère Croûte on each serving; sprinkle with thyme.

PER SERVING: about 266 cal, 11 g pro, 14 g total fat (6 g sat. fat), 26 g carb, 3 g fibre, 27 mg chol, 548 mg sodium. % RDI: 25% calcium, 6% iron, 8% vit A, 3% vit C, 18% folate.

Gruyère Croûtes: Broil 8 slices baguette on baking sheet until golden, about 2 minutes. Turn; sprinkle with 1½ cups (375 mL) shredded Gruyère cheese. Broil until crusty and cheese is melted, about 3 minutes. Float on soup. **Makes 8 croûtes.**

Cauliflower Bisque

There's just enough curry to give this smooth soup a whiff of the exotic. Do jack up the amount of curry paste if you like a bolder soup but not so much that it masks the delicate cauliflower.

4½- to 6-quart (4.5 to 6 L) slow cooker

Makes 10 to 12 servings

2 tbsp	butter or canola oil	30 mL		2 cups	18% cream, or lighter cream or milk	500 mL
1	large onion, chopped	1		¼ tsp	each salt and hot pepper sauce	1 mL
½ tsp	mild curry paste	2 mL		¼ cup	thinly sliced red onion	50 mL
1	cauliflower (2 lb/1 kg)	1		¼ cup	chopped fresh coriander	50 mL
1	large potato, peeled and diced	1				
4 cups	chicken or vegetable broth	1 L				

~ In large skillet, melt butter over low heat; fry onion and curry paste, stirring, until onion is softened, about 5 minutes. Scrape into slow cooker.

~ Trim and core cauliflower; cut into quarters. Slice cauliflower thinly; add to slow cooker along with potato and broth. Stir to combine.

~ Cover and cook on low until vegetables are tender, about 4 to 6 hours.

~ Using immersion blender, or in stand blender in batches, purée soup until smooth. (Make-ahead: Let cool for 30 minutes. Refrigerate, uncovered, in airtight containers until cold. Cover and refrigerate for up to 2 days.)

~ Stir in cream, salt and hot pepper sauce. Cover and cook on high until hot, about 10 minutes. Serve garnished with red onion and coriander.

PER EACH OF 12 SERVINGS: about 135 cal, 3 g pro, 9 g total fat (6 g sat. fat), 10 g carb, 2 g fibre, 29 mg chol, 401 mg sodium. % RDI: 5% calcium, 2% iron, 8% vit A, 38% vit C, 12% folate.

SHORTCUT

While the frying step takes a little longer, it delivers more flavour, toasting the spices and mellowing the onion. Then the fat carries these tastes over into the soup. But if you're tight on prep time, you can omit frying the butter, onion and curry powder. Simply combine in slow cooker with potato, cauliflower and broth. Continue with recipe.

Add Some Crunch to Your Soup: Croutons

Easy to make, croutons make soups sing. One ½-inch (1 cm) thick slice of bread yields about ¾ cup (175 mL) cubes.
~ In bowl, toss 2 cups (500 mL) cubed bread, such as pumpernickel, rye or sourdough; 1 tbsp (15 mL) extra-virgin olive oil; 1 small clove garlic, minced; and pinch each salt and pepper.

~ Bake in single layer on rimmed baking sheet in 400°F (200°C) oven until crisp, about 12 minutes. Let cool. (*Make-ahead: Store in airtight container for up to 3 days.*) **Makes 2 cups (500 mL).**

Variations: Omit garlic and season with dried herbs, chili powder, zaatar or freshly ground black pepper.

Hungarian Potato Soup

This is a thick, creamy soup that's good hot or cold – a vichyssoise with Eastern European accents of vinegar and sour cream.

4½- to 6-quart (4.5 to 6 L)
slow cooker

Makes 8 servings

12	black peppercorns, cracked	12
3	bay leaves	3
1 tbsp	vegetable oil	15 mL
3	stalks celery, sliced	3
2	onions, chopped	2
½ tsp	salt	2 mL

6 cups	cubed peeled potatoes (2¼ lb/1.125 kg, about 6)	1.5 L
3 cups	sodium-reduced chicken broth	750 mL
2 tbsp	white wine vinegar (approx)	30 mL
½ cup	sour cream	125 mL
3 tbsp	minced fresh parsley	45 mL

❧ In 5-inch (12 cm) square cheesecloth, tie peppercorns and bay leaves to make bag; place in slow cooker.

❧ In large skillet, heat oil over medium heat; fry celery, onions and salt, stirring occasionally, until onions are tender but not coloured, about 8 minutes. Scrape into slow cooker along with potatoes, chicken broth, vinegar and 3 cups (750 mL) water. Stir to combine.

❧ Cover and cook on low until potatoes are tender, about 5 hours. Discard spice bag.

❧ Using immersion blender, or in stand blender in batches, purée soup until smooth. (Make-ahead: Let cool for 30 minutes. Refrigerate, uncovered, in airtight containers until cold. Cover and refrigerate for up to 3 days.)

❧ Whisk in sour cream. Taste, adding a little more vinegar, if desired. Serve sprinkled with parsley.

PER SERVING: about 145 cal, 4 g pro, 4 g total fat (1 g sat. fat), 25 g carb, 2 g fibre, 6 mg chol, 392 mg sodium. % RDI: 4% calcium, 4% iron, 4% vit A, 17% vit C, 9% folate.

Leek & Carrot Soup with Chive Oil

4½- to 6-quart (4.5 to 6 L)
slow cooker

Makes 8 servings

The chive oil is a restaurant-style touch that's easy to do. Drizzled over the surface, the bright green oil both impresses visually and emboldens a pure, mild soup.

2 tbsp	butter	30 mL		½ tsp	pepper	2 mL
8 cups	chopped leeks, white and light green parts only (3 large)	2 L		¼ tsp	salt	1 mL
2 cups	chopped carrots (2 large)	500 mL		3 cups	sodium-reduced chicken broth	750 mL
2	stalks celery, chopped	2		½ cup	18% cream	125 mL
3	cloves garlic, minced	3		**CHIVE OIL:**		
2	bay leaves	2		⅓ cup	chopped fresh chives	75 mL
1 tsp	dried thyme	5 mL		¼ cup	canola oil	50 mL

❧ In large skillet, melt butter over medium heat; fry leeks, carrots, celery, garlic, bay leaves, thyme, pepper and salt, stirring often and without letting vegetables colour, until softened, about 10 minutes. Scrape into slow cooker along with broth and 1 cup (250 mL) water. Stir to combine.

❧ Cover and cook on low until vegetables are very tender, about 3 to 4 hours. Discard bay leaves.

❧ **CHIVE OIL:** Meanwhile, in blender, purée chives with oil until bright green and smooth. Strain through coffee filter into bowl. (Make-ahead: Cover and refrigerate for up to 2 days.)

❧ Using immersion blender, or in stand blender in batches, purée soup until smooth. (Make-ahead: Let cool for 30 minutes. Refrigerate, uncovered, in airtight containers until cold. Cover and refrigerate for up to 3 days or freeze for up to 1 month.)

❧ Whisk in cream. Cover and cook on high until steaming hot, about 10 minutes. Ladle into bowls; drizzle with chive oil.

PER SERVING: about 159 cal, 3 g pro, 13 g total fat (4 g sat. fat), 11 g carb, 2 g fibre, 17 mg chol, 354 mg sodium. % RDI: 6% calcium, 9% iron, 55% vit A, 12% vit C, 13% folate.

Beet & Vegetable Borscht

Gloriously colourful, the vegetables in this soup glow like jewels in a bowl. Caraway seeds add an authentic Eastern European touch to the broth.

1 tbsp	vegetable oil	15 mL
1	each large onion and carrot, chopped	1
2	stalks celery, chopped	2
1	bay leaf	1
Pinch	caraway seeds	Pinch
4	beets (with leaves)	4
2	large red-skinned potatoes	2

4 cups	beef, chicken or vegetable broth	1 L
1	can (19 oz/540 mL) tomatoes, chopped	1
4 tsp	white vinegar	20 mL
Pinch	each salt and pepper	Pinch
¼ cup	light sour cream	50 mL
2 tbsp	chopped fresh dill	30 mL

4½- to 6-quart (4.5 to 6 L) slow cooker

Makes 6 servings

TEST KITCHEN TIPS

Choose round, red-skinned waxy potatoes because they will stay in neat cubes.

Serve with lemon wedges to squeeze over top.

◞ In large skillet, heat oil over medium heat; fry onion, carrot, celery, bay leaf and caraway seeds, stirring often, until vegetables are softened, about 10 minutes. Scrape into slow cooker.

◞ Meanwhile, trim stalks from beets. Coarsely chop enough of the most tender leaves to make 2 cups (500 mL); set aside.

◞ Peel and cube beets. Peel potatoes, if desired; cut into cubes. Add beets, potatoes, broth and tomatoes to slow cooker. Stir to combine.

◞ Cover and cook on low until vegetables are tender, about 5 to 6 hours. (Make-ahead: Let cool for 30 minutes. Refrigerate, uncovered, in airtight containers until cold. Cover and refrigerate for up to 1 day.)

◞ Stir in reserved beet greens, vinegar, salt and pepper. Cover and cook on high until greens are wilted, about 15 minutes. Discard bay leaf. Garnish each bowlful with sour cream; sprinkle with dill.

PER SERVING: about 153 cal, 6 g pro, 4 g total fat (1 g sat. fat), 26 g carb, 4 g fibre, 1 mg chol, 754 mg sodium. % RDI: 8% calcium, 14% iron, 48% vit A, 37% vit C, 26% folate.

Carrot Potage

Taste buds love this soup's blend of sweet from the carrots, salty from the blue cheese and slightly bitter from the rutabaga (a.k.a. turnip).

4½- to 6-quart (4.5 to 6 L)
slow cooker

Makes 6 servings

1 tbsp	each extra-virgin olive oil and butter	15 mL
1	large onion, chopped	1
1	large clove garlic, sliced	1
½ tsp	each salt and pepper	2 mL
4 cups	chopped carrots (4 large)	1 L
2 cups	chopped potatoes (about 2)	500 mL
2 cups	cubed peeled rutabaga (one-quarter large)	500 mL
2 cups	sodium-reduced chicken broth (approx)	500 mL
2	bay leaves	2
¼ tsp	dried marjoram or thyme	1 mL
4 oz	crumbled blue cheese	125 g
2 tbsp	minced fresh chives or parsley	30 mL

In large skillet, heat oil and butter over medium heat; fry onion, garlic, salt and pepper, stirring occasionally, until softened, about 5 minutes.

Scrape into slow cooker along with carrots, potatoes, rutabaga, broth, bay leaves, marjoram and 4 cups (1 L) water. Stir to combine.

Cover and cook on low until vegetables are tender, about 4 to 6 hours.

Discard bay leaves. Using immersion blender, or in stand blender in batches, purée soup until smooth. Add up to 1 cup (250 mL) more broth or water, if desired, for thinner consistency. (Make-ahead: Let cool for 30 minutes. Refrigerate, uncovered, in airtight containers until cold. Cover and refrigerate for up to 2 days or freeze for up to 1 month.)

Ladle into bowls. Sprinkle with cheese and chives.

PER SERVING: about 190 cal, 7 g pro, 10 g total fat (5 g sat. fat), 20 g carb, 3 g fibre, 19 mg chol, 723 mg sodium. % RDI: 13% calcium, 4% iron, 135% vit A, 17% vit C, 12% folate.

Roasted Sweet Potato Soup

4½- to 6-quart (4.5 to 6 L)
slow cooker

Makes 8 servings

Roasting heightens the rich earthiness of sweet potatoes, which, by the way, are in the same calorie ballpark as white potatoes. The rosemary oil garnish adds a chef-like touch, but it can be left out and everyone will still enjoy the soup.

2	large sweet potatoes (2 lb/1 kg)	2
2 tbsp	extra-virgin olive oil	30 mL
½ tsp	salt	2 mL
1	small onion, chopped	1
1	each carrot and stalk celery, chopped	1
2	cloves garlic, minced	2
1 tsp	chopped fresh rosemary (or ¼ tsp/ 1 mL dried)	5 mL

¼ tsp	pepper	1 mL
2 cups	Homemade Chicken Broth (recipe, page 71) or sodium-reduced chicken broth	500 mL
1 tbsp	lemon juice (optional)	15 mL
8	small sprigs fresh rosemary	8
ROSEMARY OIL:		
¼ cup	extra-virgin olive oil	50 mL
2 tbsp	fresh rosemary leaves	30 mL

❧ Peel and cube sweet potatoes; toss with half each of the oil and salt. Arrange in single layer on greased rimmed baking sheet. Roast in 450°F (230°C) oven, stirring occasionally, until tender, about 20 minutes. Scrape into slow cooker.

❧ Meanwhile, in skillet, heat remaining oil over medium heat; fry onion, carrot, celery, garlic, chopped rosemary, pepper and remaining salt until vegetables are softened, about 8 minutes. Scrape into slow cooker along with broth and 3 cups (750 mL) water. Stir to combine.

❧ Cover and cook on low until vegetables are tender, about 3 to 4 hours.

❧ **ROSEMARY OIL:** Meanwhile, in small saucepan, heat oil and rosemary leaves over medium-high heat just until fragrant, about 3 minutes. Strain through fine sieve into small bowl. (Make-ahead: Refrigerate in airtight container for up to 3 days.)

❧ Stir lemon juice (if using) into soup. Using immersion blender, or in stand blender in batches, purée soup until smooth. (Make-ahead: Let cool for 30 minutes. Refrigerate, uncovered, in airtight containers until cold. Cover and refrigerate for up to 3 days or freeze for up to 1 month.)

❧ Ladle into bowls; garnish with drizzle of rosemary oil and rosemary sprig.

PER SERVING: about 111 cal, 3 g pro, 4 g total fat (1 g sat. fat), 16 g carb, trace fibre, 0 mg chol, 194 mg sodium. % RDI: 4% calcium, 7% iron, 157% vit A, 22% vit C, 6% folate.

Creamy Butternut Squash Soup with Pepper Paint

It's a large potato that gives this soup body and creaminess. For a particularly silky bowlful, strain the puréed soup through a fine sieve after puréeing.

4½- to 6-quart (4.5 to 6 L) slow cooker

Makes 6 servings

2 tbsp	butter	30 mL	4 cups	vegetable or chicken broth	1 L
1	large onion, chopped	1	1	large potato, peeled and thinly sliced	1
3	cloves garlic, minced	3	2 tbsp	tomato paste	30 mL
1 tbsp	mild curry paste	15 mL	⅓ cup	milk or 10% cream	75 mL
2 tsp	minced gingerroot	10 mL	2 tbsp	lemon juice	30 mL
½ tsp	each salt and pepper	2 mL	**RED PEPPER PAINT:**		
5 cups	cubed peeled butternut squash (half large)	1.25 L	2	sweet red peppers	2

RED PEPPER PAINT: On rimmed baking sheet, broil red peppers, turning twice, until charred, about 20 minutes. Let cool. Peel and seed peppers; purée in blender or food processor until smooth. Strain through fine sieve. Set aside. (Make-ahead: Cover and refrigerate for up to 2 days.)

In large skillet, melt butter over medium heat; fry onion, garlic, curry paste, ginger, salt and pepper, stirring, until onion is softened, about 5 minutes. Add squash; stir until coated. Scrape into slow cooker.

Add 1 cup (250 mL) of the broth to skillet; bring to boil, scraping up any brown bits from bottom of skillet. Scrape into slow cooker along with remaining broth, potato and tomato paste. Stir to combine.

Cover and cook on low until vegetables are tender, about 5 to 6 hours. Stir in cream and lemon juice.

Using immersion blender, or in stand blender in batches, purée soup until smooth. (Make-ahead: Let cool for 30 minutes. Refrigerate, uncovered, in airtight containers until cold. Cover and refrigerate for up to 3 days or freeze for up to 1 month.)

Ladle soup into bowls. Using small spoon, drop Red Pepper Paint decoratively in centre of each bowl. Using toothpick or skewer, drag through drops to make swirls.

PER SERVING: about 158 cal, 4 g pro, 5 g total fat (3 g sat. fat), 28 g carb, 4 g fibre, 11 mg chol, 669 mg sodium. % RDI: 8% calcium, 11% iron, 109% vit A, 142% vit C, 17% folate.

SUBSTITUTION

No matter what chicken broth — regular or sodium-reduced — is called for in our soup recipes, you can always substitute Homemade Chicken Broth (recipe, page 71).

Spinach Ravioli Soup

4½- to 5½-quart (4.5 to 5.5 L) slow cooker

Makes 4 servings

SUBSTITUTION

You can replace the homemade vegetable broth with 6 cups (1.5 L) store-bought. Look for sodium-reduced versions.

The broth base uses vegetables – such as carrots and celery – that are constants in the crisper. Before they get limp and past their prime, get them into a slow cooker. The dried mushrooms really deepen the flavour, but you can use a few leftover fresh mushrooms instead.

1	pkg (454 g) frozen cheese ravioli	1	2	onions (unpeeled), chopped	2
2 cups	packed fresh spinach, coarsely chopped	500 mL	1	fresh or canned plum tomato	1
1 cup	frozen peas	250 mL	3	cloves garlic, halved	3
1 cup	thinly sliced mushrooms	250 mL	1	pkg (14 g) dried mixed mushrooms	1
¼ tsp	salt	1 mL	¼ tsp	each salt and black peppercorns	1 mL
VEGETABLE BROTH:			2	bay leaves	2
2	each carrots and stalks celery, chopped	2			

❧ **VEGETABLE BROTH:** In slow cooker, combine carrots, celery, onions, tomato, garlic, dried mushrooms, salt, peppercorns, bay leaves and 7 cups (1.75 L) water.

❧ Cover and cook on low until flavourful and vegetables are soft, about 6 to 8 hours. Strain into clean saucepan, pressing vegetables to extract liquid. (Make-ahead: Let cool for 30 minutes. Refrigerate, uncovered, in airtight containers until cold. Cover and refrigerate for up to 3 days or freeze for up to 1 month.)

❧ Bring broth to boil over medium-high heat. Add ravioli; simmer for 2 minutes. Stir in spinach, peas, mushrooms and salt; simmer until spinach is wilted and ravioli are hot, about 2 minutes.

PER SERVING: about 322 cal, 13 g pro, 7 g total fat (trace sat. fat), 53 g carb, 4 g fibre, 25 mg chol, 511 mg sodium. % RDI: 6% calcium, 25% iron, 22% vit A, 8% vit C, 65% folate.

Chunky Mushroom Soup

4½- to 5-quart (4.5 to 5 L)
slow cooker

Makes 4 servings

Exotic mushrooms – cremini, oyster or, the most woodsy, shiitake – provide a stylish flourish to this fine soup. You can use all of one variety or a combination. Because the tough stems of shiitakes don't soften during cooking, leave them out. To get an accurate measure, remove the stems before slicing and measuring.

2 tbsp	vegetable oil	30 mL	½ tsp	dried thyme	2 mL
2	onions, finely chopped	2	¼ tsp	each paprika and pepper	1 mL
2	cloves garlic, minced	2	5 cups	vegetable or chicken broth	1.25 L
2	carrots, finely chopped	2	1	potato, peeled and grated	1
4 cups	sliced exotic mushrooms (about 12 oz/375 g)	1 L	2 tbsp	sherry	30 mL
3 cups	sliced button mushrooms (about 8 oz/250 g)	750 mL			

➤ In large skillet, heat oil over medium heat; fry onions, garlic and carrots, stirring occasionally, until vegetables are softened, about 5 minutes.

➤ Stir in exotic and button mushrooms, thyme, paprika and pepper; cook, stirring often, until no liquid remains, about 10 minutes. Scrape into slow cooker.

➤ Add 1 cup (250 mL) of the broth to skillet; bring to boil, scraping up brown bits from bottom of skillet. Scrape into slow cooker along with remaining broth and potato. Stir to combine.

➤ Cover and cook on low until vegetables are tender and liquid is slightly thickened, about 6 hours. (Make-ahead: Let cool for 30 minutes. Refrigerate, uncovered, in airtight containers until cold. Cover and refrigerate for up to 3 days.)

➤ Stir in sherry.

PER SERVING: about 183 cal, 4 g pro, 8 g total fat (1 g sat. fat), 24 g carb, 4 g fibre, 0 mg chol, 816 mg sodium. % RDI: 4% calcium, 17% iron, 92% vit A, 17% vit C, 15% folate.

Tomato Pepper Soup

One of the most appealing aspects of a dish is its contrasting textures. In this case, add a garnish of crunchy crumbled tortilla chips atop the smooth scarlet soup. This is a fun soup to serve before dinner, shooter-style.

4- to 5½-quart (4 to 5.5 L) slow cooker

Makes 8 to 10 servings

1	can (28 oz/796 mL) tomatoes	1	4 cups	chicken or vegetable broth	1 L
1	large onion, chopped	1	2 tbsp	tomato paste	30 mL
1	roasted red pepper, peeled, stemmed and seeded	1	1 tbsp	chili powder	15 mL
			¼ tsp	salt	1 mL
3	cloves garlic	3	1	jalapeño pepper, stemmed and seeded	1

➤ In slow cooker, combine tomatoes, onion, red pepper, garlic, broth, tomato paste, chili powder and salt.

➤ Cover and cook on low until onion is tender, about 6 hours. Add jalapeño pepper. Cover and cook on high until tender, about 15 minutes.

➤ Using immersion blender, or in stand blender in batches, purée soup until smooth. (Make-ahead: Let cool for 30 minutes. Refrigerate, uncovered, in airtight containers until cold. Cover and refrigerate for up to 3 days or freeze for up to 1 month.)

PER EACH OF 10 SERVINGS: about 45 cal, 3 g pro, 1 g total fat (trace sat. fat), 7 g carb, 1 g fibre, 0 mg chol, 515 mg sodium. % RDI: 3% calcium, 6% iron, 12% vit A, 48% vit C, 5% folate.

TEST KITCHEN TIP
Not sure how to roast a pepper? Turn to the recipe for Creamy Butternut Squash Soup with Pepper Paint (page 59) for how-tos. Or skip the roasting process by using jarred roasted whole red peppers available in supermarkets.

Fresh Soup Garnishes

Right before serving, top your soup with one of these fresh flavour hits.
➤ Shredded carrot, thinly sliced green onion or slivers of brightly coloured sweet pepper

➤ Chopped fresh herbs of any kind, such as parsley, basil, thyme, oregano, coriander, dill or sage, that match the flavours in the soup
➤ Thin slices or wedges of lemon, lime or other citrus fruit

Harira

This is the traditional soup that's typically served at day's end during Ramadan, a time of prayer and piety for Muslims. It's deliciously satisfying.

5- to 6-quart (5 to 6 L)
slow cooker

Makes 8 servings

1 tbsp	extra-virgin olive oil	15 mL
2	small onions, chopped	2
1 tsp	each ground cumin, ground ginger, turmeric and pepper	5 mL
6 cups	chicken or vegetable broth	1.5 L
1	each large bunch fresh coriander and parsley	1
1	cinnamon stick	1
1 cup	green or brown lentils	250 mL
1	can (19 oz/540 mL) chickpeas, drained and rinsed (or 2 cups/500 mL cooked chickpeas; recipe, page 213)	1
1	can (28 oz/796 mL) diced tomatoes	1
¼ cup	lemon juice	50 mL

GARNISH:

1 tsp	ground cinnamon	5 mL
1	lemon, thinly sliced	1
12	pitted dates, halved	12

TEST KITCHEN TIP
Look for plump loose dates, such as Medjool. If they're not already pitted, slit from end to end and lift out the pit.

In large skillet, heat oil over medium heat; fry onions, stirring occasionally, until softened, about 5 minutes. Add cumin, ginger, turmeric and pepper; fry, stirring, for 1 minute. Scrape into slow cooker.

Pour 1 cup (250 mL) of the broth into skillet; bring to boil, scraping up brown bits from bottom of skillet. Scrape into slow cooker.

Chop enough of the coriander and parsley to make ¼ cup (50 mL) each; set aside. Tie together remaining coriander, parsley and cinnamon stick; add to slow cooker along with remaining broth, lentils, chickpeas and tomatoes. Stir to combine.

Cover and cook on low until vegetables are tender, about 6 hours. Discard herb bundle. Stir in lemon juice and reserved chopped herbs. (Make-ahead: Let cool for 30 minutes. Refrigerate, uncovered, in airtight containers until cold. Cover and refrigerate for up to 3 days or freeze for up to 1 month.)

GARNISH: Ladle soup into bowls. Sprinkle with cinnamon; top with lemon slices and dates.

PER SERVING: about 257 cal, 14 g pro, 4 g total fat (1 g sat. fat), 44 g carb, 8 g fibre, 0 mg chol, 876 mg sodium. % RDI: 8% calcium, 34% iron, 7% vit A, 38% vit C, 79% folate.

Three-Bean & Lentil Soup

A trio of beans, supplemented by red lentils – the kind that soften and smooth out when cooked – make this soup a powerhouse of healthy eating. FYI, a bowlful provides about one-third of your day's fibre needs. It's reassuring to know that the soup also scores high on taste.

4½- to 6-quart (4.5 to 6 L)
slow cooker

Makes 10 servings

SUBSTITUTION

For each of the cans of chickpeas and beans, you can substitute 2 cups (500 mL) cooked beans (recipe, page 213).

2	onions, chopped	2	1	can (19 oz/540 mL) red kidney beans, drained and rinsed	1
2	cloves garlic, minced	2	1	can (19 oz/540 mL) black beans, drained and rinsed	1
4 tsp	mild curry paste	20 mL			
1 tbsp	minced gingerroot	15 mL	1 tbsp	chopped fresh coriander or parsley	15 mL
1	can (28 oz/796 mL) tomatoes	1			
6 cups	vegetable or chicken broth	1.5 L	1 tsp	lemon juice	5 mL
			½ tsp	salt	2 mL
¾ cup	red lentils	175 mL	¼ tsp	pepper	1 mL
1	can (19 oz/540 mL) chickpeas, drained and rinsed	1			

↜ In slow cooker, combine onions, garlic, curry paste, ginger, tomatoes, broth, 2 cups (500 mL) water and lentils.

↜ Cover and cook on low until thickened, about 8 hours. Stir in chickpeas, and kidney and black beans.

↜ Cover and cook on high until hot, about 30 minutes. (Make-ahead: Let cool for 30 minutes. Refrigerate, uncovered, in airtight containers until cold. Cover and refrigerate for up to 3 days or freeze for up to 1 month.)

↜ Stir in coriander, lemon juice, salt and pepper.

PER SERVING: about 246 cal, 14 g pro, 4 g total fat (trace sat. fat), 41 g carb, 10 g fibre, 0 mg chol, 922 mg sodium. % RDI: 6% calcium, 26% iron, 5% vit A, 18% vit C, 80% folate.

VARIATION

Chili Three-Bean and Lentil Soup: Substitute 1 tbsp (15 mL) chili powder for the ginger and curry paste. Try substituting ancho chili powder for some of the regular chili powder. It is now available among regular supermarket bottled spices.

Barley Lentil Soup

This soup is a stellar warm-up on a chilly day – and we get plenty of them in the fall, winter and even far into the Canadian spring. Omit the yogurt garnish and you have a superb vegan soup.

4½- to 5½-quart (4.5 to 5.5 L) slow cooker

Makes 4 to 6 servings

1 tbsp	vegetable oil	15 mL
1	onion, chopped	1
2	cloves garlic, minced	2
1	each large carrot and stalk celery, chopped	1
2 tsp	dried thyme	10 mL
1 tsp	each salt and pepper	5 mL
4 cups	vegetable broth	1 L

1 cup	brown or green lentils	250 mL
¼ cup	pot or pearl barley	50 mL
¼ cup	chopped fresh parsley	50 mL
TOPPING:		
¼ cup	low-fat plain yogurt	50 mL
1 tbsp	minced fresh parsley	15 mL

In large skillet, heat oil over medium heat; fry onion, garlic, carrot, celery, thyme, salt and pepper, stirring occasionally, until vegetables are softened, about 5 minutes. Scrape into slow cooker along with broth, 2 cups (500 mL) water, lentils and barley. Stir to combine.

Cover and cook on low until lentils and barley are tender, about 6 to 7 hours. (Make-ahead: Let cool for 30 minutes. Refrigerate, uncovered, in airtight containers until cold. Cover and refrigerate for up to 3 days or freeze for up to 1 month.) Stir in parsley.

TOPPING: Top each serving with yogurt; sprinkle with parsley.

PER EACH OF 6 SERVINGS: about 191 cal, 11 g pro, 3 g total fat (trace sat. fat), 34 g carb, 6 g fibre, 4 mg chol, 918 mg sodium. % RDI: 6% calcium, 31% iron, 32% vit A, 12% vit C, 84% folate.

Creamy Toppings for Soup

Sometimes soups call out for a dab of something rich and creamy on top. Try these delightful dairy garnishes.
> Tangy plain yogurt or sour cream
> Light cream or milk, swirled in a pretty pattern
> Mayonnaise seasoned with chili powder, lemon, paprika, grainy mustard or curry paste
> Shredded Asiago, Cheddar, Havarti, Gouda or any favourite firm cheese
> A spoonful of soft goat cheese or a thin slice of a slightly firmer log of goat cheese

Lemon Lentil Soup

Lemons are often used in Mediterranean cooking to give a fresh edge to lentil dishes. The lentils and kale make this soup a nutritional powerhouse, and tasty, too!

4½- to 5½-quart (4.5 to 5.5 L) slow cooker

Makes 4 to 6 servings

1	large onion, diced	1	3 cups	vegetable broth	750 mL
2	each carrots and stalks celery, thinly sliced	2	3 cups	chopped kale or spinach	750 mL
¾ cup	green or brown lentils	175 mL	2 tbsp	lemon juice	30 mL
½ tsp	dried oregano	2 mL	Dash	hot pepper sauce	Dash
1	bay leaf	1		Lemon wedges (optional)	
¼ tsp	salt	1 mL			

❧ In slow cooker, combine onion, carrots, celery, lentils, oregano, bay leaf and salt; stir in broth and 3 cups (750 mL) water.

❧ Cover and cook on low until lentils and vegetables are tender, about 5 to 7 hours.

❧ Add kale; cover and cook on high until wilted, about 20 minutes. (Make-ahead: Let cool for 30 minutes. Refrigerate, uncovered, in airtight containers until cold. Cover and refrigerate for up to 3 days.)

❧ Discard bay leaf. Stir in lemon juice and hot pepper sauce. Serve with lemon wedges (if using).

PER EACH OF 6 SERVINGS: about 128 cal, 8 g pro, 1 g total fat (trace sat. fat), 24 g carb, 5 g fibre, 0 mg chol, 418 mg sodium. % RDI: 8% calcium, 23% iron, 92% vit A, 67% vit C, 66% folate.

Turkey Broth

5½- to 6-quart (5.5 to 6 L)
slow cooker

Makes 8 cups (2 L)

Turkey soups often taste flat because the carcass for the broth, the basis for a good turkey soup, sits far too long in the refrigerator. To remedy this, remove all the meat right after a turkey dinner. Package and refrigerate the carcass and meat separately. Make broth early the next day, the easy way, in the slow cooker. You'll taste the dramatic difference in flavour.

2	onions (unpeeled), chopped	2	6	sprigs parsley	6
2	large stalks celery (with leaves), chopped	2	1	bay leaf	1
1	carrot, chopped	1	1 tsp	each salt and black peppercorns	5 mL
1 cup	sliced mushrooms	250 mL	1	cooked turkey carcass, broken into pieces	1
1	fresh or canned tomato, quartered	1	1	turkey neck, cooked or uncooked	1
2	cloves garlic (unpeeled), smashed	2			

SUBSTITUTION

To make Turkey Broth year-round, replace the carcass and neck with 3 lb (1.5 kg) uncooked turkey wings, which are available packaged in the supermarket.

❧ Place onions, celery, carrot, mushrooms, tomato, garlic, parsley, bay leaf, salt and peppercorns in slow cooker. Add turkey carcass and neck, arranging to fit. Pour in 8 cups (2 L) cold water.

❧ Cover and cook on low for 12 hours. Discard turkey carcass and neck. Strain broth through cheesecloth-lined sieve into large bowl, pressing vegetables to extract liquid.

❧ Let cool for 30 minutes. Refrigerate, uncovered, until fat hardens on surface, about 8 hours. Lift off and discard fat. (Make-ahead: Refrigerate in airtight containers for up to 3 days or freeze for up to 1 month.)

PER 1 CUP (250 mL): about 39 cal, 5 g pro, 1 g total fat (trace sat. fat), 1 g carb, 0 g fibre, 1 mg chol, 318 mg sodium. % RDI: 1% calcium, 4% iron, 2% folate.

Homemade Chicken Broth

While you can use the broth right after it has been strained, you need to skim off the fat. A far easier way to remove the fat is to refrigerate the broth until the fat hardens on top. It's easy to lift right off.

5½- to 6-quart (5.5 to 6 L) slow cooker

Makes 8 cups (2 L)

1	stewing hen (or 3 lb/ 1.5 kg chicken backs and necks)	1	1 cup	sliced mushrooms	250 mL
3	carrots (unpeeled), coarsely chopped	3	3	cloves garlic, smashed	3
3	onions (unpeeled), coarsely chopped	3	10	sprigs fresh parsley	10
3	stalks celery with leaves, coarsely chopped	3	½ tsp	dried thyme	2 mL
			½ tsp	black peppercorns	2 mL
			2	bay leaves	2

➤ Place hen in slow cooker. Add carrots, onions, celery, mushrooms, garlic, parsley, thyme, peppercorns and bay leaves. Pour in 8 cups (2 L) cold water.

➤ Cover and cook on low until richly flavoured, about 8 to 10 hours.

➤ Discard hen. Strain broth through cheesecloth-lined sieve into large bowl, pressing vegetables to extract liquid. Let cool for 30 minutes. Refrigerate, uncovered, until fat hardens on surface, about 8 hours. Lift off and discard fat. (Make-ahead: Refrigerate in airtight containers for up to 3 days or freeze for up to 1 month.)

PER 1 CUP (250 ML): about 39 cal, 5 g pro, 1 g total fat (trace sat. fat), 1 g carb, 0 g fibre, 1 mg chol, 32 mg sodium. % RDI: 1% calcium, 4% iron, 2% folate.

TEST KITCHEN TIP

While it is tempting and thrifty to use the meat from the hen for another dish, the whole point of making broth is to extract the flavour from the meat. What's left of the hen or chicken parts is flavourless and dry.

VARIATION

Homemade Vegetable Broth: Substitute 3 fresh or canned whole tomatoes for the hen.

Stews, Chilis & Curries

Boeuf Bourguignon

There's always room in a cook's repertoire for a really good stew – and that's what Boeuf Bourguignon is. For company's-coming occasions, serve in split popovers or simply with rolls or crusty baguette.

5- to 6-quart (5 to 6 L) slow cooker

Makes 8 servings

TEST KITCHEN TIPS

The secret to meltingly tender beef is all in getting the right cut: a well-marbled cross rib pot roast.

The tied bay leaf, parsley and thyme sprigs are called a bouquet garni, a classic French flavouring trio.

1	pkg (14 g) dried porcini, morel or shiitake mushrooms	1
3 lb	boneless beef cross rib pot roast	1.5 kg
4 oz	thickly sliced bacon, chopped	125 g
3 tbsp	vegetable oil	45 mL
1	onion, chopped	1
1	large carrot, chopped	1
2	cloves garlic, minced	2
½ tsp	each salt and pepper	2 mL
1½ cups	red wine	375 mL
½ cup	beef broth	125 mL
3	sprigs fresh parsley	3
2	sprigs fresh thyme	2
2	bay leaves	2
2 cups	pearl onions (one 10-oz/284 g pkg)	500 mL
1 tbsp	butter	15 mL
3 cups	button mushrooms (8 oz/250 g)	750 mL
2 tbsp	brandy	30 mL
⅓ cup	all-purpose flour	75 mL
2 tbsp	minced fresh parsley	30 mL

↜ Soak dried mushrooms in ½ cup (125 mL) hot water for 30 minutes. Meanwhile, trim beef and cut into 1½-inch (4 cm) cubes. Set aside.

↜ In large skillet, sauté bacon over medium-high heat until crisp; transfer to slow cooker.

↜ Drain fat from skillet. Add 1 tbsp (15 mL) of the oil; brown beef, in batches and adding remaining oil as necessary. Add to slow cooker.

↜ Drain fat from skillet. Fry chopped onion, carrot, garlic, salt and pepper over medium heat until softened, about 3 minutes. Reserving soaking liquid, drain mushrooms and chop; add to skillet along with soaking liquid, wine and broth. Bring to boil, scraping up brown bits from bottom of skillet. Scrape into slow cooker.

↜ Tie parsley, thyme and bay leaves together with string; add to slow cooker.

↜ In pot of boiling water, boil pearl onions for 1 minute; drain and chill in cold water. Peel and trim, leaving root ends intact. In skillet, melt butter over medium heat; brown pearl onions, about 5 minutes. With slotted spoon, transfer to slow cooker. Set skillet with remaining butter aside.

>

~ Cover and cook on low until beef is fork-tender, about 6 to 8 hours. Skim off any fat.

~ In skillet with remaining butter, sauté button mushrooms over medium-high heat until browned, about 5 minutes. Scrape into slow cooker along with brandy. Move meat and vegetables to 1 side of slow cooker. Discard herbs.

~ Whisk flour with ½ cup (125 mL) water; whisk into liquid in slow cooker. Stir to redistribute ingredients.

~ Cover and cook on high until thickened, about 15 minutes. (Make-ahead: Let cool for 30 minutes. Refrigerate, uncovered, in airtight containers until cold. Cover and refrigerate for up to 3 days or freeze for up to 1 month.)

~ Sprinkle with parsley.

PER SERVING: about 398 cal, 40 g pro, 20 g total fat (6 g sat. fat), 12 g carb, 2 g fibre, 91 mg chol, 390 mg sodium. % RDI: 3% calcium, 29% iron, 30% vit A, 7% vit C, 15% folate.

Potato Primer

Unlike apples, where consumers can choose between a Mac to eat out of hand or a Spy to bake, potatoes aren't usually labelled with variety names. So which potato should you use in the slow cooker? Here are some guidelines.

> **LONG:** These "baking potatoes" are high-starch, with a dry, fluffy texture. Excellent for baking and fries, they're the slow cooker choice for mashing. They're also great at thickening and adding body to soups. Long potatoes have white interiors and skins that range from brown and rough to buff-colour and smooth.

> **ROUND OR OVAL:** You'll find these under the name "all-purpose." Lower in starch, these round or oval spuds are firm and waxy – ideal for slow cooker soups, pot roasts and stews where distinct cubes or chunks are needed. The skins can be light, buff-colour or red, with white or yellow flesh, depending on the variety.

> **NEW POTATOES:** These petite spuds are harvested immature or bred for size and come in a rainbow of colours. Their solid texture works well in stews or pot roasts. They're also lovely as a side dish, simply cooked with a little broth, seasoning and olive oil.

Beef Stew with Pan-Roasted Garlic

It takes longer to pan-roast garlic for this aromatic stew, but it's time tastily spent.

4½- to 6-quart (4.5 to 6 L) slow cooker

Makes 8 servings

12	cloves garlic, peeled	12
2 tbsp	vegetable oil	30 mL
2	each carrots, parsnips and Yukon Gold potatoes	2
1½ lb	stewing beef cubes	750 g
½ tsp	each salt and pepper	2 mL
1	onion, chopped	1
1½ tsp	each dried thyme and sage	7 mL
1½ cups	sodium-reduced beef broth	375 mL
1 cup	red wine or beef broth	250 mL
¼ cup	tomato paste	50 mL
1 cup	frozen peas	250 mL
¼ cup	chopped fresh parsley	50 mL

SHORTCUT
If time is short, substitute raw garlic for the pan-roasted.

➤ In small saucepan, cover and fry garlic in oil over low heat, shaking pan occasionally, until softened and golden, about 30 minutes. With slotted spoon, transfer garlic to plate; drain and reserve oil.

➤ Meanwhile, peel carrots, parsnips and potatoes; cut into 1-inch (2.5 cm) chunks. Add to slow cooker; top with garlic.

➤ Season beef with salt and pepper. In large skillet, heat 1 tbsp (15 mL) of the reserved oil over medium-high heat; brown beef, in batches. Transfer to slow cooker.

➤ Drain fat from skillet; add remaining reserved oil. Fry onion and 1 tsp (5 mL) each of the thyme and sage over medium heat, stirring occasionally, until light golden, about 5 minutes. Scrape into slow cooker.

➤ Add broth, wine and tomato paste to skillet; bring to boil, scraping up brown bits from bottom of skillet. Scrape into slow cooker. Stir to combine.

➤ Cover and cook on low until beef and vegetables are tender, about 6 to 8 hours. (Make-ahead: Let cool for 30 minutes. Refrigerate, uncovered, in airtight containers until cold. Cover and refrigerate for up to 3 days.)

➤ Stir in peas and remaining thyme and sage; cover and cook on high until steaming hot, about 10 minutes. Sprinkle with parsley.

PER SERVING: about 275 cal, 22 g pro, 10 g total fat (3 g sat. fat), 24 g carb, 4 g fibre, 42 mg chol, 355 mg sodium. % RDI: 5% calcium, 24% iron, 38% vit A, 27% vit C, 23% folate.

Soy-Braised Beef

Dishes like this one belong to the family of Chinese dishes called "red cooked." Thick, dark soy sauce gives the dish its vibrant flavour and colour.

5- to 6-quart (5 to 6 L) slow cooker

Makes 6 to 8 servings

3 lb	boneless beef cross rib pot roast	1.5 kg	1/3 cup	dark soy sauce	75 mL
4	each carrots and green onions	4	2 tbsp	rice wine or dry sherry	30 mL
2	whole star anise	2	1 tsp	granulated sugar	5 mL
1 tsp	peppercorns	5 mL	1	can (28 oz/796 mL) tomatoes, coarsely chopped	1
1	piece (2 inches/5 cm) cinnamon stick, broken	1	1 tbsp	cornstarch	15 mL
1	piece (1½ inches/4 cm) gingerroot, sliced	1	1 tbsp	Chinese black vinegar or balsamic vinegar	15 mL
3	cloves garlic	3	2 tsp	grated orange rind	10 mL

❧ Cut beef and carrots into 2-inch (5 cm) chunks. Place in slow cooker. Thinly slice white parts of green onions; add to slow cooker. Slice green parts into ½-inch (1 cm) lengths; set aside.

❧ In 7-inch (18 cm) square cheesecloth, tie star anise, peppercorns, cinnamon stick and ginger to form bag. Add to slow cooker with garlic, soy sauce, rice wine, sugar, tomatoes and ¼ cup (50 mL) water. Stir to combine.

❧ Cover and cook on low until beef is tender, about 5 to 6 hours. Discard spice bag. Move meat to 1 side of slow cooker.

❧ In small bowl, whisk cornstarch with ¼ cup (50 mL) water; whisk into liquid in slow cooker. Stir to redistribute ingredients.

❧ Cover and cook on high until thickened, about 10 minutes. (Make-ahead: Let cool for 30 minutes. Refrigerate, uncovered, in airtight containers until cold. Cover and refrigerate for up to 3 days or freeze for up to 1 month.)

❧ Stir in vinegar and orange rind; sprinkle with green parts of onions.

PER EACH OF 8 SERVINGS: about 361 cal, 37 g pro, 18 g total fat (7 g sat. fat), 11 g carb, 2 g fibre, 90 mg chol, 858 mg sodium. % RDI: 6% calcium, 35% iron, 66% vit A, 28% vit C, 10% folate.

Greek Stew with Feta

Bold flavours and its crumbled feta cheese topping are the hallmarks of this stew. Look for creamy feta and taste it before buying, if possible, and certainly before using. Some feta cheese is very salty and needs to soak for a few minutes in cold water before topping the stew. Instead of stewing beef, you can also cut up a cross rib pot roast.

5- to 6-quart (5 to 6 L) slow cooker

Makes 6 to 8 servings

3 lb	stewing beef cubes	1.5 kg	2 tbsp	red wine vinegar	30 mL
7	small onions (1½ lb/750 g)	7	2 tsp	dried oregano	10 mL
3	cloves garlic, minced	3	½ tsp	each salt and pepper	2 mL
1	can (28 oz/796 mL) tomatoes	1	½ cup	all-purpose flour	125 mL
½ cup	beef broth	125 mL	1	sweet green pepper, diced	1
1	can (5½ oz/156 mL) tomato paste	1	½ cup	crumbled feta cheese	125 mL
			2 tbsp	minced fresh parsley	30 mL

➤ Trim beef and cut into 1-inch (2.5 cm) cubes; place in slow cooker. Cut onions lengthwise into wedges, leaving root end intact; add to slow cooker along with garlic and tomatoes.

➤ Combine beef broth, tomato paste, vinegar, oregano, salt and pepper; pour into slow cooker. Stir to combine.

➤ Cover and cook on low until beef is tender, about 8 to 9 hours. Skim off any fat. Move beef and vegetables to 1 side of slow cooker.

➤ In small bowl, whisk flour with ½ cup (125 mL) cold water; whisk in ½ cup (125 mL) of the hot liquid. Whisk back into liquid in slow cooker. Stir to redistribute ingredients.

➤ Stir in green pepper; cover and cook on high until thickened, about 10 minutes. (Make-ahead: Omit green pepper until time to reheat. Let cool for 30 minutes. Refrigerate, uncovered, in airtight containers until cold. Cover and refrigerate for up to 3 days or freeze for up to 1 month.) Sprinkle with feta and parsley.

PER EACH OF 8 SERVINGS: about 214 cal, 18 g pro, 6 g total fat (3 g sat. fat), 23 g carb, 4 g fibre, 35 mg chol, 494 mg sodium. % RDI: 9% calcium, 23% iron, 13% vit A, 57% vit C, 14% folate.

TEST KITCHEN TIP
If you prefer a thinner sauce, reduce the amount of flour to ¼ cup (50 mL).

Southwestern Beef Stew

You can treat this chili-inspired stew as a model for pork or lamb. Feel free to replace the lima beans with peas if they're handier or better liked.

5- to 6-quart (5 to 6 L)
slow cooker

Makes 6 to
8 servings

2 lb	stewing beef cubes	1 kg
2 tbsp	vegetable oil	30 mL
2	onions, chopped	2
2 tbsp	chili powder	30 mL
1 tsp	each salt and pepper	5 mL
4	each large carrots and stalks celery, cut in 1-inch (2.5 cm) chunks	4

1 tbsp	each cider vinegar and liquid honey	15 mL
1¾ cups	beef broth	425 mL
⅓ cup	all-purpose flour	75 mL
1½ cups	each frozen corn and lima beans	375 mL

✎ Trim beef and cut into bite-size cubes, if necessary.

✎ In large skillet, heat half of the oil over medium-high heat; brown beef, in batches. Transfer to slow cooker.

✎ Drain fat from skillet; add remaining oil. Fry onions, chili powder, salt and pepper over medium heat, stirring occasionally, until onion is softened, about 4 minutes. Scrape into slow cooker along with carrots, celery, vinegar and honey.

✎ Add 1 cup (250 mL) of the broth to skillet; bring to boil, scraping up brown bits from bottom of skillet. Scrape into slow cooker along with remaining broth. Stir to combine.

✎ Cover and cook on low until beef is tender, about 6 to 8 hours. Skim off any fat. Move beef and vegetables to 1 side of slow cooker.

✎ In small bowl, whisk flour with ½ cup (125 mL) water; whisk into liquid in slow cooker. Stir to redistribute ingredients.

✎ Cover and cook on high until thickened, about 15 minutes. (Make-ahead: Let cool for 30 minutes. Refrigerate, uncovered, in airtight containers until cold. Cover and refrigerate for up to 3 days or freeze for up to 1 month.)

✎ Add corn and lima beans; cover and cook until steaming hot.

PER EACH OF 8 SERVINGS: about 342 cal, 31 g pro, 12 g total fat (3 g sat. fat), 28 g carb, 4 g fibre, 55 mg chol, 596 mg sodium. % RDI: 5% calcium, 29% iron, 119% vit A, 13% vit C, 21% folate.

Braised Beef in Wine

Known as *boeuf en daube*, this is a traditional Provençale dish of chunks of beef marinated in wine and braised in a sealed casserole. The slow cooker approximates the gentle cooking of this method. And, speaking of cooking traditions, the optional but highly recommended pig's foot (trotter) gives the sauce extra body by adding natural gelatin. Ask the butcher to halve it lengthwise.

5- to 6-quart (5 to 6 L)
slow cooker

Makes 6 to
8 servings

3 lb	boneless beef cross rib pot roast	1.5 kg	4	thick slices lean bacon, coarsely chopped	4
1	pig's foot, halved (optional)	1	2 cups	halved mushrooms	500 mL
1¼ cups	dry red or white wine	300 mL	2 cups	thickly sliced carrots	500 mL
2 tsp	dried thyme	10 mL	2	onions, chopped	2
½ tsp	each salt and pepper	2 mL	4	cloves garlic, minced	4
1	can (28 oz/796 mL) tomatoes	1	¼ cup	tomato paste	50 mL
			½ cup	chopped fresh parsley	125 mL
			2 tsp	grated orange rind	10 mL

❧ Cut beef into 8 chunks; place in glass bowl. Add pig's foot (if using), wine, thyme, salt and pepper; mix well. Cover and marinate in refrigerator for 24 hours, turning occasionally.

❧ Drain tomatoes, reserving juice for another use, such as soup. Halve tomatoes; squeeze out seeds. Add seeded tomatoes to slow cooker along with bacon, mushrooms, carrots, onions and garlic. Stir to combine.

❧ With slotted spoon, transfer beef and pig's foot to slow cooker. Mix tomato paste into marinade; pour into slow cooker. Stir to combine.

❧ Cover and cook on low until beef is tender, about 5 to 6 hours. Skim off fat. (Make-ahead: Let cool for 30 minutes. Refrigerate, uncovered, in airtight containers until cold. Cover and refrigerate for up to 3 days or freeze for up to 1 month.)

❧ Stir in parsley and orange rind.

PER EACH OF 8 SERVINGS: about 427 cal, 39 g pro, 24 g total fat (11 g sat. fat), 12 g carb, 3 g fibre, 100 mg chol, 458 mg sodium. % RDI: 6% calcium, 39% iron, 53% vit A, 30% vit C, 13% folate.

Jamaican Beef Pepper Pot

There are as many variations of this chunky soup as there are kitchens in Jamaica. You may want to add more or less hot pepper sauce, depending on your passion for hot and spicy foods.

4½- to 6-quart (4.5 to 6 L) slow cooker

Makes 8 to 10 servings

2	sweet potatoes, peeled and cubed	2	¼ cup	tomato paste	50 mL
1 tbsp	vegetable oil	15 mL	1 tsp	dried thyme	5 mL
2 lb	stewing beef cubes	1 kg	½ tsp	each salt and pepper	2 mL
6	slices bacon, chopped	6	¼ cup	all-purpose flour	50 mL
2	onions, chopped	2	1	each sweet red and green pepper, chopped	1
4	cloves garlic, minced	4	1 tbsp	wine vinegar	15 mL
6 cups	beef broth	1.5 L	1 tsp	hot pepper sauce	5 mL

❧ Place sweet potatoes in slow cooker.

❧ In large skillet, heat oil over medium-high heat; brown beef, in batches. Add to slow cooker.

❧ Add bacon to skillet; fry over medium heat until crisp, about 5 minutes. Using slotted spoon, transfer to slow cooker.

❧ Drain fat from skillet. Fry onions and garlic, stirring occasionally, until softened, about 5 minutes. Add 1 cup (250 mL) of the broth to skillet; bring to boil, scraping up brown bits from bottom of skillet. Scrape into slow cooker along with remaining broth, 1½ cups (375 mL) water, tomato paste, thyme, salt and pepper. Stir to combine.

❧ Cover and cook on low until beef and potatoes are tender, about 7 to 8 hours. Skim off fat. Move meat and vegetables to 1 side of slow cooker. Whisk flour with ½ cup (125 mL) water; whisk into liquid in slow cooker. Stir in red and green peppers.

❧ Cover and cook on high until thickened, about 15 minutes. Stir in vinegar and hot pepper sauce. (Make-ahead: Let cool for 30 minutes. Refrigerate, uncovered, in airtight containers until cold. Cover and refrigerate for up to 3 days or freeze for up to 1 month.)

PER EACH OF 10 SERVINGS: about 289 cal, 25 g pro, 10 g total fat (3 g sat. fat), 24 g carb, 3 g fibre, 48 mg chol, 715 mg sodium. % RDI: 4% calcium, 22% iron, 149% vit A, 80% vit C, 15% folate.

Beef with Beer & Onions

4½- to 6-quart (4.5 to 6 L)
slow cooker

Makes 8 servings

This stew is known as *carbonnade de boeuf* in Belgium, its country of origin. As it cooks, it fills the kitchen with heady aromas – an invitation to sit down and partake. Carbonnade reheats well, so it's no-fuss party fare. Spoon it over noodles, mashed russet or sweet potatoes, polenta, barley, rice or wild rice.

5	large onions (2 lb/1 kg)	5	1 tsp	crumbled dried thyme	5 mL
3 lb	stewing beef cubes	1.5 kg	½ tsp	each crumbled dried basil, oregano and sage	2 mL
⅓ cup	all-purpose flour	75 mL	1	bay leaf	1
1 tsp	salt	5 mL	1	bottle (12 oz/341 mL) lager beer	1
½ tsp	pepper	2 mL	1 tbsp	Dijon mustard	15 mL
3 tbsp	vegetable oil (approx)	45 mL	¼ cup	finely chopped fresh parsley	50 mL
4	thick slices bacon, chopped	4			

TEST KITCHEN TIP

When choosing bacon for stews or beans, you will get a lot more flavour if you pick double-smoked. In a slab or sliced, this bacon is drier, often leaner and shrinks less.

❧ Peel onions. Cut in half lengthwise; slice thinly crosswise to make 8 cups (2 L). Set aside.

❧ Trim fat from beef. In large bowl, stir flour, salt and pepper. One-third at a time, toss beef cubes in flour mixture; reserve any remaining flour mixture.

❧ In large skillet, heat 1 tbsp (15 mL) of the oil over medium-high heat; brown beef, in 3 batches, adding and heating more oil between batches as necessary. Transfer beef to slow cooker.

❧ Return skillet to medium heat; add any remaining oil or enough extra oil to coat bottom of skillet; fry bacon just until starting to crisp. Add onions, thyme, basil, oregano, sage, bay leaf and any remaining flour mixture. Cook, stirring, until onions are softened, about 8 minutes. Scrape into slow cooker.

❧ Add beer to skillet; bring to boil, scraping up brown bits from bottom of skillet. Scrape into slow cooker along with mustard. Stir to combine.

❧ Cover and cook on low until beef is tender and liquid has turned into slightly thickened gravy, about 7 to 8 hours. Discard bay leaf. (Make-ahead: Let cool for 30 minutes. Refrigerate, uncovered, in airtight containers until cold. Cover and refrigerate for up to 3 days or freeze for up to 1 month.)

❧ Serve sprinkled with parsley.

PER SERVING: about 479 cal, 37 g pro, 29 g total fat (11 g sat. fat), 17 g carb, 2 g fibre, 110 mg chol, 525 mg sodium. % RDI: 5% calcium, 31% iron, 2% vit A, 5% vit C, 16% folate.

Old-Fashioned Beef & Root Vegetable Stew

Simple ingredients, easy cooking and memorable flavours are the hallmarks of a traditional beef stew. Serve this lovely version with biscuits or crusty bread.

5- to 6-quart (5 to 6 L)
slow cooker

Makes 8 to
10 servings

2 lb	stewing beef cubes	1 kg		1 cup	cubed peeled rutabaga	250 mL
½ cup	all-purpose flour	125 mL		3 cups	beef broth	750 mL
1 tbsp	vegetable oil	15 mL		2	bay leaves	2
2	each onions, carrots and parsnips, peeled and cubed	2		2 tsp	dried marjoram or thyme	10 mL
2	potatoes, peeled and cubed	2		¾ tsp	each salt and pepper	4 mL
				2 cups	frozen chopped green beans or peas	500 mL

❧ Trim beef and cut into 1-inch (2.5 cm) cubes, if necessary. In large bowl, toss beef with ¼ cup (50 mL) of the flour. In large skillet, heat oil over medium-high heat; brown beef, in batches. Transfer to slow cooker.

❧ Add ½ cup (125 mL) water to skillet; bring to boil, scraping up brown bits from bottom of skillet. Scrape into slow cooker along with onions, carrots, parsnips, potatoes and rutabaga. Stir in broth, bay leaves, marjoram, salt and pepper.

❧ Cover and cook on low until beef and vegetables are tender, about 7 to 8 hours. Skim off any fat. Move meat and vegetables to 1 side of slow cooker.

❧ Whisk remaining flour with ⅓ cup (75 mL) water; whisk into liquid in slow cooker. Stir in beans.

❧ Cover; cook on high until thickened and steaming hot, about 15 minutes. Discard bay leaves. (Make-ahead: Let cool for 30 minutes. Refrigerate, uncovered, in airtight containers until cold. Cover; refrigerate for up to 3 days.)

PER EACH OF 10 SERVINGS: about 256 cal, 23 g pro, 8 g total fat (3 g sat. fat), 22 g carb, 3 g fibre, 44 mg chol, 480 mg sodium. % RDI: 5% calcium, 21% iron, 38% vit A, 18% vit C, 21% folate.

TEST KITCHEN TIP

When a stew contains sweet vegetables, such as onions, carrots and parsnips, it may need a splash of lemon juice, cider vinegar or balsamic vinegar to balance the flavours. Taste before you serve and decide.

Wine-Braised Veal Shanks

6-quart (6 L) slow cooker

Makes 8 servings

Osso bucco is the Italian name for both veal shanks and the rustic dish made from them. The shanks for this no-tomato version tend to be expensive, making it a bit of a splurge. But it's a splurge to remember. Serve with crusty bread.

3 tbsp	all-purpose flour	45 mL	¾ cup	white wine	175 mL
½ tsp	each salt and pepper	2 mL	¾ cup	sodium-reduced chicken broth	175 mL
8	pieces veal hind shank (1½ inches/4 cm thick), about 4½ lb (2.25 kg)	8	1 tsp	grated lemon rind	5 mL
4 tsp	extra-virgin olive oil	20 mL	½ cup	halved pitted green olives	125 mL
1	onion, chopped	1	1 tbsp	capers, drained and rinsed	15 mL
4	cloves garlic, minced	4	1 tbsp	lemon juice	15 mL
1 tsp	dried rosemary	5 mL	2 tbsp	chopped fresh parsley	30 mL

SUBSTITUTION

If you don't have — or don't want to use — white wine in this recipe, you can substitute an equal amount of sodium-reduced chicken broth and 1½ tsp (7 mL) wine vinegar.

↜ In shallow dish, stir together flour and half each of the salt and pepper. Firmly tie kitchen string around each veal shank; press into flour mixture to coat. Reserve remaining flour mixture.

↜ In large skillet, heat 1 tbsp (15 mL) of the oil over medium-high heat; brown veal, in batches. Transfer to slow cooker.

↜ Drain fat from skillet; add remaining oil. Fry onion, garlic, rosemary and remaining salt and pepper over medium heat, stirring occasionally, until softened, about 5 minutes. Scrape into slow cooker.

↜ Add wine to skillet; bring to boil, scraping up brown bits from bottom. Scrape into slow cooker along with broth and lemon rind. Stir to combine.

↜ Cover; cook on low until shanks are tender, 6 to 8 hours. Skim off any fat. Stir in olives, capers and lemon juice. Move veal and vegetables to 1 side.

↜ Whisk remaining flour with 3 tbsp (45 mL) water; whisk into liquid in slow cooker. Stir to redistribute ingredients.

↜ Cover and cook on high until thickened, about 15 minutes. (Make-ahead: Let cool for 30 minutes. Refrigerate, uncovered, in airtight containers until cold. Cover and refrigerate for up to 3 days or freeze for up to 1 month.)

↜ Sprinkle with parsley.

PER SERVING: about 258 cal, 35 g pro, 10 g total fat (3 g sat. fat), 5 g carb, 1 g fibre, 148 mg chol, 540 mg sodium. % RDI: 4% calcium, 14% iron, 1% vit A, 5% vit C, 12% folate.

Company Veal & Mushroom Stew

Mushrooms always make meat or poultry taste better, and flavour-packed shiitakes bring the taste up another notch. Shiitakes are more expensive than other mushrooms. However, like a lot of good things in life, they are worth every penny.

5- to 6-quart (5 to 6 L) slow cooker

Makes 8 servings

2½ lb	stewing veal cubes	1.25 kg	½ tsp	dried thyme	2 mL
⅓ cup	all-purpose flour	75 mL	¼ tsp	grated nutmeg	1 mL
2 tbsp	vegetable oil	30 mL	2½ cups	chicken broth	625 mL
2 tbsp	butter	30 mL	4 cups	small button or cremini mushrooms (12 oz/375 g)	1 L
1	onion, chopped	1			
3	leeks (white and light green parts only), chopped	3	2 cups	shiitake mushroom caps (8 oz/250 g)	500 mL
2	cloves garlic, chopped	2	2 tbsp	lemon juice	30 mL
1	bay leaf	1	½ cup	whipping cream (optional)	125 mL
¾ tsp	each salt and pepper	4 mL	¼ cup	chopped fresh parsley	50 mL

Trim veal. In large bowl, toss veal with flour to coat. In large skillet, heat oil over medium-high heat; brown veal, in batches. Transfer to slow cooker.

Drain fat from skillet; add 1 tbsp (15 mL) of the butter. Fry onion, leeks, garlic and bay leaf over medium heat, stirring, until vegetables are softened, 5 minutes. Add ½ tsp (2 mL) each of the salt and pepper, thyme and nutmeg.

Stir in broth; bring to boil, scraping up any brown bits from bottom of skillet. Scrape over veal; stir to combine.

Cover and cook on low until veal is tender, about 6 to 7 hours. Skim off any fat. Discard bay leaf. (Make-ahead: Let cool for 30 minutes. Refrigerate, uncovered, in airtight containers until cold. Cover and refrigerate for up to 3 days or freeze for up to 1 month.)

Meanwhile, in large skillet, heat remaining butter over medium-high heat; sauté button and shiitake mushrooms with remaining salt and pepper until lightly browned, 10 minutes. Add to slow cooker with lemon juice.

Cover and cook on high until flavours are blended and mushrooms are softened, 15 minutes. Stir in cream (if using) and parsley.

PER SERVING: about 302 cal, 31 g pro, 14 g total fat (5 g sat. fat), 12 g carb, 2 g fibre, 137 mg chol, 630 mg sodium. % RDI: 6% calcium, 21% iron, 4% vit A, 12% vit C, 19% folate.

Chunky Beef & Chickpea Chili

With lots of spice and chunks of beef, it's no wonder that this comforting, nourishing chili is a big favourite.

4½- to 6-quart (4.5 to 6 L)
slow cooker

Makes 4 to
6 servings

2 lb	stewing beef cubes	1 kg
1 tbsp	vegetable oil	15 mL
1 cup	beef broth	250 mL
2	each onions and carrots, chopped	2
2	stalks celery, sliced	2
1	can (19 oz/540 mL) stewed tomatoes	1
1	can (19 oz/540 mL) chickpeas, drained and rinsed (or 2 cups/ 500 mL cooked chickpeas; recipe, page 213)	1
1	can (5½ oz/156 mL) tomato paste	1
2 tbsp	chili powder	30 mL
1 tsp	each ground cumin and dried oregano	5 mL
¾ tsp	salt	4 mL
1	sweet red pepper, chopped	1

SUBSTITUTION
Feel free to change the chickpeas to red kidney beans or another bean you have on hand.

❧ Trim beef and cut into ½-inch (1 cm) cubes. In large skillet, heat oil over medium-high heat; brown beef, in batches. Transfer to slow cooker.

❧ Add broth to skillet; bring to boil, scraping up brown bits from bottom of skillet. Scrape into slow cooker along with onions, carrots, celery, tomatoes, chickpeas, tomato paste, chili powder, cumin, oregano and salt. Stir to combine.

❧ Cover and cook on low until meat is tender, about 7 to 8 hours. Skim off any fat. (Make-ahead: Let cool for 30 minutes. Refrigerate, uncovered, in airtight containers until cold. Cover and refrigerate for up to 3 days or freeze for up to 1 month.)

❧ Add red pepper. Cover and cook on high until pepper is tender-crisp, about 15 minutes.

PER EACH OF 6 SERVINGS: about 441 cal, 41 g pro, 15 g total fat (4 g sat. fat), 37 g carb, 8 g fibre, 74 mg chol, 980 mg sodium. % RDI: 10% calcium, 46% iron, 89% vit A, 105% vit C, 35% folate.

Picadillo

Try this saucy ground beef stew over rice or potatoes or roll up with cheese in tortillas for quick burritos.

4½- to 6-quart (4.5 to 6 L)
slow cooker

Makes 6 servings

2 lb	lean ground beef	1 kg	2 tsp	dried oregano	10 mL
2	onions, chopped	2	½ tsp	salt	2 mL
2	cloves garlic, minced	2	¼ tsp	pepper	1 mL
1	can (5½ oz/156 mL) tomato paste	1	½ cup	sliced pimiento-stuffed green olives	125 mL
2 tbsp	Worcestershire sauce	30 mL	1	sweet green pepper, diced	1
2 tbsp	red wine vinegar	30 mL			
1 tbsp	finely chopped fresh or pickled jalapeño pepper	15 mL			

In large skillet, sauté beef over medium-high heat, breaking up with fork until crumbly and no longer pink, about 5 minutes. With slotted spoon, transfer beef to slow cooker.

To slow cooker, add onions, garlic, tomato paste, 1 cup (250 mL) water, Worcestershire sauce, vinegar, jalapeño pepper, oregano, salt and pepper. Stir to combine.

Cover and cook on low until thickened, about 6 to 8 hours. Skim off any fat. (Make-ahead: Let cool for 30 minutes. Refrigerate, uncovered, in airtight containers until cold. Cover and refrigerate for up to 3 days or freeze for up to 1 month.)

Stir in olives and green pepper; cover and cook on high until pepper is tender-crisp, about 15 minutes.

PER SERVING: about 319 cal, 32 g pro, 17 g total fat (6 g sat. fat), 12 g carb, 3 g fibre, 80 mg chol, 661 mg sodium. % RDI: 4% calcium, 31% iron, 10% vit A, 55% vit C, 6% folate.

Sausage Sloppy Joes

Sloppy **isn't a food word that automatically makes your mouth water, but when connected to Joe – whoever he was – it brings back memories of a saucy dish that never goes out of style. We recommend the kid-friendly method of eating this dish: spoon the Sausage Sloppy Joes onto buns and serve with carrot and celery sticks, and crunchy pickles.**

3½- to 5½-quart (3.5 to 5.5 L) slow cooker

Makes 8 servings

1 lb	sweet Italian sausages	500 mL	1	sweet red pepper, chopped	1
2 tbsp	vegetable oil	30 mL	2 tsp	dried oregano	10 mL
1 lb	lean ground beef	500 mL	½ tsp	salt	2 mL
3	onions, chopped	3	¼ tsp	pepper	1 mL
4	cloves garlic, minced	4	¼ cup	tomato paste	50 mL
4 cups	sliced mushrooms (12 oz/375 g)	1 L	1	can (28 oz/796 mL) tomatoes	1

❧ Remove casings from sausages. In large skillet, heat half of the oil over medium-high heat; sauté sausage meat and beef, breaking up with fork until crumbly and no longer pink, about 8 minutes. Using slotted spoon, transfer meat to slow cooker.

❧ Drain fat from skillet; add remaining oil. Sauté onions, garlic, mushrooms, red pepper, oregano, salt and pepper over medium-high heat until vegetables are softened, about 8 minutes. Stir in tomato paste; cook for 2 minutes.

❧ Scrape onion mixture into slow cooker along with tomatoes. Using fork, break up tomatoes into bite-size pieces. Stir to combine.

❧ Cover and cook on low until sauce is thick enough to mound on spoon, about 4 to 6 hours.

PER SERVING: about 304 cal, 22 g pro, 19 g total fat (6 g sat. fat), 13 g carb, 3 g fibre, 55 mg chol, 677 mg sodium. % RDI: 6% calcium, 24% iron, 8% vit A, 68% vit C, 10% folate.

DID YOU KNOW?

This American recipe is thought to have originated in an Iowa restaurant in the 1920s and got its name from a Florida bar a decade later.

Fennel & Tomato Pork Stew

Fennel is the bulbous vegetable with dill-like fronds emerging from the top. It is also an aromatic spice that goes beautifully with pork. It is the seeds that add their licorice notes to this delicious Mediterranean-inspired ragout.

4½- to 6-quart (4.5 to 6 L) slow cooker

Makes 4 servings

2 lb	boneless pork shoulder blade roast	1 kg	½ cup	sodium-reduced chicken broth	125 mL
½ tsp	each salt and pepper	2 mL	2 cups	bottled strained tomatoes	500 mL
2 tbsp	vegetable oil	30 mL	3	sprigs fresh thyme (or 1 tsp/5 mL dried)	3
1	onion, chopped	1	1 tbsp	all-purpose flour	15 mL
2	each carrots and stalks celery, chopped	2	⅓ cup	chopped pitted black olives	75 mL
4	cloves garlic	4	¼ cup	chopped fresh parsley	50 mL
2 tsp	fennel seeds, crushed	10 mL			

➤ Trim pork and cut into 1-inch (2.5 cm) cubes; sprinkle with half each of the salt and pepper. In large skillet, heat half of the oil over medium-high heat; brown pork, in batches and adding more of the remaining oil as necessary. Transfer to slow cooker.

➤ Drain fat from skillet; add remaining oil. Fry onion, carrots, celery, garlic, fennel seeds and remaining salt and pepper over medium heat until vegetables are softened, about 8 minutes. Add broth; bring to boil, scraping up brown bits from bottom of skillet. Scrape into slow cooker along with tomatoes and thyme. Stir to combine.

➤ Cover and cook on low until pork is tender, about 6 to 7 hours. Skim off fat. Move pork and vegetables to 1 side of slow cooker.

➤ In small bowl, whisk flour with 2 tbsp (30 mL) water; whisk into liquid in slow cooker. Stir to redistribute ingredients.

➤ Cover and cook on high until thickened, about 15 minutes. Stir in olives; sprinkle with parsley.

PER SERVING: about 355 cal, 37 g pro, 15 g total fat (3 g sat. fat), 17 g carb, 3 g fibre, 104 mg chol, 640 mg sodium. % RDI: 10% calcium, 36% iron, 77% vit A, 33% vit C, 18% folate.

SUBSTITUTION
You can replace the strained tomatoes with an equal amount of chopped seeded canned tomatoes.

Pork & Pearl Onion Adobo

Adobo is the Philippine national dish and can be made with chicken and seafood as well. The flavour combination traditionally includes soy sauce, vinegar, garlic and bay leaves. Serve over rice.

5- to 6-quart (5 to 6 L)
slow cooker

Makes 8 servings

3 lb	boneless pork shoulder blade roast	1.5 kg	½ cup	rice vinegar or cider vinegar	125 mL
1 tbsp	vegetable oil	15 mL	¼ cup	soy sauce	50 mL
2 cups	pearl onions (one 10-oz/284 g pkg), peeled	500 mL	3	thin slices gingerroot	3
			3	each bay leaves and whole cloves	3
2	onions, chopped	2	1	cinnamon stick, broken	1
6	carrots, cut into chunks	6	2 tsp	peppercorns	10 mL
4	cloves garlic, minced	4	1 tbsp	cornstarch	15 mL
			1	stalk celery, thinly sliced	1

❧ Trim pork and cut into 1½-inch (4 cm) cubes. In large skillet, heat oil over medium-high heat; brown pork, in batches. Transfer to slow cooker.

❧ Drain fat from skillet. Fry pearl onions, chopped onions, carrots and garlic over medium heat, stirring occasionally, until chopped onions are golden, about 6 minutes. Scrape into slow cooker.

❧ Add 1 cup (250 mL) water, vinegar and soy sauce to skillet; bring to boil, scraping up brown bits from bottom of skillet. Scrape into slow cooker.

❧ In 6-inch (15 cm) square cheesecloth, tie ginger, bay leaves, cloves, cinnamon and peppercorns to form bag. Nestle into slow cooker.

❧ Cover and cook until pork is tender, about 6 to 8 hours. Discard spice bag. Skim off any fat. Move meat and vegetables to 1 side of slow cooker.

❧ Whisk cornstarch with 2 tbsp (30 mL) water; whisk into liquid in slow cooker. Stir in celery.

❧ Cover and cook on high until thickened, about 20 minutes. (Make-ahead: Let cool for 30 minutes. Refrigerate, uncovered, in airtight containers until cold. Cover and refrigerate for up to 3 days or freeze for up to 1 month.)

PER SERVING: about 327 cal, 38 g pro, 13 g total fat (4 g sat. fat), 13 g carb, 2 g fibre, 107 mg chol, 677 mg sodium. % RDI: 6% calcium, 20% iron, 137% vit A, 8% vit C, 11% folate.

Zesty Lemon Pork Stew

It's all here – chunks of pork and sweet potatoes, even a green vegetable. Serve with a salad and call it dinner.

5- to 6-quart (5 to 6 L) slow cooker

Makes 4 to 6 servings

2 lb	boneless pork shoulder blade roast	1 kg
1 tbsp	vegetable oil	15 mL
3 cups	chicken broth	750 mL
2	onions, chopped	2
2	sweet potatoes, peeled and cubed	2
2	stalks celery, sliced	2
1 tsp	grated lemon rind	5 mL
1 tbsp	lemon juice	15 mL
2 tsp	dried thyme	10 mL
¾ tsp	salt	4 mL
¼ cup	all-purpose flour	50 mL
1	can (14 oz/398 mL) artichoke hearts, drained	1
2 cups	frozen green beans or peas	500 mL

➤ Trim pork and cut into ¾-inch (2 cm) cubes. In large skillet, heat oil over medium-high heat; brown pork, in batches. Transfer to slow cooker.

➤ Drain fat from skillet; add 1 cup (250 mL) of the chicken broth. Bring to boil, scraping up brown bits from bottom of skillet. Scrape into slow cooker along with remaining broth, onions, sweet potatoes, celery, lemon rind and juice, thyme and salt. Stir to combine.

➤ Cover and cook on low until pork and vegetables are tender, about 6 to 8 hours. Skim off any fat. Move meat and vegetables to 1 side of slow cooker.

➤ Whisk flour with ⅓ cup (75 mL) water; whisk into liquid in slow cooker. Stir to redistribute ingredients.

➤ Cover and cook on high until thickened, about 15 minutes. (Make-ahead: Let cool for 30 minutes. Refrigerate, uncovered, in airtight containers until cold. Cover and refrigerate for up to 3 days or freeze for up to 1 month.)

➤ Add artichokes and green beans; cover and cook on high until steaming hot, about 10 to 15 minutes.

PER EACH OF 6 SERVINGS: about 392 cal, 38 g pro, 13 g total fat (4 g sat. fat), 29 g carb, 5 g fibre, 95 mg chol, 946 mg sodium. % RDI: 10% calcium, 29% iron, 97% vit A, 33% vit C, 27% folate.

Pork Stew with Fennel & Squash

5½- to 6-quart (5.5 to 6 L)
slow cooker

Makes 8 servings

It's not hard to eat local and in-season in the fall, when squash is piled high at every farmer's market. Butternut squash is a good choice for stews and soups because it's so easy to peel and seed. If you don't use a whole squash, wrap what you don't need and refrigerate for up to a few days.

3 lb	boneless pork shoulder blade roast	1.5 kg
¾ tsp	salt	4 mL
¼ tsp	pepper	1 mL
1	fennel bulb	1
3 tbsp	vegetable oil	45 mL
1	onion, chopped	1
2	cloves garlic, minced	2
1½ tsp	dried Italian herb seasoning or crumbled dried sage	7 mL
2	bay leaves	2
½ cup	dry white wine	125 mL
2 tbsp	tomato paste	30 mL
1	can (28 oz/796 mL) tomatoes	1
3 cups	cubed peeled butternut squash	750 mL
½ cup	sodium-reduced chicken broth	125 mL
¼ cup	all-purpose flour	50 mL
2 tbsp	chopped fresh parsley	30 mL

❧ Trim pork and cut into 1½-inch (4 cm) cubes. Toss with ¼ tsp (1 mL) of the salt and pepper.

❧ Remove fronds from fennel stems; chop fronds coarsely, discarding stems. Cut fennel lengthwise into 1-inch (2.5 cm) thick wedges. Set fronds and fennel wedges aside separately.

❧ In large skillet, heat 2 tbsp (30 mL) of the oil over medium-high heat; brown pork, in batches. Transfer to slow cooker.

❧ Drain any fat from skillet; add remaining oil. Fry fennel, onion, garlic, Italian herb seasoning, bay leaves and remaining salt over medium heat until vegetables are softened, about 10 minutes. Scrape into slow cooker.

❧ Add wine to skillet; bring to boil, scraping up brown bits from bottom of skillet. Add tomato paste; cook, stirring, until combined, about 1 minute. Scrape into slow cooker along with tomatoes. Using fork, break tomatoes into bite-size chunks. Stir in squash, ½ cup (125 mL) water and broth.

❧ Cover and cook on low until pork and vegetables are tender, about 6 to 7 hours. Skim off fat. Move pork and vegetables to 1 side of slow cooker.

>

﹏ In small bowl, whisk flour with ⅓ cup (75 mL) water; whisk into liquid in slow cooker. Stir to redistribute ingredients.

﹏ Cover and cook on high until thickened, about 15 minutes. (Make-ahead: Let cool for 30 minutes. Refrigerate, uncovered, in airtight containers until cold. Cover and refrigerate for up to 3 days.)

﹏ Sprinkle with parsley and reserved fennel fronds.

PER SERVING: about 261 cal, 26 g pro, 10 g total fat (2 g sat. fat), 18 g carb, 3 g fibre, 72 mg chol, 484 mg sodium. % RDI: 8% calcium, 26% iron, 68% vit A, 48% vit C, 18% folate.

Keep Herbs and Spices Fresh

Stale dried herbs and spices will ruin a perfectly good recipe. Here's how to keep them fresh.

> Store herbs and spices in the dark, away from heat.

> Buy in small quantities that suit your needs.

> Every six months, check through stored herbs and spices and discard any musty or dull ones.

> Buy whole spices. They keep their flavour longer. Use an inexpensive hand grater for small things, like fresh nutmeg, and a clean coffee grinder to make short work of seeds and bark.

> Buy herbs in as whole a form as possible, such as thyme leaves. Avoid powdered herbs.

Smoky Pork Stew

Paprika, which gives this stew a goulash flavour, is available in many forms these days: smoked, unsmoked, sweet, bittersweet and hot. For the smoked, you may need to go to a specialty food store, but more and more supermarkets are stocking this Spanish specialty. Once you have a tin of it, you'll find yourself using it whenever you want to give a whiff of sweet or hot peppery smoke to a dish, whether it's eggs, fish, poultry, legumes or meats. This stew is delightful topped with sour cream and served with egg noodles and tender-crisp green beans.

4½- to 6-quart (4.5 to 6 L) slow cooker

Makes 4 to 6 servings

2	onions, sliced	2	1 tbsp	smoked or regular sweet paprika	15 mL
2	cloves garlic, minced	2	1 tsp	dried oregano	5 mL
2 lb	boneless pork shoulder blade roast	1 kg	½ tsp	each dry mustard and salt	2 mL
½ cup	salsa or tomato sauce	125 mL	¼ tsp	pepper	1 mL
2 tbsp	packed brown sugar	30 mL	3 tbsp	all-purpose flour	45 mL
2 tbsp	Worcestershire sauce	30 mL			

❧ Place onions and garlic in slow cooker. Trim pork and cut into 1-inch (2.5 cm) cubes; place on onion mixture.

❧ Combine 1 cup (250 mL) water, salsa, sugar, Worcestershire sauce, paprika, oregano, mustard, salt and pepper; pour into slow cooker. Stir to combine.

❧ Cover and cook on low until meat is fork-tender, about 6 to 7 hours. Skim off fat. Move meat and vegetables to 1 side of slow cooker.

❧ In small bowl, whisk flour with ¼ cup (50 mL) cold water; whisk into liquid in slow cooker. Stir to redistribute ingredients.

❧ Cover and cook on high until sauce is thickened, 10 to 15 minutes. (Make-ahead: Let cool for 30 minutes. Refrigerate, uncovered, in airtight containers until cold. Cover and refrigerate for up to 3 days or freeze for up to 1 month.)

PER EACH OF 6 SERVINGS: about 187 cal, 22 g pro, 4 g total fat (2 g sat. fat), 15 g carb, 2 g fibre, 64 mg chol, 453 mg sodium. % RDI: 4% calcium, 18% iron, 6% vit A, 5% vit C, 10% folate.

VARIATION

Paprika Beef Stew: Replace pork with 2 lb (1 kg) stewing beef cubes, salsa with chili sauce, and smoked paprika with regular sweet paprika.

Pork & Black Bean Chili

Strained tomatoes are available in bottles alongside the usual array of canned tomato products. In this recipe, you can replace them with seeded canned tomatoes or tomato sauce.

4½- to 5½-quart (4.5 to 5.5 L) slow cooker

Makes 4 servings

4	thick slices bacon, sliced crosswise into strips	4
1¼ lb	boneless pork loin centre roast, cubed	625 g
1 tbsp	vegetable oil	15 mL
2	onions, diced	2
1	each carrot and sweet green pepper, diced	1
4	cloves garlic, minced	4
1½ tsp	each dried oregano and ground cumin	7 mL
¼ tsp	each salt and pepper	1 mL

2	cans (each 19 oz/ 540 mL) black beans, drained and rinsed (or 4 cups/1 L cooked beans; recipe, page 213)	2
½ cup	bottled strained tomatoes	125 mL
SALSA:		
½ cup	chopped cherry or grape tomatoes	125 mL
Half	sweet yellow or orange pepper, diced	Half
1	green onion, thinly sliced	1
1 tbsp	lime juice	15 mL

➤ In large skillet, fry bacon over medium heat until crisp. With slotted spoon, transfer to paper towel–lined plate. Discard all but 1 tbsp (15 mL) of the fat in skillet; brown pork, in batches. Transfer bacon and pork to slow cooker.

➤ Drain fat from skillet; add oil. Fry onions, carrot, green pepper, garlic, oregano, cumin, salt and pepper over medium heat until onions are golden, about 10 minutes. Scrape into slow cooker.

➤ Add 1 cup (250 mL) water to skillet; bring to boil, scraping up brown bits from bottom of skillet. Add to slow cooker along with 1 cup (250 mL) water, beans and strained tomatoes. Stir to combine.

➤ Cover and cook on low until pork is tender, about 6 to 8 hours. Skim off any fat. (Make-ahead: Let cool for 30 minutes. Refrigerate, uncovered, in airtight containers until cold. Cover and refrigerate for up to 3 days or freeze for up to 1 month.)

➤ SALSA: In bowl, combine tomatoes, yellow pepper, green onion and lime juice; serve with chili.

PER SERVING: about 545 cal, 50 g pro, 16 g total fat (5 g sat. fat), 51 g carb, 18 g fibre, 98 mg chol, 1,172 mg sodium. % RDI: 14% calcium, 47% iron, 38% vit A, 105% vit C, 67% folate.

Sausage Tomato Stew

4½- to 6-quart (4.5 to 6 L)
slow cooker

Makes 4 to
6 servings

Instead of the sweet green pepper, added at the end of cooking time to preserve its freshness, try a Cubanelle pepper. Compared to a sweet bell pepper, it's longer and pointier, with thinner flesh, and much tastier without being bitter. Another alternative is a sweet banana pepper or two.

1 tbsp	vegetable oil	15 mL	¼ cup	tomato paste	50 mL
2 lb	mild or hot Italian sausages, sliced	1 kg	2 tsp	dried Italian herb seasoning	10 mL
2 cups	chicken broth	500 mL	2	cloves garlic, minced	2
4	carrots, sliced	4	¼ cup	all-purpose flour	50 mL
2	onions, chopped	2	1	sweet green pepper, diced	1
1	can (19 oz/540 mL) Italian stewed tomatoes	1			

❧ In large skillet, heat oil over medium-high heat; brown sausages, in batches if necessary. Transfer to slow cooker.

❧ Drain fat from skillet. Add 1 cup (250 mL) of the broth; bring to boil, scraping up brown bits from bottom of skillet. Scrape into slow cooker along with remaining broth, carrots, onions, tomatoes, tomato paste, Italian herb seasoning and garlic. Stir to combine.

❧ Cover and cook on low until vegetables are tender, about 4 to 6 hours. Skim off any fat. Move sausage and vegetables to 1 side of slow cooker.

❧ Whisk flour with ⅓ cup (75 mL) water; whisk into liquid in slow cooker. Stir in green pepper.

❧ Cover and cook on high until pepper is tender-crisp and sauce is thickened, about 15 minutes. (Make-ahead: Let cool for 30 minutes. Refrigerate, uncovered, in airtight containers until cold. Cover and refrigerate for up to 3 days or freeze for up to 1 month.)

PER EACH OF 6 SERVINGS: about 419 cal, 27 g pro, 24 g total fat (8 g sat. fat), 24 g carb, 4 g fibre, 64 mg chol, 1,463 mg sodium. % RDI: 9% calcium, 26% iron, 130% vit A, 57% vit C, 15% folate.

Braised Pork, Potatoes & Beans in White Wine Sauce

So many one-pot stews feature tomatoes in one form or another – whole, diced, sauce, etc. Here's a change: a sauce of just broth and wine, with a creamy velvet finish. The best part is how deliciously it mashes with the potatoes.

4½- to 6-quart (4.5 to 6 L) slow cooker

Makes 8 servings

3 lb	boneless pork shoulder butt	1.5 kg	1 cup	sodium-reduced chicken broth	250 mL
½ tsp	each salt and white pepper	2 mL	1 cup	dry white wine	250 mL
2 tbsp	vegetable oil	30 mL	5 cups	small potatoes, halved (about 1¼ lb/625 g)	1.25 L
1 tbsp	butter or vegetable oil	15 mL	⅓ cup	whipping cream	75 mL
2	each onions and stalks celery, chopped	2	¼ cup	all-purpose flour	50 mL
¼ tsp	grated nutmeg	1 mL	2 cups	frozen lima beans or peas, thawed	500 mL
			1 tbsp	chopped fresh dill	15 mL

Trim pork and cut into 1½-inch (4 cm) cubes. Sprinkle with half each of the salt and pepper.

In large skillet, heat oil over medium-high heat; brown pork, in batches. Transfer to slow cooker.

Drain fat from skillet; add butter. Fry onions, celery, remaining salt and pepper and nutmeg over medium heat until vegetables are softened, about 6 minutes. Scrape into slow cooker.

Add broth and wine to skillet; bring to boil, scraping up brown bits from bottom. Scrape into slow cooker along with potatoes. Stir to combine.

Cover and cook on low until potatoes and pork are tender, about 6 to 7 hours. Skim off fat. Move pork and vegetables to 1 side of slow cooker. Whisk cream with flour; whisk into liquid in slow cooker. Stir in lima beans.

Cover and cook on high until thickened, about 15 minutes. (Make-ahead: Let cool for 30 minutes. Refrigerate, uncovered, in airtight containers until cold. Cover and refrigerate for up to 3 days.)

Stir in dill.

PER SERVING: about 399 cal, 36 g pro, 15 g total fat (6 g sat. fat), 28 g carb, 4 g fibre, 112 mg chol, 364 mg sodium. % RDI: 5% calcium, 27% iron, 6% vit A, 20% vit C, 16% folate.

TEST KITCHEN TIP
If small potatoes are unavailable, use new or waxy red-skinned potatoes and cut into 2-inch (5 cm) cubes. Peel potatoes, if you like, but keep in mind that the peel contains fibre and helps keep the potatoes intact.

SUBSTITUTION
You can replace the white pepper with black pepper.

Lamb Stew with Squash & Mint

5- to 6-quart (5 to 6 L) slow cooker

Makes 6 servings

Leg of lamb becomes meltingly tender as it braises in a slow cooker. You can save yourself some work by buying cubed lamb, either shoulder or leaner leg.

3 lb	boneless leg of lamb	1.5 kg	1	can (19 oz/540 mL) chickpeas, drained and rinsed (or 2 cups/ 500 mL cooked chickpeas; recipe, page 213)	1
2 tbsp	vegetable oil	30 mL			
2	onions, chopped	2			
4	cloves garlic, minced	4			
1 tbsp	dried mint	15 mL	¼ cup	tomato paste	50 mL
½ tsp	each salt and pepper	2 mL	2 tbsp	all-purpose flour	30 mL
1½ cups	sodium-reduced beef broth	375 mL	2 tbsp	chopped fresh parsley	30 mL
			1 tbsp	lemon juice	15 mL
2 cups	cubed (1 inch/2.5 cm) peeled butternut squash	500 mL	½ tsp	hot pepper sauce	2 mL

TEST KITCHEN TIP

For a smaller crowd, this recipe is easy to halve. Use 2½-quart (2.5 L) slow cooker and cook for 5 to 6 hours. Makes 2 to 4 servings.

❧ Trim lamb and cut into 1-inch (2.5 cm) cubes. In large skillet, heat oil over medium-high heat; brown lamb, in batches. Transfer to slow cooker.

❧ Drain fat from skillet. Fry onions, garlic, mint, salt and pepper over medium heat, stirring occasionally, until onions are softened, about 5 minutes. Scrape into slow cooker.

❧ Add half of the broth to skillet; bring to boil, scraping up brown bits from bottom of skillet. Scrape into slow cooker along with remaining broth, squash, chickpeas and tomato paste. Stir to combine.

❧ Cover and cook on low until lamb is tender, about 6 to 8 hours. Skim off fat. Move meat and vegetables to 1 side of slow cooker.

❧ Whisk flour with ¼ cup (50 mL) water; whisk into liquid in slow cooker. Stir to redistribute ingredients.

❧ Cover and cook on high until thickened, about 15 minutes. (Make-ahead: Let cool for 30 minutes. Refrigerate, uncovered, in airtight containers until cold. Cover and refrigerate for up to 3 days or freeze for up to 1 month.)

❧ Stir in parsley, lemon juice and hot pepper sauce.

PER SERVING: about 367 cal, 43 g pro, 8 g total fat (3 g sat. fat), 30 g carb, 5 g fibre, 132 mg chol, 630 mg sodium. % RDI: 6% calcium, 36% iron, 40% vit A, 33% vit C, 30% folate.

Greek Lamb Stew with Artichokes

It's the touch of cinnamon and allspice that give this robust stew an exotic allure. Pick flat-leaf parsley for its superior flavour as an ingredient or a garnish.

5- to 6-quart (5 to 6 L) slow cooker

Makes 6 to 8 servings

3 lb	boneless lamb shoulder roast	1.5 kg	Pinch	each ground allspice and cinnamon	Pinch
1 tbsp	extra-virgin olive oil	15 mL	2 tbsp	all-purpose flour	30 mL
3	onions, sliced	3	1½ cups	beef broth	375 mL
6	cloves garlic, minced	6	¼ cup	tomato paste	50 mL
1 tbsp	dried oregano	15 mL	1	can (14 oz/398 mL) artichoke hearts, drained and quartered	1
1 tbsp	grated lemon rind	15 mL			
¼ tsp	salt	1 mL	½ cup	crumbled feta cheese	125 mL
			2 tbsp	chopped fresh parsley	30 mL

❧ Trim lamb and cut into 1-inch (2.5 cm) cubes. In large skillet, heat oil over medium-high heat; brown lamb, in batches. Transfer to slow cooker.

❧ Drain fat from skillet. Fry onions, garlic, oregano, lemon rind, salt, allspice and cinnamon over medium heat, stirring occasionally, until onions are softened, about 5 minutes.

❧ Sprinkle with flour; cook, stirring, for 1 minute. Add beef broth and tomato paste; bring to boil, stirring and scraping up brown bits from bottom of skillet. Scrape into slow cooker. Stir to combine.

❧ Cover and cook on low until lamb is tender, about 6 to 8 hours. (Make-ahead: Let cool for 30 minutes. Refrigerate, uncovered, in airtight containers until cold. Cover and refrigerate for up to 3 days or freeze for up to 1 month.)

❧ Stir in artichokes; cover and cook until steaming hot, about 15 minutes. Serve sprinkled with feta cheese and parsley.

PER EACH OF 8 SERVINGS: about 242 cal, 25 g pro, 11 g total fat (4 g sat. fat), 11 g carb, 3 g fibre, 77 mg chol, 535 mg sodium. % RDI: 8% calcium, 21% iron, 4% vit A, 18% vit C, 21% folate.

Lamb Cuts for the Slow Cooker

> **ROASTS:** Choose shoulder roasts for their rich marbling and flavour.
> **SHANKS:** Lamb shanks are another excellent option for long, moist cooking.

> **STEWING CUBES:** For stews, opt for shoulder cubes over cubed leg of lamb.

Pearl Onion Lamb Tagine

This is a wonderful lamb stew, enhanced with a whisper of saffron and cinnamon, plus a touch of sweetness from golden raisins. Serve with whole wheat couscous, whole grain (brown) rice or crusty bread.

5- to 6-quart (5 to 6 L) slow cooker

Makes 6 servings

3 lb	boneless lamb shoulder roast	1.5 kg	2 cups	chicken broth	500 mL
¾ tsp	salt	4 mL	1 cup	white wine	250 mL
½ tsp	pepper	2 mL	1 tbsp	sweet paprika	15 mL
3 tbsp	vegetable oil	45 mL	1 tsp	cinnamon	5 mL
1	onion, chopped	1	¼ tsp	saffron threads	1 mL
3 cups	pearl onions, peeled (see Tip, right)	750 mL	¼ cup	all-purpose flour	50 mL
			1 cup	golden raisins	250 mL

❧ Trim lamb and cut into 1½-inch (4 cm) cubes; sprinkle with salt and pepper. In skillet, heat 2 tbsp (30 mL) of the oil over medium-high heat; brown lamb, in batches. Transfer to slow cooker.

❧ Drain fat from skillet; add remaining oil. Fry chopped onion and pearl onions over medium heat, stirring often, until starting to turn golden, about 5 minutes. Scrape into slow cooker.

❧ Add half of the broth to skillet; bring to boil, scraping up brown bits from bottom of skillet. Scrape into slow cooker along with remaining broth, wine, paprika, cinnamon and saffron. Stir to combine.

❧ Cover and cook on low until lamb is tender, about 6 to 8 hours. Skim off any fat. Move lamb and onions to 1 side of slow cooker.

❧ Whisk flour with ⅓ cup (75 mL) water; whisk into liquid in slow cooker. Stir in raisins.

❧ Cover and cook on high until thickened, about 15 minutes. (Make-ahead: Let cool for 30 minutes. Refrigerate, uncovered, in airtight containers until cold. Cover and refrigerate for up to 3 days or freeze for up to 1 month.)

TEST KITCHEN TIPS

Pearl onions come in 10-oz (284 g) net bags, which yield 2 cups (500 mL), so you'll need about 1½ packages for this recipe. Pop leftover onions in with roasting vegetables and chops. Leave whole in chilis and stews that call for chopped onions.

To peel pearl onions, blanch in boiling water for 1 minute; drain and chill in cold water. Drain and peel.

PER SERVING: about 520 cal, 50 g pro, 21 g total fat (7 g sat. fat), 31 g carb, 3 g fibre, 168 mg chol, 630 mg sodium. % RDI: 5% calcium, 37% iron, 7% vit A, 7% vit C, 7% folate.

Lamb Stew with Lima Beans

There are 10 spices in this stew, but once you get past the idea that it will take you a couple of minutes to measure them out, they do produce a beautifully balanced flavour. The lima beans are especially delicious with the mellow spicing. If you are not yet a lima bean fan, replace with an equal amount of cooked chickpeas – or leave them out. The stew is perfectly delectable with or without them.

4½- to 6-quart (4.5 to 6 L) slow cooker

Makes 6 to 8 servings

3 lb	boneless leg of lamb	1.5 kg	Pinch	each saffron threads, cayenne pepper and ground cloves	Pinch
1 tbsp	vegetable oil	15 mL	1	can (28 oz/796 mL) tomatoes	1
2	onions, chopped	2	¼ cup	tomato paste	50 mL
3	cloves garlic, smashed	3	2	strips lemon rind	2
½ tsp	each salt, ground cumin, coriander and ginger	2 mL	3 cups	cooked large lima beans (recipe, page 213)	750 mL
¼ tsp	each turmeric, cinnamon and ground cardamom	1 mL	½ cup	quartered pitted green olives	125 mL
¼ tsp	pepper	1 mL	⅓ cup	chopped fresh parsley	75 mL

❧ Trim lamb; cut into 1-inch (2.5 cm) cubes. In large skillet, heat half of the oil over medium-high heat; brown lamb, in batches. Transfer to slow cooker.

❧ Drain fat from skillet; add remaining oil. Fry onions and garlic over medium heat, stirring occasionally, until onions are softened, 6 minutes.

❧ Stir in salt, cumin, coriander, ginger, turmeric, cinnamon, cardamom, pepper, saffron, cayenne and cloves; cook, stirring, for 2 minutes.

❧ Stir in 1 cup (250 mL) water; bring to boil, scraping up brown bits from bottom of skillet. Scrape into slow cooker along with tomatoes; using fork, break tomatoes into bite-size pieces. Stir in tomato paste and lemon rind.

❧ Cover and cook on low until lamb is tender, about 6 to 8 hours. (Make-ahead: Let cool for 30 minutes. Refrigerate, uncovered, in airtight containers until cold. Cover and refrigerate for up to 3 days or freeze for up to 1 month.)

❧ Stir in lima beans and olives; cover and cook on high until steaming hot, about 15 minutes. Stir in parsley.

PER EACH OF 8 SERVINGS: about 333 cal, 37 g pro, 10 g total fat (3 g sat. fat), 24 g carb, 7 g fibre, 93 mg chol, 504 mg sodium. % RDI: 7% calcium, 43% iron, 5% vit A, 32% vit C, 43% folate.

Chicken with 40 Cloves of Garlic

This slow cooker version of a classic French oven-braised chicken is delicious with green beans and buttermilk mashed potatoes. To ease the chore of peeling 40 cloves of garlic, lay them in groups of four on a cutting board and press down on them with the flat side of a chef's knife to loosen the skins. The peel doesn't exactly pop off but is broken and much easier to remove.

4½- to 6-quart (4.5 to 6 L)
slow cooker

Makes 4 servings

1 tbsp	vegetable oil	15 mL	¼ tsp	crumbled dried sage	1 mL
8	chicken thighs	8	¼ tsp	pepper	1 mL
40	cloves garlic (about 4 heads)	40	Pinch	salt	Pinch
			1 cup	chicken broth	250 mL
½ tsp	crumbled dried thyme	2 mL	3 tbsp	all-purpose flour	45 mL
½ tsp	crumbled dried rosemary	2 mL	2 tbsp	minced fresh parsley	30 mL

TEST KITCHEN TIP

Regular skin-on, bone-in chicken thighs are our choice for braising. The bone adds flavour, and the skin helps keep the meat intact. However, the skin adds calories and fat to the dish (some estimates are as high as 3 grams of fat for every 100 grams of chicken). The skin also gets flabby when braised in the slow cooker, making it unappealing to eat and look at. We suggest removing it, either before serving or at the table as family and guests cut the meat away from the bone.

➤ In large skillet, heat oil over medium-high heat; brown chicken, in batches if necessary. Transfer to slow cooker.

➤ Drain fat from skillet. Fry garlic, thyme, rosemary, sage, pepper and salt over medium heat, stirring occasionally, until garlic is pale golden, about 5 minutes. Add broth; bring to boil, scraping up brown bits from bottom of skillet. Scrape into slow cooker. Stir to combine.

➤ Cover and cook on low until juices run clear when chicken is pierced, about 4 hours. Skim off fat. Move chicken and garlic to 1 side of slow cooker.

➤ In small bowl, whisk flour with ¼ cup (50 mL) water; whisk into liquid in slow cooker. Stir to redistribute ingredients.

➤ Cover and cook on high until thickened, about 15 minutes. (Make-ahead: Let cool for 30 minutes. Refrigerate, uncovered, in airtight containers until cold. Cover and refrigerate for up to 1 day or freeze for up to 1 month.)

➤ Sprinkle with parsley.

PER SERVING (WITHOUT SKIN): about 338 cal, 25 g pro, 20 g total fat (5 g sat. fat), 15 g carb, 1 g fibre, 112 mg chol, 345 mg sodium. % RDI: 7% calcium, 18% iron, 6% vit A, 22% vit C, 11% folate.

Saucy Mushroom Chicken

The perfect combination of ease, taste and economy, chicken thighs have it all. In the slow cooker, they stay moist much better than chicken breasts.

4½- to 6-quart (4.5 to 6 L)
slow cooker

Makes 4 servings

1 tbsp	vegetable oil	15 mL	½ tsp	salt	2 mL
8	chicken thighs	8	¼ tsp	pepper	1 mL
3 cups	sliced white or cremini mushrooms	750 mL	1 cup	2% evaporated milk or low-sodium chicken broth	250 mL
1	onion, chopped	1	1 tbsp	Dijon mustard	15 mL
2	cloves garlic, minced	2	¼ cup	all-purpose flour	50 mL
1 tsp	dried thyme	5 mL	2	green onions, sliced	2

❧ In large skillet, heat oil over medium-high heat; brown chicken, in batches if necessary. Transfer to slow cooker.

❧ Drain fat from skillet. Sauté mushrooms, onion, garlic, thyme, salt and pepper until mushrooms are golden and no liquid remains, about 8 minutes. Scrape into slow cooker.

❧ Add milk to skillet; bring to boil, scraping up brown bits from bottom of skillet. Scrape into slow cooker along with mustard. Stir to combine.

❧ Cover; cook on low until juices run clear when chicken is pierced, about 4 hours. Skim off fat. Move chicken and mushrooms to 1 side of slow cooker.

❧ In small bowl, whisk flour with ⅓ cup (75 mL) water; whisk into liquid in slow cooker. Stir to redistribute ingredients.

❧ Cover and cook on high until thickened, about 15 minutes. (Make-ahead: Let cool for 30 minutes. Refrigerate, uncovered, in airtight containers until cold. Cover and refrigerate for up to 1 day or freeze for up to 1 month.)

❧ Sprinkle with green onions.

PER SERVING (WITHOUT SKIN): about 384 cal, 29 g pro, 21 g total fat (6 g sat. fat), 19 g carb, 2 g fibre, 117 mg chol, 518 mg sodium. % RDI: 20% calcium, 22% iron, 9% vit A, 20% vit C, 20% folate.

Chicken & Sausage Gumbo

4½- to 6-quart (4.5 to 6 L) slow cooker

Makes 4 to 6 servings

This is a chicken dish waiting for friends to come over to watch a game, play cards or just visit. You can easily double the ingredients to suit the crowd. The cooking time is about the same. Rice is the starch of choice alongside.

2 tbsp	vegetable oil	30 mL		¼ tsp	each salt and pepper	1 mL
4	boneless skinless chicken thighs, cubed	4		½ cup	dry white wine or sodium-reduced chicken broth	125 mL
4	chorizo or mild Italian sausages, sliced	4		1	can (28 oz/796 mL) diced tomatoes	1
2	each onions and stalks celery, diced	2		½ cup	sodium-reduced chicken broth	125 mL
1	sweet red pepper, diced	1		3 tbsp	tomato paste	45 mL
4	cloves garlic, minced	4		1	pkg (250 g) frozen okra, thawed and sliced	1
1 tsp	each sweet paprika and dried thyme	5 mL		¼ cup	chopped fresh parsley	50 mL
2	bay leaves	2				

SUBSTITUTION

One cup (250 mL) frozen peas or edamame are handy substitutes for the frozen okra.

➤ In large skillet, heat half of the oil over medium-high heat; brown chicken and sausages, in batches if necessary. Transfer to slow cooker.

➤ Drain fat from skillet; add remaining oil. Fry onions, celery, red pepper, garlic, paprika, thyme, bay leaves, salt and pepper until vegetables are softened, about 8 minutes. Scrape into slow cooker.

➤ Add wine to skillet; bring to boil, scraping up brown bits from bottom of skillet. Scrape into slow cooker along with tomatoes, broth, tomato paste and ½ cup (125 mL) water. Stir to combine.

➤ Cover and cook on low until juices run clear when chicken is pierced, about 4 hours. Skim off fat; discard bay leaves. (Make-ahead: Let cool for 30 minutes. Refrigerate, uncovered, in airtight containers until cold. Cover and refrigerate for up to 1 day or freeze for up to 1 month.)

➤ Stir in okra. Cover and cook on high until steaming hot, about 15 minutes. Sprinkle with parsley.

PER EACH OF 6 SERVINGS: about 344 cal, 20 g pro, 22 g total fat (7 g sat. fat), 17 g carb, 4 g fibre, 67 mg chol, 869 mg sodium. % RDI: 10% calcium, 26% iron, 17% vit A, 103% vit C, 35% folate.

Black Bean Garlic Chicken

The primary colour of the sweet bell pepper adds to the vibrant look of this dish. The signature ingredient, black bean garlic sauce, is found in East Asian grocery stores and the condiments aisle of most supermarkets.

4½- to 6-quart (4.5 to 6 L)
slow cooker

Makes 4 servings

1 tbsp	vegetable oil	15 mL		1 tbsp	soy sauce	15 mL
8	boneless chicken thighs (skin-on)	8		1 tbsp	cornstarch	15 mL
1	onion, sliced	1		Half	sweet yellow or red pepper, diced	Half
2	cloves garlic, minced	2		2 tbsp	minced fresh coriander or parsley	30 mL
¾ cup	chicken broth	175 mL				
3 tbsp	black bean garlic sauce	45 mL				

TEST KITCHEN TIP
Chicken thighs are often sold skin-on, bone-in – or boneless skinless. For this recipe, you may have to buy skin-on, bone-in. To bone, slit meat on skinless side through to the bone. With kitchen knife slanted toward the bone, cut meat away from bone.

➤ In large skillet, heat oil over medium-high heat; brown chicken, in batches if necessary. Transfer to slow cooker.

➤ Drain fat from skillet. Fry onion and garlic over medium heat, stirring occasionally, until onion is softened, 5 minutes. Scrape into slow cooker.

➤ In skillet, mix together broth, black bean garlic sauce and soy sauce; bring to boil, scraping up brown bits from bottom of skillet. Scrape into slow cooker. Stir to combine.

➤ Cover and cook on low until juices run clear when chicken is pierced, about 4 hours. Skim off fat. Move chicken to 1 side of slow cooker.

➤ In small bowl, whisk cornstarch with 2 tbsp (30 mL) water; whisk into liquid in slow cooker. Stir in yellow pepper.

➤ Cover and cook on high until thickened and pepper is tender-crisp, about 10 to 15 minutes. (Make-ahead: Let cool for 30 minutes. Refrigerate, uncovered, in airtight containers until cold. Cover and refrigerate for up to 1 day or freeze for up to 1 month.)

➤ Sprinkle with coriander.

PER SERVING (WITHOUT SKIN): about 239 cal, 24 g pro, 10 g total fat (2 g sat. fat), 12 g carb, 1 g fibre, 94 mg chol, 689 mg sodium. % RDI: 2% calcium, 11% iron, 3% vit A, 27% vit C, 7% folate.

Charmoula Chicken

Charmoula is a Moroccan seasoning mixture of fresh herbs (parsley and coriander, which is also known as cilantro) and spices (paprika, cumin and cinnamon). Adding the herbs at the end gives the freshest, brightest flavour.

4½- to 6-quart (4.5 to 6 L)
slow cooker

Makes 4 servings

1 tbsp	vegetable oil	15 mL	Pinch	cinnamon	Pinch
8	chicken thighs	8	1 cup	chicken broth	250 mL
1	onion, chopped	1	¼ cup	all-purpose flour	50 mL
2	cloves garlic, minced	2	2 tbsp	minced fresh coriander or parsley	30 mL
1 tsp	sweet paprika	5 mL	1 tbsp	minced fresh parsley	15 mL
½ tsp	ground cumin	2 mL	2 tsp	lemon juice	10 mL
¼ tsp	each salt and pepper	1 mL			

❧ In large skillet, heat oil over medium-high heat; brown chicken, in batches if necessary. Transfer to slow cooker.

❧ Drain fat from skillet. Fry onion, garlic, paprika, cumin, salt, pepper and cinnamon over medium heat, stirring occasionally, until onion is softened, about 5 minutes. Add broth; bring to boil, scraping up brown bits on bottom of skillet. Scrape into slow cooker. Stir to combine.

❧ Cover and cook on low until juices run clear when chicken is pierced, about 4 hours. Skim off fat. Move chicken to 1 side of slow cooker.

❧ In small bowl, whisk flour with ⅓ cup (75 mL) water. Stir into liquid in slow cooker. Stir to redistribute ingredients.

❧ Cover and cook on high until thickened, about 15 minutes. (Make-ahead: Let cool for 30 minutes. Refrigerate, uncovered, in airtight containers until cold. Cover and refrigerate for up to 1 day or freeze for up to 1 month.)

❧ Stir in coriander, parsley and lemon juice.

PER SERVING (WITHOUT SKIN): about 316 cal, 24 g pro, 20 g total fat (5 g sat. fat), 10 g carb, 1 g fibre, 112 mg chol, 485 mg sodium. % RDI: 3% calcium, 16% iron, 8% vit A, 10% vit C, 14% folate.

Easy Chicken Curry

The fresh red onion topping makes this dish special. The onion is salted then rinsed, so nothing remains of the harsh flavour normally associated with raw onions.

5- to 6-quart (5 to 6 L)
slow cooker

Makes 6 servings

1 tbsp	vegetable oil	15 mL		3 tbsp	all-purpose flour	45 mL
12	chicken thighs	12		**TOPPING:**		
4 cups	thinly sliced onions (about 4)	1 L		⅔ cup	thinly sliced red onion	150 mL
½ cup	each orange juice and sodium-reduced chicken broth	125 mL		½ tsp	salt	2 mL
				2 tbsp	lime or lemon juice	30 mL
2 tbsp	mild curry paste	30 mL		¾ cup	plain Balkan-style yogurt	175 mL
3	cloves garlic, minced	3		2 tbsp	chopped fresh coriander	30 mL
1 tbsp	grated gingerroot	15 mL				

⌐ In large skillet, heat oil over medium-high heat; brown chicken, in batches. Transfer to slow cooker.

⌐ Drain fat from skillet. Fry onions over medium heat, stirring occasionally, until almost softened, about 10 minutes. Transfer to slow cooker.

⌐ In skillet, bring orange juice, broth, curry paste, garlic and ginger to boil, blending curry paste into liquid and scraping up brown bits from bottom of skillet. Scrape into slow cooker. Stir to combine.

⌐ Cover and cook on low until juices run clear when chicken is pierced, about 4 to 6 hours. Skim off fat.

⌐ Scrape onions off chicken and back into sauce. With slotted spoon, transfer chicken to platter. Cover and keep warm.

⌐ In small bowl, whisk flour with ¼ cup (50 mL) water; whisk into liquid in slow cooker. Cover and cook on high until thickened, about 15 minutes. Pour over chicken. (Make-ahead: Let cool for 30 minutes. Refrigerate, uncovered, in airtight containers until cold. Cover and refrigerate for up to 1 day or freeze for up to 1 month.)

⌐ **TOPPING:** Meanwhile, sprinkle onion with salt; let stand for 15 minutes. Rinse in cold water; pat dry. In small bowl, toss onion with lime juice. Top each serving with yogurt then red onion mixture. Sprinkle with coriander.

PER SERVING (WITHOUT SKIN): about 276 cal, 26 g pro, 12 g total fat (2 g sat. fat), 17 g carb, 2 g fibre, 98 mg chol, 321 mg sodium. % RDI: 8% calcium, 12% iron, 3% vit A, 25% vit C, 17% folate.

TEST KITCHEN TIP
For a smaller crowd, this recipe is easy to halve. Use 2½-quart (2.5 L) slow cooker; cook until juices run clear when chicken is pierced, about 4 hours. Makes 2 to 4 servings.

Paprika Chicken

**4½- to 6-quart (4.5 to 6 L)
slow cooker**

Makes 4 servings

For this dish, look for sweet Hungarian paprika. If your paprika has been lurking in your spice drawer for more than a year, it's time to get a new bottle.

1 tbsp	vegetable oil	15 mL	1	can (19 oz/540 mL) tomatoes	1
8	chicken thighs	8	2 tbsp	tomato paste	30 mL
1	onion, chopped	1	1	sweet green pepper, diced	1
2	cloves garlic, minced	2			
1 tbsp	sweet paprika	15 mL	½ cup	light sour cream	125 mL
¼ tsp	each salt and pepper	1 mL	2 tbsp	minced fresh parsley	30 mL

➤ In large skillet, heat oil over medium-high heat; brown chicken, in batches if necessary. Transfer to slow cooker.

➤ Drain fat from skillet. Fry onion, garlic, paprika, salt and pepper over medium heat, stirring often, until onion is softened, about 5 minutes.

➤ Add tomatoes; mash with potato masher or fork into bite-size pieces. Bring to boil, scraping up brown bits from bottom of skillet. Scrape into slow cooker. Stir to combine.

➤ Cover; cook on low until juices run clear when chicken is pierced, about 4 hours. Skim off fat. Stir tomato paste and green pepper into slow cooker.

➤ Cover and cook on high until thickened, about 15 minutes. (Make-ahead: Let cool for 30 minutes. Refrigerate, uncovered, in airtight containers until cold. Cover and refrigerate for up to 1 day or freeze for up to 1 month.)

➤ Garnish with sour cream and parsley.

PER SERVING (WITHOUT SKIN): about 268 cal, 26 g pro, 11 g total fat (3 g sat. fat), 17 g carb, 3 g fibre, 99 mg chol, 478 mg sodium. % RDI: 12% calcium, 21% iron, 26% vit A, 87% vit C, 14% folate.

Chicken Cuts for the Slow Cooker

For the slow cooker, thighs are the best cut. While shoppers often opt for boneless skinless, our preference is bone-in (for flavour) and skin-on (to keep the meat intact). No one needs the extra calories from fatty chicken skin, so trim off any visible pads of fat before cooking and remove the flabby skin after cooking.

Sweet & Sour Chicken

This family-friendly chicken needs lots of rice to soak up its tangy orange sauce. With youngsters, this recipe will feed six.

4½- to 6-quart (4.5 to 6 L)
slow cooker

Makes 4 servings

2	green onions	2
1	each sweet red and green pepper	1
3	carrots, thinly sliced	3
3	cloves garlic, sliced	3
8	chicken thighs	8
½ tsp	each salt and pepper	2 mL

1 tbsp	vegetable oil	15 mL
1 cup	orange juice	250 mL
½ cup	each liquid honey and soy sauce	125 mL
3 tbsp	tomato paste	45 mL
3 tbsp	cornstarch	45 mL

❧ Chop white parts of onions; place in slow cooker. Thinly slice green parts; set aside.

❧ Seed, core and cut red and green peppers into ½-inch (1 cm) pieces. Add red pepper to slow cooker; set green pepper aside. Add carrots and garlic to slow cooker.

❧ Sprinkle chicken with salt and pepper. In large skillet, heat oil over medium-high heat; brown chicken, in batches if necessary. Transfer to slow cooker.

❧ Drain fat from skillet. Add orange juice; bring to boil, scraping up brown bits from bottom of skillet. Whisk in honey, soy sauce and tomato paste; scrape into slow cooker. Stir to combine.

❧ Cover; cook on low until juices run clear when chicken is pierced, about 4 hours. Skim off fat. Move chicken and peppers to 1 side of slow cooker.

❧ Whisk cornstarch with ¼ cup (50 mL) water; stir into liquid in slow cooker. Stir in green pepper.

❧ Cover and cook on high until thickened and green pepper is tender-crisp, about 15 minutes. (Make-ahead: Let cool for 30 minutes. Refrigerate, uncovered, in airtight containers until cold. Cover and refrigerate for up to 1 day.)

❧ Sprinkle with reserved green onions.

PER SERVING (WITHOUT SKIN): about 516 cal, 27 g pro, 19 g total fat (5 g sat. fat), 63 g carb, 4 g fibre, 93 mg chol, 2,470 mg sodium. % RDI: 6% calcium, 26% iron, 154% vit A, 158% vit C, 22% folate.

Chicken Zarzuela

6-quart (6 L) slow cooker

Makes 8 servings

The word *zarzuela* in Spanish means both a comic opera in which song is intermingled with spoken word, and a delicious stew often made with seafood. Here, zarzuela features chicken, with signature Spanish ingredients such as olive oil, saffron, olives and almonds.

16	chicken thighs	16	4 tsp	sweet paprika	20 mL
1 tsp	salt	5 mL	1 tsp	dried marjoram or oregano	5 mL
½ tsp	pepper	2 mL			
2 tbsp	olive oil	30 mL	¼ tsp	saffron threads	1 mL
2	Spanish onions, chopped	2	⅓ cup	ground almonds	75 mL
			1 tbsp	lemon juice	15 mL
6	cloves garlic, minced	6	1 cup	large green olives, pitted and halved	250 mL
½ cup	dry white wine	125 mL			
1	can (28 oz/796 mL) tomatoes	1	¼ cup	chopped fresh parsley	50 mL
			2 tbsp	tomato paste	30 mL

SUBSTITUTION

No white wine? Pour 2 tbsp (30 mL) white wine vinegar into measuring cup. Fill to ½ cup (125 mL) with chicken broth.

❧ Sprinkle chicken with ½ tsp (2 mL) of the salt and pepper. In large skillet, heat 1 tbsp (15 mL) of the oil over medium-high heat; brown chicken, in batches. Transfer to slow cooker.

❧ Drain fat from skillet; heat remaining oil over medium heat. Fry onions and 4 of the garlic cloves until softened, about 4 minutes. Add wine; bring to boil, scraping up brown bits from bottom of skillet. Scrape into slow cooker along with tomatoes, paprika, marjoram and remaining salt. Mash tomatoes with fork until slightly chunky. Stir to combine.

❧ Cover and cook on low until juices run clear when chicken is pierced, about 4 to 5 hours. Skim off fat.

❧ Meanwhile, crumble saffron into bowl; pour in 2 tbsp (30 mL) hot water and let stand for 5 minutes. Stir almonds, remaining garlic and lemon juice into bowl; stir into slow cooker along with olives, parsley and tomato paste.

❧ Cover and cook on high until thickened, about 20 minutes. (Make-ahead: Let cool for 30 minutes. Refrigerate, uncovered, in airtight containers until cold. Cover and refrigerate for up to 1 day.)

PER SERVING (WITHOUT SKIN): about 351 cal, 35 g pro, 17 g total fat (3 g sat. fat), 16 g carb, 3 g fibre, 138 mg chol, 1,028 mg sodium. % RDI: 9% calcium, 26% iron, 18% vit A, 48% vit C, 18% folate.

Chicken & Cornmeal Dumplings

Keep this recipe in mind for Sunday dinners, when the family takes time to enjoy one another's company and some good cooking.

6-quart (6 L) slow cooker

Makes 6 to
8 servings

3 lb	chicken thighs	1.5 kg	2	potatoes, peeled and cut in 1-inch (2.5 cm) cubes	2
1 tbsp	vegetable oil	15 mL	3 tbsp	all-purpose flour	45 mL
2	each carrots and stalks celery, cut into chunks	2	**DUMPLINGS:**		
1	onion, chopped	1	¾ cup	all-purpose flour	175 mL
2	cloves garlic, minced	2	¼ cup	cornmeal	50 mL
2	bay leaves	2	1 tsp	baking powder	5 mL
1 tsp	dried thyme	5 mL	¼ tsp	baking soda	1 mL
½ tsp	each salt and pepper	2 mL	Pinch	salt	Pinch
¼ tsp	dried marjoram	1 mL	2 tbsp	cold butter, cubed	30 mL
1 cup	sodium-reduced chicken broth	250 mL	⅔ cup	buttermilk	150 mL
			2 tbsp	chopped fresh parsley	30 mL

TEST KITCHEN TIP

In this recipe, we recommend removing the thighs from the slow cooker and letting them cool slightly. Pull off the skin, then return them to the slow cooker and top the stew off with the dumplings.

❧ Trim fat from chicken; place in slow cooker.

❧ In large skillet, heat oil over medium heat; fry carrots, celery, onion, garlic, bay leaves, thyme, salt, pepper and marjoram, stirring occasionally, until vegetables are softened, about 5 minutes. Scrape into slow cooker.

❧ Add 1½ cups (375 mL) water to skillet; bring to boil, scraping up brown bits. Scrape into slow cooker along with broth and potatoes. Stir to combine.

❧ Cover and cook on low until juices run clear when chicken is pierced, about 3 to 4 hours. Discard bay leaves. Skim off fat.

❧ Move chicken and vegetables to 1 side. In bowl, whisk flour with ⅓ cup (75 mL) water until smooth; whisk into liquid in slow cooker. Stir gently.

❧ DUMPLINGS: Meanwhile, in bowl, whisk flour, cornmeal, baking powder, baking soda and salt. Using pastry blender, cut in butter until in coarse crumbs. Add buttermilk and parsley; stir to make sticky spoonable dough.

❧ Drop 8 spoonfuls of dumpling batter onto stew. Cover and cook on high until dumplings are no longer doughy underneath, about 20 minutes.

PER EACH OF 8 SERVINGS (WITHOUT SKIN): about 385 cal, 25 g pro, 19 g total fat (6 g sat. fat), 28 g carb, 2 g fibre, 113 mg chol, 458 mg sodium. % RDI: 8% calcium, 19% iron, 40% vit A, 15% vit C, 26% folate.

Saucy Peanut Chicken

The sauce for this chicken is a delectable blend of peanuts and coconut milk, with a blush of hot peppers. It's a wonderful party dish to serve over rice, with sugar snap peas, asparagus or broccoli.

6-quart (6 L) slow cooker

Makes 8 servings

¼ cup	vegetable oil	50 mL		1 cup	coconut milk	250 mL
1	onion, chopped	1		3 tbsp	smooth peanut butter	45 mL
4	cloves garlic, chopped	4		16	chicken thighs	16
3 tbsp	tomato paste	45 mL		¼ cup	chopped fresh coriander or parsley	50 mL
2 tbsp	sweet paprika	30 mL		2 tbsp	minced hot red or jalapeño pepper	30 mL
¾ tsp	each salt and pepper	4 mL				
½ tsp	ground ginger	2 mL				

❧ In large skillet, heat half of the oil over medium-high heat; sauté onion and garlic until softened, about 4 minutes.

❧ Stir in tomato paste, paprika, 2 tbsp (30 mL) water, ½ tsp (2 mL) each of the salt and pepper and ginger; cook, stirring, for 1 minute.

❧ Stir in coconut milk and peanut butter; let cool slightly. Transfer to food processor; purée until smooth. (Make-ahead: Let cool to room temperature. Refrigerate in airtight container for up to 2 days.)

❧ Sprinkle chicken with remaining salt and pepper. In large skillet, heat remaining oil over medium-high heat; brown chicken, in batches. Transfer to slow cooker. Pour sauce over top.

❧ Cover and cook on low until juices run clear when chicken is pierced, about 4 hours. Skim off fat.

❧ Stir in coriander and hot pepper. Cover and cook on high until flavours are blended, about 20 minutes.

PER SERVING: about 514 cal, 41 g pro, 36 g total fat (12 g sat. fat), 6 g carb, 1 g fibre, 149 mg chol, 399 mg sodium. % RDI: 4% calcium, 25% iron, 19% vit A, 15% vit C, 8% folate.

Chicken with Lemon, Fennel & Garlic

The mild licorice flavour of a fennel bulb is, like tarragon, a superb match with chicken. Fennel is also delicious roasted in wedges or sliced paper-thin in a salad.

4½- to 6-quart (4.5 to 6 L) slow cooker

Makes 6 servings

1	large fennel bulb	1
⅓ cup	all-purpose flour	75 mL
¼ tsp	each salt and pepper	1 mL
8	chicken thighs	8
2 tbsp	vegetable oil	30 mL

20	large cloves garlic (about 2 heads)	20
1 cup	chicken broth	250 mL
½ cup	white wine	125 mL
2 tbsp	chopped fresh dill	30 mL
2 tbsp	lemon juice	30 mL

❧ Remove fronds from fennel stems; chop fronds coarsely, discarding stems. Cut fennel in half lengthwise and core; cut lengthwise into ¼-inch (5 mm) thick slices. Set fronds and fennel slices aside separately.

❧ In shallow dish, combine flour, salt and pepper; add chicken and turn to coat. Reserve remaining flour mixture.

❧ In large skillet, heat oil over medium-high heat; brown chicken, in batches if necessary. Transfer to slow cooker.

❧ Drain fat from skillet. Fry garlic and sliced fennel over medium-low heat, stirring occasionally, until fennel is softened, about 10 minutes. Scrape into slow cooker. Add broth to skillet; bring to boil, scraping up brown bits from bottom of skillet. Scrape into slow cooker. Stir in wine.

❧ Cover and cook on low until juices run clear when chicken is pierced and fennel is tender, about 4 to 5 hours. Skim off fat. Move chicken and vegetables to 1 side. In small bowl, whisk reserved flour mixture with ⅓ cup (75 mL) water; whisk into liquid in slow cooker. Stir to redistribute.

❧ Cover and cook on high until slightly thickened, about 15 minutes. (Make-ahead: Let cool for 30 minutes. Refrigerate, uncovered, in airtight containers until cold. Cover and refrigerate for up to 1 day.)

❧ Stir in dill, lemon juice and reserved fennel fronds.

PER SERVING (WITHOUT SKIN): about 266 cal, 18 g pro, 15 g total fat (3 g sat. fat), 15 g carb, 3 g fibre, 62 mg chol, 315 mg sodium. % RDI: 6% calcium, 15% iron, 2% vit A, 18% vit C, 13% folate.

Soy-Glazed Chicken Hot Pot

Soy sauce is key to the flavour and colour of this dish. To cut extra salt, we have chosen sodium-reduced soy sauce rather than regular and gone a step further with sodium-reduced chicken broth. This cuts the sodium by more than half.

4½- to 6-quart (4.5 to 6 L)
slow cooker

Makes 4 servings

2 tsp	vegetable oil	10 mL
8	chicken thighs	8
1 cup	halved mushrooms	250 mL
1	onion, sliced	1
1	piece (2 inches/5 cm) gingerroot, sliced	1
2	cloves garlic, minced	2
Pinch	hot pepper flakes	Pinch
1 cup	sodium-reduced chicken broth	250 mL
¼ cup	sodium-reduced soy sauce	50 mL
1 tbsp	granulated sugar	15 mL
3 tbsp	cornstarch	45 mL
1	sweet yellow or green pepper, chopped	1
	Coriander or parsley sprigs	

❧ In large skillet, heat oil over medium-high heat; brown chicken, in batches if necessary. Transfer to slow cooker.

❧ Drain fat from skillet. Fry mushrooms, onion, ginger, garlic and hot pepper flakes over medium heat, stirring occasionally, until onion is softened, about 5 minutes. Scrape into slow cooker.

❧ Add chicken broth, soy sauce and sugar to skillet; bring to boil, scraping up brown bits from bottom of skillet. Scrape into slow cooker. Stir to combine.

❧ Cover and cook on low until juices run clear when chicken is pierced, about 4 to 5 hours. Skim off fat. Move chicken and vegetables to 1 side.

❧ In small bowl, whisk cornstarch with ¼ cup (50 mL) water; whisk into liquid in slow cooker. Stir in yellow pepper.

❧ Cover and cook on high until thickened and pepper is tender-crisp, about 15 minutes. (Make-ahead: Let cool for 30 minutes. Refrigerate, uncovered, in airtight containers until cold. Cover and refrigerate for up to 1 day or freeze for up to 1 month.)

❧ Garnish with coriander.

PER SERVING (WITHOUT SKIN): about 244 cal, 25 g pro, 8 g total fat (2 g sat. fat), 17 g carb, 1 g fibre, 95 mg chol, 853 mg sodium. % RDI: 3% calcium, 15% iron, 2% vit A, 82% vit C, 10% folate.

Thai Green Curry Chicken

This dish is hot and spicy, as you would expect in a good Thai restaurant. For those sensitive to hot food, reduce the curry paste to 2 tsp (10 mL) or use mild Indian curry paste. Serve with lots of rice.

4½- to 6-quart (4.5 to 6 L)
slow cooker

Makes 6 servings

6	boneless skinless chicken thighs	6
2 tbsp	vegetable oil	30 mL
3	small Asian eggplants (or 1 large eggplant), cut into 2-inch (5 cm) chunks	3
1	large onion, diced	1
2	cloves garlic, minced	2
1	piece (2 inches/5 cm) gingerroot, sliced	1
1	can (400 mL) coconut milk	1
2 tbsp	fish sauce	30 mL
1 tbsp	granulated sugar	15 mL
1 tbsp	Thai green curry paste	15 mL
½ tsp	grated lime rind	2 mL
1 tbsp	lime juice	15 mL
2	sweet green peppers, diced	2
½ cup	lightly packed fresh basil (Thai basil if available)	125 mL
½ cup	lightly packed fresh coriander leaves	125 mL

❧ Cut chicken into bite-size pieces. In wok or large skillet, heat 1 tbsp (15 mL) of the oil over high heat; stir-fry chicken, in batches, until browned, about 3 minutes. Transfer to slow cooker.

❧ Add remaining oil to wok; stir-fry eggplants, onion, garlic and ginger until onion is softened, about 5 minutes. Scrape into slow cooker.

❧ In wok, whisk together coconut milk, fish sauce, sugar, curry paste, and lime rind and juice; bring to boil, scraping up brown bits from bottom of wok. Pour into slow cooker; stir to combine.

❧ Cover and cook on low until chicken and eggplant are tender, about 4 to 5 hours. Skim off fat.

❧ Stir in green peppers and three-quarters each of the basil and coriander; cover and cook on high until peppers are tender-crisp, about 15 minutes. Sprinkle with remaining basil and coriander.

PER SERVING: about 336 cal, 18 g pro, 23 g total fat (13 g sat. fat), 17 g carb, 4 g fibre, 63 mg chol, 543 mg sodium. % RDI: 4% calcium, 26% iron, 6% vit A, 58% vit C, 19% folate.

Chicken Chili

4½- to 6-quart (4.5 to 6 L)
slow cooker

Makes 4 servings

This chili is seasoned with just a touch of chipotle chili powder, which is hotter than regular chili powder. Chipotle peppers are smoked ripe jalapeño peppers, which are then ground to make this seasoning. When combined with two other spices, ground coriander and cumin, they make for an interesting new twist on tomato-less chili. Serve with tortillas (corn if you can find them) or cornbread.

2 tbsp	vegetable oil	30 mL	1	can (19 oz/540 mL) white kidney beans, drained and rinsed	1
8	boneless skinless chicken thighs	8	2	cans (each 4½ oz/ 127 mL) chopped green chilies	2
1	onion, chopped	1			
3	cloves garlic, minced	3	2 tbsp	all-purpose flour	30 mL
2 tsp	ground coriander	10 mL	⅓ cup	chopped fresh coriander	75 mL
1½ tsp	ground cumin	7 mL			
1 tsp	chipotle chili powder	5 mL	2 tbsp	lime juice	30 mL
¼ tsp	each salt and pepper	1 mL			

SUBSTITUTIONS

If you want to cook your own beans, feel free. Substitute 2 cups (500 mL) cooked beans (see recipe, page 213) for the canned. You can also use regular chili powder instead of chipotle chili powder.

➤ In large skillet, heat half of the oil over medium-high heat; brown chicken, in batches if necessary. Transfer to slow cooker.

➤ Drain fat from skillet; add remaining oil. Fry onion, garlic, coriander, cumin, chili powder, salt and pepper over medium heat, stirring occasionally, until onion is softened, about 6 minutes. Scrape into slow cooker along with beans and green chilies. Stir to combine.

➤ Cover and cook on low until juices run clear when chicken is pierced, about 4 to 5 hours.

➤ Remove chicken from sauce; cube and set aside. Skim off fat. Move beans to 1 side of slow cooker. In small bowl, whisk flour with 3 tbsp (45 mL) water; whisk into liquid in slow cooker.

➤ Cover and cook on high until thickened, about 15 minutes. Stir in chicken. (Make-ahead: Let cool for 30 minutes. Refrigerate, uncovered, in airtight containers until cold. Cover and refrigerate for up to 1 day.)

➤ Cover and cook on high until hot, about 5 minutes. Stir in coriander and lime juice.

PER SERVING: about 352 cal, 30 g pro, 14 g total fat (2 g sat. fat), 28 g carb, 9 g fibre, 95 mg chol, 708 mg sodium. % RDI: 8% calcium, 29% iron, 5% vit A, 32% vit C, 35% folate.

Indonesian Chicken in Peanut Sauce

This quick, saucy chicken dish is characteristic of Southeast Asian cooking, which pairs peanuts so deliciously with chicken. Serve with plenty of rice.

4½- to 6-quart (4.5 to 6 L)
slow cooker

Makes 4 servings

8	chicken thighs	8	½ tsp	ground ginger	2 mL
5	carrots, sliced	5	¼ tsp	hot pepper flakes	1 mL
2	onions, chopped	2	1 cup	frozen peas	250 mL
2	cloves garlic, minced	2	1 tsp	white wine vinegar	5 mL
¾ cup	smooth peanut butter	175 mL	2	green onions, sliced	2
¼ cup	soy sauce	50 mL	½ cup	chopped unsalted peanuts	125 mL

Pull skin off chicken thighs and discard. Place chicken, carrots, onions and garlic in slow cooker.

In small bowl, whisk together 1¼ cups (300 mL) water, peanut butter, soy sauce, ginger and hot pepper flakes; pour into slow cooker. Stir to combine.

Cover and cook on low until vegetables are tender and juices run clear when chicken is pierced, about 4 to 5 hours. Skim off fat. (Make-ahead: Let cool for 30 minutes. Refrigerate, uncovered, in airtight containers until cold. Cover and refrigerate for up to 1 day.)

Add peas and vinegar; cover and cook on high until steaming hot, about 10 minutes. Serve garnished with green onions and peanuts.

PER SERVING: about 655 cal, 48 g pro, 39 g total fat (8 g sat. fat), 34 g carb, 9 g fibre, 115 mg chol, 1,467 mg sodium. % RDI: 10% calcium, 31% iron, 232% vit A, 17% vit C, 51% folate.

Turkey Black Bean Chili

This is a handsome veggie-rich supper in a bowl. The recipe uses canned beans, but check page 213 for details on soaking and cooking dried beans. Freeze in 2-cup (500 mL) freezer bags to cut the cost of a batch of chili.

4½- to 6-quart (4.5 to 6 L) slow cooker

Makes 4 to 6 servings

2 tbsp	vegetable oil	30 mL	1	can (28 oz/796 mL) diced tomatoes	1
1 lb	ground turkey or chicken	500 g	1	can (19 oz/540 mL) black beans, drained and rinsed	1
1	onion, chopped	1	1	small zucchini, cubed	1
2	cloves garlic, minced	2	½ cup	corn kernels	125 mL
3 tbsp	chili powder	45 mL	¼ cup	minced fresh coriander or parsley	50 mL
2 tsp	dried oregano	10 mL		Sour cream and sliced jalapeño peppers (optional)	
½ tsp	salt	2 mL			
¼ tsp	pepper	1 mL			
2 tbsp	tomato paste	30 mL			

❧ In large skillet, heat 1 tbsp (15 mL) of the oil over medium-high heat; sauté turkey, breaking up with fork until crumbly and no longer pink, about 8 minutes. Using slotted spoon, transfer turkey to slow cooker.

❧ Drain fat from skillet; add remaining oil. Fry onion, garlic, chili powder, oregano, salt and pepper over medium heat until onion is softened, about 4 minutes. Stir in tomato paste; cook for 1 minute. Add tomatoes; bring to boil, scraping up brown bits from bottom of skillet. Scrape into slow cooker along with black beans, zucchini and corn. Stir to combine.

❧ Cover and cook on low until thick enough to mound on spoon, about 4 hours. Skim off fat. (Make-ahead: Let cool for 30 minutes. Refrigerate, uncovered, in airtight containers until cold. Cover and refrigerate for up to 3 days or freeze for up to 1 month.)

❧ Stir in coriander. Serve garnished with sour cream and jalapeño peppers (if using).

PER EACH OF 6 SERVINGS: about 281 cal, 20 g pro, 12 g total fat (3 g sat. fat), 26 g carb, 9 g fibre, 60 mg chol, 717 mg sodium. % RDI: 9% calcium, 33% iron, 16% vit A, 42% vit C, 30% folate.

Sausage & Seafood Ragout

The sausage is savoury, the fish is flaky, and the sauce is thick – what more hearty meal could you ask for to feed hungry family and friends?

4½- to 6-quart (4.5 to 6 L) slow cooker

Makes 8 to 10 servings

1 tbsp	extra-virgin olive oil	15 mL	1	small eggplant, cut into 1-inch (2.5 cm) cubes	1
1 lb	chorizo or mild Italian sausages, cut into chunks	500 g	1	can (28 oz/796 mL) diced tomatoes	1
1	onion, diced	1	¼ cup	tomato paste	50 mL
2	cloves garlic, minced	2	1 tbsp	sweet paprika	15 mL
½ cup	diced celery	125 mL	2 lb	mussels	1 kg
½ tsp	dried thyme	2 mL	12 oz	catfish fillets	375 g
¾ cup	dry white wine	175 mL	2 tbsp	chopped fresh parsley	30 mL

❧ In large skillet, heat oil over medium-high heat; brown sausages. Transfer to slow cooker.

❧ Drain fat from skillet. Fry onion, garlic, celery and thyme over medium heat, stirring often, until softened, about 5 minutes. Scrape into slow cooker.

❧ Add wine to skillet; bring to boil, scraping up brown bits from bottom of skillet. Scrape into slow cooker along with eggplant, tomatoes, tomato paste and paprika. Stir to combine.

❧ Cover and cook on low until eggplant is tender, about 5 to 6 hours. Skim off fat.

❧ Meanwhile, scrub mussels; trim off any beards. Discard any that do not close when tapped. Cut fish into 2-inch (5 cm) pieces. Nestle mussels and fish into liquid.

❧ Cover and cook on high until steaming hot and mussels open, about 20 minutes. Discard any that do not open. Sprinkle with parsley.

PER EACH OF 10 SERVINGS: about 313 cal, 22 g pro, 20 g total fat (7 g sat. fat), 11 g carb, 2 g fibre, 63 mg chol, 781 mg sodium. % RDI: 5% calcium, 23% iron, 11% vit A, 27% vit C, 11% folate.

Vegetable Curry with Chopped Eggs

4½- to 5½-quart (4.5 to 5.5 L) slow cooker

Makes 4 to 6 servings

This mild curry is delicious spooned over basmati rice (try whole grain for added nutrition) and accompanied by lime wedges to squeeze over top.

2 tbsp	vegetable oil	30 mL
1	large onion, sliced	1
1	small eggplant, cubed	1
3	cloves garlic, minced	3
1 tbsp	minced gingerroot	15 mL
½ tsp	salt	2 mL
3 cups	cauliflower florets	750 mL
2	potatoes, peeled and cubed	2
2 cups	vegetable broth	500 mL
¼ cup	tomato paste	50 mL
3 tbsp	mild curry paste	45 mL
1½ cups	frozen peas	375 mL
4	hard-cooked eggs, diced	4
¼ cup	fresh coriander sprigs	50 mL

In large skillet, heat oil over medium heat; fry onion, eggplant, garlic, ginger and salt until eggplant is softened, about 6 minutes. Scrape into slow cooker along with cauliflower, potatoes, broth, tomato paste and curry paste. Stir to combine.

Cover and cook until vegetables are tender, about 4 hours.

Stir in peas. Cover and cook on high until steaming hot, about 15 minutes. Ladle curry into bowls; sprinkle with eggs and coriander.

PER EACH OF 6 SERVINGS: about 245 cal, 9 g pro, 13 g total fat (2 g sat. fat), 26 g carb, 6 g fibre, 124 mg chol, 698 mg sodium. % RDI: 5% calcium, 13% iron, 11% vit A, 58% vit C, 33% folate.

Chinese Braised Tofu

This is the popular Chinese dish *ma po tofu* with ground soy protein replacing the usual ground pork. Serve over rice.

4½- to 5½-quart (4.5 to 5.5 L) slow cooker

Makes 4 to 6 servings

1	pkg (454 g) medium-firm tofu, drained	1	1	pkg (12 oz/340 g) precooked ground soy protein mixture	1	
6	green onions	6	1½ cups	vegetable broth	375 mL	
1 tbsp	vegetable oil	15 mL	2 tbsp	dry sherry or vegetable broth	30 mL	
3 cups	sliced mushrooms (8 oz/250 g)	750 mL	2 tbsp	soy sauce	30 mL	
2	carrots, diced	2	2 tbsp	black bean garlic sauce	30 mL	
3	cloves garlic, minced	3	1 tsp	sesame oil	5 mL	
1 tbsp	minced gingerroot	15 mL	3 tbsp	cornstarch	45 mL	
Pinch	each hot pepper flakes and ground cloves	Pinch	1 cup	frozen peas	250 mL	

Cut tofu into ¾-inch (2 cm) cubes; drain in colander for 15 minutes.

Meanwhile, chop white and green parts of green onions separately. In large skillet, heat oil over medium-high heat; sauté white parts of onions, mushrooms, carrots, garlic, ginger, hot pepper flakes and cloves until no liquid remains, 8 minutes. Scrape into slow cooker. Add soy protein mixture.

Add broth to skillet; bring to boil, scraping up brown bits on bottom of skillet. Scrape into slow cooker along with sherry, soy sauce, black bean garlic sauce and sesame oil; stir well. Nestle tofu into sauce.

Cover and cook on low until bubbly and vegetables are tender, about 3 hours. Skim off fat. Move tofu and vegetables to 1 side of slow cooker.

In small bowl, whisk cornstarch with ½ cup (125 mL) water; whisk into liquid in slow cooker. Gently stir in peas, redistributing ingredients.

Cover and cook on high until thickened, about 20 minutes. (Make-ahead: Let cool for 30 minutes. Refrigerate, uncovered, in airtight containers until cold. Cover and refrigerate for up to 1 day.)

Sprinkle with green parts of onions.

PER EACH OF 6 SERVINGS: about 214 cal, 18 g pro, 7 g total fat (1 g sat. fat), 21 g carb, 6 g fibre, 0 mg chol, 908 mg sodium. % RDI: 14% calcium, 35% iron, 63% vit A, 10% vit C, 28% folate.

4½- to 5½-quart (4.5 to 5.5 L) slow cooker

Makes 4 servings

Thai Green Curry with Vegetables & Tofu

If you like mild curry, reduce the curry paste to 2 tsp (10 mL). Serve over rice with lime wedges to squeeze over top.

1	pkg (1 lb/500 g) firm tofu, drained	1
1 tbsp	vegetable oil	15 mL
1	onion, coarsely chopped	1
1	large eggplant (1 lb/ 500 g), cubed	1
1	sweet red pepper, cut into chunks	1
1	zucchini, cut into chunks	1
3	cloves garlic, minced	3
1 tbsp	minced gingerroot	15 mL
1	can (400 mL) coconut milk	1
½ cup	chopped fresh coriander	125 mL
1 tbsp	green curry paste	15 mL
1 tbsp	soy sauce	15 mL
½ tsp	grated lime rind	2 mL
1 tbsp	lime juice	15 mL
1	sweet green pepper, cut into chunks	1
⅓ cup	chopped peanuts	75 mL

❧ Cut tofu into ¾-inch (2 cm) cubes; drain in colander for 15 minutes.

❧ Meanwhile, in large skillet, heat oil over medium heat; fry onion, eggplant, red pepper, zucchini, garlic and ginger, stirring occasionally, until eggplant is tender, about 8 minutes. Scrape into slow cooker.

❧ Stir together coconut milk, 1 tbsp (15 mL) of the coriander, curry paste, soy sauce, and lime rind and juice; stir into eggplant mixture. Add tofu. Stir gently to combine.

❧ Cover and cook until vegetables are tender, about 4 hours.

❧ Gently stir in green pepper and remaining coriander. Cover and cook on high until thickened and green pepper is tender-crisp, about 15 minutes. Sprinkle with peanuts.

PER SERVING: about 467 cal, 17 g pro, 37 g total fat (20 g sat. fat), 26 g carb, 7 g fibre, 0 mg chol, 443 mg sodium. % RDI: 22% calcium, 43% iron, 15% vit A, 130% vit C, 46% folate.

Black Bean Chili with Avocado Salsa

Avocado salsa adds its modern, fresh zing to a comforting, crowd-pleasing classic. Buy avocados a few days ahead and let ripen at room temperature until they give to light pressure. The skin of a nobbly Haas avocado turns almost black as it ripens.

4½- to 6-quart (4.5 to 6 L) slow cooker

Makes 8 servings

1 tbsp	vegetable oil	15 mL
2	onions, chopped	2
2	cloves garlic, minced	2
2	carrots, chopped	2
1	jalapeño pepper, seeded and minced	1
1 tbsp	chili powder	15 mL
1 tsp	each ground cumin and dried oregano	5 mL
¼ tsp	salt	1 mL
2	cans (each 28 oz/ 796 mL) stewed tomatoes	2
¼ cup	tomato paste	50 mL

2	cans (each 19 oz/ 540 mL) black beans, drained and rinsed (or 4 cups/1 L cooked beans; recipe, page 213)	2
2	sweet red peppers, chopped	2
AVOCADO SALSA:		
2	avocados, peeled, pitted and diced	2
2 tbsp	minced red onion	30 mL
2 tbsp	chopped fresh coriander	30 mL
2 tbsp	lime juice	30 mL
Pinch	each salt and pepper	Pinch

➷ In large skillet, heat oil over medium heat; fry onions, garlic, carrots, jalapeño pepper, chili powder, cumin, oregano and salt, stirring occasionally, until onions are softened, about 5 minutes.

➷ Add juice from 1 of the cans of tomatoes; bring to boil, scraping up brown bits from bottom of skillet. Scrape into slow cooker along with tomatoes and remaining juice, tomato paste, black beans and red peppers. Stir to combine. Cover and cook until carrots are tender, about 4 to 6 hours. (Make-ahead: Let cool for 30 minutes. Refrigerate, uncovered, in airtight containers until cold. Cover and refrigerate for up to 3 days or freeze for up to 1 month.)

➷ **AVOCADO SALSA:** In bowl, combine avocados, onion, coriander, lime juice, salt and pepper. Spoon over each serving of chili.

PER SERVING: about 294 cal, 11 g pro, 10 g total fat (2 g sat. fat), 45 g carb, 14 g fibre, 0 mg chol, 934 mg sodium. % RDI: 12% calcium, 34% iron, 77% vit A, 148% vit C, 50% folate.

TVP Tacos

4½- to 6-quart (4.5 to 6 L)
slow cooker

Makes 12 tacos, or
8 to 12 servings

TVP, or textured vegetable protein, is a dried soy product available in granules or chunks. Cooked TVP resembles the texture of ground meat. Available in the health food section of grocery stores, bulk food stores and health food stores, TVP is an economical vegetarian protein. Like tofu, TVP has a mild flavour and absorbs the tastes that cook with it. Vegetarians and meat eaters alike will enjoy its versatility.

12	taco shells	12	2	onions, finely diced	2
2 cups	shredded iceberg lettuce	500 mL	2	stalks celery, finely diced	2
2	plum tomatoes, chopped	2	6	cloves garlic, minced	6
1	avocado (optional), peeled, pitted and cubed	1	2 tbsp	chili powder	30 mL
			4 tsp	each ground cumin and coriander	20 mL
1 cup	shredded Cheddar cheese	250 mL	1 tsp	dried oregano	5 mL
FILLING:			½ tsp	chipotle chili powder (or ½ tsp/2 mL hot pepper sauce)	2 mL
2 cups	vegetable broth	500 mL	½ tsp	salt	2 mL
2 cups	TVP granules	500 mL	1	can (28 oz/796 mL) tomatoes	1
2 tbsp	vegetable oil	30 mL			

SUBSTITUTION

This recipe works nicely with meat, too. For Beef Tacos, omit vegetable broth and replace TVP granules with 2 lb (1 kg) lean ground beef. In skillet over medium-high heat, sauté beef, breaking up with fork until crumbly and no longer pink, about 12 minutes. Drain fat from pan. Proceed with recipe.

❧ FILLING: In saucepan, bring 1½ cups (375 mL) of the broth to boil. Place TVP in slow cooker; pour in hot broth. Cover; let stand for 10 minutes.

❧ In large skillet, heat oil over medium heat; fry onions, celery and garlic until softened, 5 minutes. Add chili powder, cumin, coriander, oregano, chipotle powder and salt; cook, stirring, for 1 minute. Scrape into slow cooker.

❧ Add remaining broth and tomatoes to skillet. Mash tomatoes with potato masher or fork into small bite-size pieces. Bring to boil over medium heat, scraping up brown bits on bottom of skillet. Scrape into slow cooker.

❧ Cover and cook on low until thick enough to mound on spoon, about 4 to 6 hours. (Make-ahead: Let cool for 30 minutes. Refrigerate, uncovered, in airtight containers until cold. Cover and refrigerate for up to 3 days or freeze for up to 1 month.)

❧ Fill each taco shell with about ¼ cup (50 mL) filling. Top with lettuce, tomatoes, avocado (if using), and cheese.

PER TACO: about 210 cal, 13 g pro, 9 g total fat (3 g sat. fat), 21 g carb, 5 g fibre, 11 mg chol, 443 mg sodium. % RDI: 17% calcium, 26% iron, 10% vit A, 22% vit C, 12% folate.

Ratatouille with Chickpeas

This fresh-tasting dish is a colourful main course that can double as a side dish. Enjoy with whole grain baguette.

4½- to 5½-quart (4.5 to 5.5 L) slow cooker

Makes 6 servings

1 tbsp	vegetable oil	15 mL
1	onion, chopped	1
2	cloves garlic, minced	2
6 cups	cubed eggplant (1 large)	1.5 L
2 tsp	dried basil	10 mL
1 tsp	dried oregano	5 mL
½ tsp	each salt and pepper	2 mL
1	each sweet red and yellow pepper	1

2	zucchini	2
⅓ cup	tomato paste	75 mL
1	can (19 oz/540 mL), chickpeas, drained and rinsed (or 2 cups/ 500 mL cooked chickpeas; recipe, page 213)	1
1	can (28 oz/796 mL) tomatoes	1
¼ cup	chopped fresh basil or parsley	50 mL

❧ In large skillet, heat oil over medium heat; fry onion, garlic, eggplant, basil, oregano, salt and pepper, stirring occasionally, until onion is softened, about 10 minutes. Scrape into slow cooker.

❧ Halve, core and seed red and yellow peppers; cut into 1-inch (2.5 cm) pieces. Cut zucchini in half lengthwise; cut crosswise into 1½-inch (4 cm) chunks. Add peppers, zucchini, tomato paste, chickpeas and tomatoes to slow cooker. Mash tomatoes with fork until slightly chunky. Stir to combine.

❧ Cover and cook on low until vegetables are tender, about 4 hours. (Make-ahead: Let cool for 30 minutes. Refrigerate, uncovered, in airtight containers until cold. Cover and refrigerate for up to 3 days or freeze for up to 1 month.)

❧ Stir in basil.

PER SERVING: about 192 cal, 7 g pro, 4 g total fat (trace sat. fat), 36 g carb, 8 g fibre, 0 mg chol, 589 mg sodium. % RDI: 9% calcium, 21% iron, 21% vit A, 155% vit C, 37% folate.

Three-Bean Chili

Just stir, cover and turn the slow cooker on. Nothing could be simpler.

1	can (28 oz/796 mL) tomatoes	1
¼ cup	tomato paste	50 mL
1 tbsp	chili powder	15 mL
1 tsp	each dried oregano and ground cumin	5 mL
¼ tsp	each salt, pepper and granulated sugar	1 mL

1	onion, chopped	1
2	cloves garlic, minced	2
1	each carrot and stalk celery, chopped	1
1	each can (19 oz/ 540 mL) red kidney beans, black beans and chickpeas, drained and rinsed	1

4½- to 5½-quart (4.5 to 5.5 L) slow cooker

Makes 6 servings

In slow cooker, mash tomatoes with potato masher or fork until slightly chunky. Add tomato paste, chili powder, oregano, cumin, salt, pepper and sugar. Stir to blend well.

Add onion, garlic, carrot, celery, kidney beans, black beans and chickpeas. Stir to combine.

Cover and cook on low until thick enough to mound on spoon, about 4 to 6 hours. (Make-ahead: Let cool for 30 minutes. Refrigerate, uncovered, in airtight containers until cold. Cover and refrigerate for up to 3 days or freeze for up to 1 month.)

PER SERVING: about 297 cal, 18 g pro, 3 g total fat (trace sat. fat), 55 g carb, 14 g fibre, 0 mg chol, 838 mg sodium. % RDI: 10% calcium, 32% iron, 45% vit A, 37% vit C, 76% folate.

SUBSTITUTION

If you like to cook your own beans, substitute 2 cups (500 mL) each cooked red kidney beans, black beans and chickpeas for the canned. Our easy recipe for cooking dried beans is on page 213.

Storing Staples

> On a regular basis, make a note to use up any supplies before they expire.
> At least once a year, clean out your pantry. Check expiry dates and chuck any over-the-hill items.
> Store pasta, rice, lentils, beans, cornmeal and flour in resealable containers or freezer bags, not their tattered packaging.
> Label containers with name of contents and date purchased.
> Use the refrigerator or freezer to keep whole grains, such as rolled oats, barley and flour, from going rancid.

Pot Roasts, Braised Steaks & Ribs

Spanish Pot Roast

While most pot roasts are on the delicious but homey side, this one is comfortably exotic. It features a touch of prosciutto, a splash of sherry and, in keeping with Spanish tradition, ground almonds to give body to the gravy.

5- to 6-quart (5 to 6 L) slow cooker

Makes 8 servings

3 lb	boneless beef cross rib pot roast	1.5 kg
¼ tsp	each salt and pepper	1 mL
2 tbsp	vegetable oil (approx)	30 mL
1	onion, thinly sliced	1
2	cloves garlic, minced	2
4 oz	prosciutto, diced	125 g
½ tsp	dried marjoram	2 mL
1 cup	sodium-reduced beef broth	250 mL
½ cup	sherry or sodium-reduced beef broth	125 mL
1	can (28 oz/796 mL) tomatoes, drained	1
1 cup	sliced roasted red peppers	250 mL
2 tbsp	all-purpose flour	30 mL
¼ cup	ground almonds	50 mL
2 tbsp	tomato paste	30 mL
1	sweet green pepper, thinly sliced	1

❧ Sprinkle beef with salt and pepper. In Dutch oven, heat half of the oil over medium-high heat; brown beef all over, adding more of the remaining oil, if necessary. Transfer to slow cooker.

❧ Drain fat from Dutch oven; add remaining oil. Fry onion, garlic, prosciutto and marjoram over medium heat until onion is softened, about 5 minutes. Add broth and sherry; bring to boil, scraping up brown bits from bottom of pan. Scrape into slow cooker along with tomatoes and red peppers. Stir to combine.

❧ Cover and cook on low until beef is tender, about 6 to 8 hours.

❧ Transfer beef to cutting board; cover and keep warm for about 15 minutes before slicing across the grain.

❧ Meanwhile, skim fat from liquid in slow cooker. In small bowl, whisk flour with ¼ cup (50 mL) water; whisk into liquid along with almonds and tomato paste. Stir in green pepper.

❧ Cover and cook on high until thickened, about 15 minutes. Serve with beef.

PER SERVING: about 397 cal, 36 g pro, 23 g total fat (7 g sat. fat), 12 g carb, 2 g fibre, 110 mg chol, 565 mg sodium. % RDI: 6% calcium, 38% iron, 9% vit A, 90% vit C, 12% folate.

TEST KITCHEN TIP
Jars of roasted red peppers are a great resource, especially when sweet pepper prices exceed the price of meat. Refrigerate any leftover peppers in their liquid and use up within a few days in salads, stews or pasta sauces, or as a garnish atop soups.

Braised Ginger Hoisin Pot Roast

You can substitute 1 tsp (5 mL) ground ginger for the gingerroot.

5- to 6-quart (5 to 6 L)
slow cooker

Makes 6 to
8 servings

4 lb	boneless beef cross rib or blade pot roast	2 kg	½ cup	hoisin sauce	125 mL
½ tsp	pepper	2 mL	½ cup	beef broth	125 mL
2 tbsp	vegetable oil	30 mL	¼ cup	packed brown sugar	50 mL
1	onion, chopped	1	¼ cup	sodium-reduced soy sauce	50 mL
5	cloves garlic, minced	5	2 tbsp	all-purpose flour	30 mL
1 tbsp	minced gingerroot	15 mL	2	green onions, thinly sliced	2

TEST KITCHEN TIP

Pot roasts reheat beautifully and are easier to carve when cold. Cool, wrap and refrigerate separately from the gravy. Once the gravy is cold, remove the solidified fat on top. Slice meat thinly, trimming off fat. Nestle in gravy and reheat.

❧ Sprinkle beef with pepper. In Dutch oven, heat oil over medium-high heat; brown beef all over. Transfer to slow cooker.

❧ Drain fat from Dutch oven. Fry onion, garlic and ginger over medium heat, stirring occasionally, until onion is softened, about 2 minutes. Add hoisin sauce, broth, brown sugar, soy sauce and ¼ cup (50 mL) water; bring to boil, scraping up brown bits from bottom of pan. Scrape over beef.

❧ Cover and cook on low until beef is tender, about 6 hours.

❧ Transfer beef to cutting board; cover and keep warm for about 10 to 15 minutes before slicing across the grain.

❧ Meanwhile, skim fat from liquid. In small bowl, whisk flour with ¼ cup (50 mL) water; whisk into liquid. Cover and cook on high, stirring once, until thickened, about 15 minutes. Serve with beef. Sprinkle with green onions.

PER EACH OF 8 SERVINGS: about 473 cal, 50 g pro, 21 g total fat (7 g sat. fat), 18 g carb, 1 g fibre, 116 mg chol, 754 mg sodium. % RDI: 4% calcium, 33% iron, 3% vit C, 13% folate.

Beef Cuts for the Slow Cooker

> **POT ROASTS:** Slow cooking imitates braising (simmering in liquid in a closed pot on the stove or in the oven). The following economical roasts are best braised and therefore a perfect fit: blade, cross rib, top blade, boneless bottom blade or brisket, and shoulder cuts. Cook until well-done and fork-tender.
> **RIBS:** Simmering short ribs are another rich, delicious stewing option.

> **STEWING BEEF CUBES:** While handy, these can be a mix of different cuts with varied cooking times. When you can, cut up a whole roast, such as a boneless cross rib, instead. You get the cube size you like, and you can trim fat and a few bucks by doing the knife work yourself.
> **SIMMERING STEAKS:** Try blade, top blade, boneless bottom blade and cross rib steaks.

Tangy Beef Pot Roast

This sweet-and-sour roast is truly a one-pot meal, but you might want to add a touch of colour with a side of carrots and/or a green vegetable cooked separately while the gravy thickens.

5- to 6-quart (5 to 6 L) slow cooker

Makes 6 to 8 servings

3 cups	sliced onions (see Tip, right)	750 mL	1½ tsp	ground ginger	7 mL
8	potatoes, halved	8	½ tsp	each salt and pepper	2 mL
1 tbsp	vegetable oil	15 mL	¼ tsp	ground cloves	1 mL
3 lb	boneless beef cross rib or blade pot roast	1.5 kg	1	bay leaf	1
			1 cup	light sour cream	250 mL
1½ cups	beef broth or water	375 mL	3 tbsp	all-purpose flour	45 mL
¼ cup	packed brown sugar	50 mL	1	sweet green pepper, diced	1
¼ cup	red wine vinegar	50 mL			

❧ Arrange onions and potatoes over bottom of slow cooker. In Dutch oven, heat oil over medium-high heat; brown beef all over. Place on vegetables.

❧ Drain fat from Dutch oven. Add ½ cup (125 mL) of the broth; bring to boil, scraping up brown bits from bottom of pan. Scrape into slow cooker.

❧ Mix together remaining broth, brown sugar, vinegar, ginger, salt, pepper, cloves and bay leaf; pour over beef.

❧ Cover and cook on low until beef is tender, about 7 to 8 hours. Discard bay leaf.

❧ Transfer beef to cutting board; cover and keep warm for about 15 minutes before slicing across the grain.

❧ Meanwhile, skim fat from liquid in slow cooker. Move vegetables to 1 side. In bowl, whisk sour cream with flour; whisk in ½ cup (125 mL) of the cooking liquid. Gently stir into slow cooker along with green pepper.

❧ Cover and cook on high until thickened, about 15 minutes. Serve with beef.

PER EACH OF 8 SERVINGS: about 530 cal, 41 g pro, 16 g total fat (6 g sat. fat), 54 g carb, 4 g fibre, 89 mg chol, 531 mg sodium. % RDI: 10% calcium, 39% iron, 2% vit A, 55% vit C, 17% folate.

TEST KITCHEN TIP
How many onions? An average golden-beige-skinned cooking onion weighs about 4 oz (125 g) and makes close to 1 cup (250 mL) chopped onion or 1 cup (250 mL) lightly packed sliced onion. For stews, sauces and pot roasts, a little more or less onion is not going to matter.

Mushroom Pot Roast

A mushroom sauce adds class – without a lot of cost – to a budget-friendly pot roast. Leftovers are awfully good the next day.

5- to 6-quart (5 to 6 L)
slow cooker

Makes 6 servings

3 lb	boneless beef cross rib pot roast	1.5 kg	3	cloves garlic, minced	3
½ tsp	each salt and pepper	2 mL	1 tsp	each dried marjoram and oregano	5 mL
2 tbsp	vegetable oil	30 mL	⅓ cup	sodium-reduced beef broth	75 mL
4 cups	button mushrooms (12 oz/375 g)	1 L	2 tbsp	tomato paste	30 mL
2	each carrots and stalks celery, sliced	2	2 tsp	Worcestershire sauce	10 mL
1	onion, diced	1	3 tbsp	all-purpose flour	45 mL

TEST KITCHEN TIP

Carving a pot roast is easy. Here's how.
1. Transfer the roast to a carving board. Cover and keep warm for about 15 minutes to allow the juices to redistribute throughout the meat. Remove any strings.
2. Carve across the grain as thinly as possible. This shortens the long muscle fibres, maximizing tenderness.

⤷ Sprinkle beef with salt and pepper. In Dutch oven, heat half of the oil over medium-high heat; brown beef all over. Transfer to slow cooker.

⤷ Drain fat from Dutch oven; add remaining oil. Fry mushrooms, carrots, celery, onion, garlic, marjoram and oregano over medium heat until vegetables are softened, about 10 minutes. Scrape into slow cooker.

⤷ Add broth to Dutch oven; bring to boil, scraping up brown bits from bottom of pan. Scrape into slow cooker along with tomato paste and Worcestershire sauce. Stir to combine.

⤷ Cover and cook on low until beef is tender, about 5 to 7 hours.

⤷ Transfer beef to cutting board; cover and keep warm for about 15 minutes before slicing across the grain.

⤷ Meanwhile, skim fat from liquid in slow cooker. Move vegetables to 1 side. In small bowl, whisk flour with ¼ cup (50 mL) water; whisk into liquid. Stir to redistribute ingredients.

⤷ Cover and cook on high until thickened, 15 minutes. Serve with beef.

PER SERVING: about 454 cal, 47 g pro, 23 g total fat (8 g sat. fat), 11 g carb, 2 g fibre, 114 mg chol, 347 mg sodium. % RDI: 4% calcium, 42% iron, 44% vit A, 8% vit C, 15% folate.

Pot Roast with Parsnips & Turnips

A pot roast is an ideal weekend dinner. It makes enough leftovers to reheat another night – and maybe some extra to make sandwiches. Available year-round, root vegetables, such as parsnips and carrots, are economical, tasty and nutritious.

5- to 6-quart (5 to 6 L)
slow cooker

Makes 8 to
10 servings

2	each large parsnips and carrots	2
2	white turnips	2
3	onions	3
3 lb	boneless beef blade or cross rib pot roast	1.5 kg
½ tsp	each salt and pepper	2 mL
2 tbsp	vegetable oil	30 mL

3	cloves garlic, sliced	3
1 cup	sodium-reduced beef broth	250 mL
1	can (28 oz/796 mL) tomatoes	1
½ tsp	dried marjoram or thyme	2 mL
2	bay leaves	2
2 tbsp	all-purpose flour	30 mL

❧ Peel and cut parsnips and carrots in half lengthwise; cut into 2-inch (5 cm) long pieces. Peel and quarter turnips. Place vegetables in slow cooker.

❧ Leaving root end intact, cut onions into 6 wedges each. Set aside.

❧ Sprinkle beef with salt and pepper. In Dutch oven, heat half of the oil over medium-high heat; brown beef all over. Transfer to slow cooker.

❧ Drain fat from Dutch oven; add remaining oil. Fry onions over medium heat, turning once, until golden, about 5 minutes. Transfer to slow cooker.

❧ Add garlic to Dutch oven; fry, stirring, for 1 minute. Add broth; bring to boil, scraping up brown bits from bottom of pan. Scrape into slow cooker along with tomatoes, marjoram and bay leaves. Stir to combine.

❧ Cover and cook on low until beef is tender, about 7 to 8 hours.

❧ Transfer beef to cutting board; cover and keep warm for about 15 minutes before slicing across the grain. Discard bay leaves.

❧ Meanwhile, skim fat from liquid in slow cooker. Move vegetables to 1 side. In small bowl, whisk flour with ¼ cup (50 mL) water; whisk into liquid. Stir to redistribute ingredients.

❧ Cover and cook on high until thickened, about 10 minutes. Serve with beef.

PER EACH OF 10 SERVINGS: about 327 cal, 28 g pro, 16 g total fat (4 g sat. fat), 19 g carb, 4 g fibre, 77 mg chol, 407 mg sodium. % RDI: 7% calcium, 28% iron, 33% vit A, 37% vit C, 21% folate.

Beer-Braised Brisket

Brisket is a large, tasty, reasonably priced cut of boneless beef that's great for a big guest list. Serve it right away or make it ahead; just slice and reheat in its sauce.

4½- to 6-quart (4.5 to 6 L) slow cooker

Makes 10 to 12 servings

1	bottle (341 mL) beer	1	6	cloves garlic, minced	6
¾ cup	sodium-reduced beef broth	175 mL	¼ tsp	pepper	1 mL
2 tbsp	Dijon mustard	30 mL	4 lb	double beef brisket pot roast (see All About Brisket, below)	2 kg
1 tbsp	prepared horseradish	15 mL			
4	onions, sliced	4	¼ cup	all-purpose flour	50 mL

❧ In slow cooker, combine beer, broth, mustard, horseradish, onions, garlic and pepper. Add brisket; spoon some of the liquid and about one-third of the onions over top.

❧ Cover and cook on low until fork-tender, about 5 to 6 hours.

❧ Transfer brisket to cutting board; cover and keep warm for 15 minutes.

❧ Meanwhile, skim fat from liquid in slow cooker. In small bowl, whisk flour with ⅓ cup (75 mL) water; whisk into liquid. Cover and cook on high until thickened and saucy, about 15 minutes. (Make-ahead: Let brisket and sauce cool separately for 30 minutes. Combine brisket and sauce in uncovered airtight container; refrigerate until cold. Cover and refrigerate for up to 2 days or freeze for up to 1 month.)

❧ Slice brisket across grain. Arrange slices in sauce; spoon sauce over top.

PER EACH OF 12 SERVINGS: about 352 cal, 28 g pro, 23 g total fat (9 g sat. fat), 8 g carb, 1 g fibre, 95 mg chol, 176 mg sodium. % RDI: 2% calcium, 20% iron, 2% vit C, 8% folate.

All About Brisket

A whole brisket is made up of two muscles: the triangular flat and the point, the raised muscle at one end of the flat. You can buy a whole brisket, just the point, just the flat or a double brisket, which includes the point and part of the flat. This cut contains lean and juicier not-so-lean meat all in one pot roast.

Brisket is ideal to make ahead. Let meat and gravy cool separately, according to the recipe, then refrigerate overnight. Lift fat off gravy. The meat firms up as it cools, making slicing across the grain neater and easier. You can refrigerate or freeze the slices in the gravy in the amounts you need. Reheat gently in the oven or on the stove top.

Wine-Braised Brisket

Red wine permeates this fork-tender meat, while soy sauce and cranberry juice add a nice balance of saltiness and sweetness. For this pot roast, choose either a double beef brisket (which includes part of the flat and the point) or a regular brisket (just the flat). You may need to cut the brisket in half to fit it into the slow cooker.

5- to 6-quart (5 to 6 L)
slow cooker

Makes 10 servings

1¼ tsp	salt	6 mL	¾ cup	dry red wine	175 mL
¾ tsp	pepper	4 mL	½ cup	beef broth	125 mL
¾ tsp	crumbled dried rosemary	4 mL	½ cup	thawed cranberry cocktail concentrate	125 mL
¼ tsp	cayenne pepper	1 mL	¼ cup	soy sauce	50 mL
4 lb	double beef brisket pot roast (see All About Brisket, page 151)	2 kg	4	large cloves garlic, minced	4
2	large onions, sliced	2	¼ cup	all-purpose flour	50 mL

➤ In large bowl, combine salt, pepper, rosemary and cayenne pepper; rub about half over brisket. Toss onions in remaining spice mixture. Arrange brisket on onions in bowl, fat side up.

➤ In separate bowl, stir together wine, broth, cranberry concentrate, soy sauce and garlic; pour over brisket. Cover and refrigerate for at least 12 hours or for up to 24 hours.

➤ Transfer onions and liquid to slow cooker; top with brisket. Cover and cook on low until meat is fall-apart tender, about 5 to 6 hours.

➤ Transfer brisket to cutting board; cover and keep warm for 20 minutes.

➤ Meanwhile, skim fat from liquid in slow cooker. In small bowl, whisk flour with ⅓ cup (75 mL) water; whisk into liquid.

➤ Cover and cook on high until thickened, about 20 minutes. (Make-ahead: Let brisket and sauce cool separately for 30 minutes. Combine brisket and sauce in uncovered airtight container; refrigerate until cold. Cover and refrigerate for up to 2 days or freeze for up to 1 month.)

➤ Slice brisket across the grain. Serve with sauce.

PER SERVING: about 306 cal, 29 g pro, 15 g total fat (6 g sat. fat), 13 g carb, 1 g fibre, 73 mg chol, 805 mg sodium. % RDI: 2% calcium, 23% iron, 17% vit C, 7% folate.

Corned Beef Dinner

5- to 6-quart (5 to 6 L) slow cooker

Makes 4 servings

Accompany this easy corned beef dinner with grainy mustard and steamed cabbage or a cabbage salad. While the recipe serves four generously, it can stretch to six servings – or you can make any leftovers into sandwiches.

3	potatoes, quartered	3	1 tsp	dried thyme	5 mL
2	each carrots and stalks celery, cut into chunks	2	1 tsp	black peppercorns	5 mL
2	onions, quartered	2	½ tsp	caraway seeds, crushed	2 mL
2	cloves garlic, crushed	2	2 lb	corned beef brisket	1 kg
Half	small rutabaga, peeled and cut into chunks	Half	1¼ cups	sodium-reduced chicken broth or water	300 mL
1	bay leaf	1			

❧ Place potatoes, carrots, celery, onions, garlic, rutabaga, bay leaf, thyme, peppercorns and caraway seeds in slow cooker. Rinse corned beef; place on top of vegetables. Add broth and 1¼ cups (300 mL) water.

❧ Cover; cook on low until corned beef is fork-tender, about 8 to 10 hours.

❧ Transfer corned beef to cutting board; slice thinly. Arrange beef and vegetables on platter. Moisten with a little strained cooking liquid, if desired.

PER SERVING: about 441 cal, 34 g pro, 17 g total fat (6 g sat. fat), 37 g carb, 5 g fibre, 156 mg chol, 1,920 mg sodium. % RDI: 8% calcium, 29% iron, 95% vit A, 42% vit C, 20% folate.

Simply Delicious: BBQ Brisket

Need another quick brisket recipe? How about a saucy one made with your favourite barbecue sauce? (We recommend our chili and maple versions on pages 216 and 217.) Tuck slices of this divinely easy brisket into crusty buns for scrumptious sandwiches.

❧ Cut 4-lb (2 kg) boneless beef brisket pot roast (flat only) crosswise in half if necessary. In 4½- to 6-quart (4.5 to 6 L) slow cooker, combine brisket with 2 cups (500 mL) barbecue sauce; turn to coat. Place 1 half on top of the other, if necessary.

❧ Cover and cook on low, turning once halfway through, until fork-tender, about 5 to 6 hours.

❧ Transfer brisket to cutting board; cover and keep warm for 10 minutes.

❧ Meanwhile, skim fat off liquid in slow cooker. *(Make-ahead: Let brisket and sauce cool separately for 30 minutes. Combine in uncovered airtight container; refrigerate until cold. Cover and refrigerate for up to 2 days or freeze for up to 1 month.)*

❧ Slice brisket across grain; serve with sauce. **Makes 10 servings.**

Ropa Vieja

This is a Cuban cousin of Mexican pulled beef or pork. It's called *ropa vieja* – old clothes or rags – because of the tattered appearance of the well cooked beef. Serve it with the traditional Rice & Black Beans (recipe, page 234) or pair it with tortillas. It's also delicious over baked and split russet potatoes.

4½- to 6-quart (4.5 to 6 L) slow cooker

Makes 6 servings

2 lb	flank steak	1 kg	1 tsp	dried oregano	5 mL
½ tsp	each salt and pepper	2 mL	1 cup	beef broth	250 mL
1 tbsp	vegetable oil (approx)	15 mL	¼ cup	chopped fresh coriander	50 mL
1	onion, halved and sliced	1	1	can (398 mL) tomato sauce	1
1	Cubanelle or sweet red pepper	1	2 tbsp	tomato paste	30 mL
4	cloves garlic, chopped	4	1 tbsp	white vinegar	15 mL
1 tsp	ground cumin	5 mL	2	bay leaves	2

❧ Sprinkle both sides of steak with salt and pepper. In Dutch oven, heat oil over medium-high heat; brown steak on both sides. Transfer to slow cooker.

❧ Adding a little more oil if necessary, fry onion, Cubanelle pepper, garlic, cumin and oregano over medium heat until softened, about 5 minutes. Scrape over steak.

❧ Add broth and ½ cup (125 mL) water to Dutch oven; bring to boil, scraping up brown bits from bottom of pan. Stir in 1 tbsp (15 mL) of the coriander, tomato sauce and paste, vinegar and bay leaves. Scrape over steak.

❧ Cover and cook on low until steak is tender enough to pull apart with 2 forks, about 5 hours.

❧ Discard bay leaves. Cut steak across the grain into quarters; shred with 2 forks. Garnish with remaining coriander. Return to sauce and stir to coat.

PER SERVING: about 340 cal, 35 g pro, 16 g total fat (6 g sat. fat), 11 g carb, 2 g fibre, 64 mg chol, 868 mg sodium. % RDI: 3% calcium, 29% iron, 11% vit A, 65% vit C, 10% folate.

Saucy Cajun Round Steak

4½- to 6-quart (4.5 to 6 L) slow cooker

Makes 4 servings

Less tender cuts of meat, such as round steak, are not only inexpensive but also lean and high in protein and iron. They taste good, too.

¼ cup	all-purpose flour	50 mL	2	cloves garlic, minced	2
¼ tsp	each salt and pepper	1 mL	2	stalks celery, sliced	2
1 lb	inside round marinating steak	500 g	2 tsp	Cajun seasoning	10 mL
1 tbsp	vegetable oil	15 mL	1 tsp	dried thyme	5 mL
¼ cup	tomato paste	50 mL	1	sweet green pepper, chopped	1
2 cups	beef broth	500 mL	2	green onions, chopped	2
2	slices bacon, chopped	2	2 tbsp	chopped fresh parsley	30 mL
2	onions, sliced	2			

In large heavy plastic bag, shake together flour, salt and pepper. Cut steak into 8 pieces. One piece at a time, seal steak in bag; pound with meat mallet to ¼-inch (5 mm) thickness, working flour mixture into meat.

In large skillet, heat oil over medium-high heat; brown steak well, in batches, if necessary. Transfer to slow cooker.

In same skillet, whisk tomato paste into beef broth; bring to boil, scraping up brown bits from bottom of skillet. Scrape into slow cooker along with bacon, onions, garlic, celery, Cajun seasoning and thyme. Stir to combine.

Cover and cook on low until steaks are tender, about 6 to 8 hours. (Make-ahead: Let cool for 30 minutes. Refrigerate, uncovered, in airtight containers until cold. Cover and refrigerate for up to 3 days or freeze for up to 1 month.)

Add green pepper; cover and cook on high until pepper is tender-crisp, about 15 minutes. Stir in green onions and parsley.

PER SERVING: about 310 cal, 31 g pro, 13 g total fat (4 g sat. fat), 18 g carb, 3 g fibre, 55 mg chol, 630 mg sodium. % RDI: 5% calcium, 30% iron, 11% vit A, 60% vit C, 20% folate.

Herb & Onion Swiss Steak

With a retro feel, this dish is deliciously fashionable once again, and the slow cooker makes it even easier.

4½- to 6-quart (4.5 to 6 L)
slow cooker

Makes 4 servings

2	onions, sliced	2	¼ cup	tomato paste	50 mL
2	carrots, sliced	2	¾ cup	beef broth	175 mL
¼ cup	all-purpose flour	50 mL	½ cup	dry white wine	125 mL
¼ tsp	each salt and pepper	1 mL	2	cloves garlic, sliced	2
1 lb	inside round marinating steak	500 g	1½ tsp	dried marjoram	7 mL
1 tbsp	vegetable oil	15 mL	¼ cup	chopped fresh parsley	50 mL

TEST KITCHEN TIP
In any recipe that calls for broth, you can substitute the sodium-reduced version.

❧ Place onions and carrots in slow cooker. In large heavy plastic bag, shake together flour, salt and pepper. Cut steak into 8 pieces. One piece at a time, seal steak in bag; pound with meat mallet to ¼-inch (5 mm) thickness, working flour mixture into meat.

❧ In large skillet, heat oil over medium-high heat; brown steaks well, in batches, if necessary. Place on vegetables in slow cooker.

❧ In same skillet, whisk tomato paste into broth; add wine. Bring to boil, scraping up brown bits from bottom of pan; add garlic and marjoram. Scrape into slow cooker.

❧ Cover and cook on low until steaks are tender, about 6 to 8 hours. (Make-ahead: Let cool for 30 minutes. Refrigerate, uncovered, in airtight containers until cold. Cover and refrigerate for up to 3 days or freeze for up to 1 month.)

❧ Serve sprinkled with parsley.

PER SERVING: about 272 cal, 29 g pro, 9 g total fat (2 g sat. fat), 19 g carb, 3 g fibre, 50 mg chol, 391 mg sodium. % RDI: 5% calcium, 28% iron, 97% vit A, 25% vit C, 17% folate.

Barbecue Sauce Short Ribs

Baked potatoes or rice are a must to accompany these richly sauced beef ribs.

5- to 6-quart (5 to 6 L)
slow cooker

Makes 6 servings

3 lb	beef simmering short ribs	1.5 kg	2 tbsp	Worcestershire sauce	30 mL
2	onions, chopped	2	2 tsp	dried thyme	10 mL
4	cloves garlic, minced	4	1 tsp	dry mustard	5 mL
1 cup	ketchup	250 mL	¾ tsp	each salt and pepper	4 mL
¼ cup	fancy molasses	50 mL	¼ cup	all-purpose flour	50 mL
			2 tsp	cider vinegar	10 mL

❧ Cut ribs into 2-rib pieces, trimming off fat; place in slow cooker. Sprinkle with onions and garlic.

❧ In small bowl, whisk together 1 cup (250 mL) water, ketchup, molasses, Worcestershire sauce, thyme, mustard, salt and pepper; pour over ribs.

❧ Cover and cook on low until meat is fork-tender, about 7 to 8 hours. Skim off fat.

❧ Move ribs to 1 side of slow cooker. In small bowl, whisk flour with ½ cup (125 mL) water; whisk in ½ cup (125 mL) of the cooking liquid. Whisk back into liquid in slow cooker. Stir to redistribute ingredients.

❧ Cover and cook on high until thickened, about 15 minutes. Stir in vinegar. (Make-ahead: Let cool for 30 minutes. Refrigerate, uncovered, in airtight containers until cold. Cover and refrigerate for up to 3 days or freeze for up to 1 month.)

TEST KITCHEN TIP

If gravy or sauce is too thick, adjust by adding more boiling water or broth at end of cooking time. Taste and adjust seasoning.

If too thin, transfer liquid to saucepan and boil hard to desired thickness.

PER SERVING: about 331 cal, 25 g pro, 12 g total fat (5 g sat. fat), 31 g carb, 2 g fibre, 56 mg chol, 933 mg sodium. % RDI: 6% calcium, 27% iron, 5% vit A, 15% vit C, 7% folate.

Short Ribs with Mushrooms & Red Wine

Short ribs are utterly delicious but fatty. Here, we cut back the fat at three stages: trimming when cutting the strips into portions, by broiling, then by skimming off the fat that rises to the top of the almost-finished dish.

5- to 6-quart (5 to 6 L) slow cooker

Makes 6 to 8 servings

1	pkg (14 g) dried porcini or shiitake mushrooms	1
3 lb	beef simmering short ribs	1.5 kg
1 tbsp	vegetable oil	15 mL
2 cups	button mushrooms	500 mL
2	onions, chopped	2
3	cloves garlic, minced	3
2	carrots, diced	2
1 tbsp	crumbled dried rosemary	15 mL

¾ tsp	salt	4 mL
½ tsp	pepper	2 mL
¾ cup	red wine	175 mL
2 tbsp	tomato paste	30 mL
1	can (28 oz/796 mL) diced tomatoes	1
¼ cup	all-purpose flour	50 mL
2 tbsp	balsamic or wine vinegar	30 mL
2 tbsp	minced fresh parsley	30 mL

SUBSTITUTION

No wine? You can substitute an equal amount of sodium-reduced beef broth mixed with 1 tbsp (15 mL) wine vinegar.

TEST KITCHEN TIP

For a smaller crowd, this recipe is easy to halve. Use 2½-quart (2.5 L) slow cooker and cook for 6 to 7 hours. Makes 2 to 4 servings.

Place porcini mushrooms in heatproof bowl; cover with 1 cup (250 mL) boiling water. Let stand for 20 minutes. Strain, reserving liquid; set mushrooms and liquid aside separately.

Cut ribs into 2-rib pieces, trimming off fat; broil, turning once, until well browned, about 5 minutes. Place in slow cooker.

In large skillet, heat oil over medium-high heat; sauté porcini and button mushrooms, onions, garlic, carrots, rosemary, salt and pepper until onions are softened, about 5 minutes. Scrape into slow cooker.

In skillet, whisk together reserved soaking liquid, wine and tomato paste; bring to boil, scraping up brown bits from bottom of skillet. Scrape into slow cooker along with tomatoes. Stir to combine.

Cover and cook on low until meat is tender, about 7 to 8 hours.

Skim fat from liquid. Move ribs to 1 side. In small bowl, whisk flour, vinegar and ⅓ cup (75 mL) water; whisk into liquid. Stir to redistribute. Cover and cook on high until thickened, about 15 minutes. Stir in parsley.

PER EACH OF 8 SERVINGS: about 468 cal, 20 g pro, 36 g total fat (15 g sat. fat), 17 g carb, 3 g fibre, 69 mg chol, 441 mg sodium. % RDI: 6% calcium, 21% iron, 53% vit A, 33% vit C, 14% folate.

Pork Roast in Onion Gravy

Here's a perfect match for mashed potatoes any night of the week. You can substitute a boneless pork rib roast and reduce the cooking time to five hours.

5- to 6-quart (5 to 6 L) slow cooker

Makes 8 to 12 servings

½ tsp	whole cloves	2 mL	¼ cup	tomato paste	50 mL
4 lb	pork rib roast	2 kg	2 tbsp	cider vinegar	30 mL
½ tsp	pepper	2 mL	4	cloves garlic, minced	4
2 tbsp	vegetable oil	30 mL	2	bay leaves	2
4	onions, sliced	4	½ tsp	salt	2 mL
1 tsp	cumin or caraway seeds	5 mL	¼ cup	cornstarch	50 mL
1 cup	each white wine and chicken broth (or 2 cups/500 mL chicken broth)	250 mL	¼ cup	minced fresh parsley	50 mL

➤ Stick cloves into pork; sprinkle with pepper. In Dutch oven, heat half of the oil over medium-high heat; brown pork all over. Transfer to slow cooker.

➤ Drain fat from Dutch oven; add remaining oil. Sauté onions and cumin seeds until golden, about 8 minutes. Scrape into slow cooker. Add wine to Dutch oven; bring to boil, scraping up brown bits from bottom of pan. Scrape into slow cooker along with broth, tomato paste, vinegar, garlic, bay leaves and salt. Stir to combine.

➤ Cover and cook on low until pork is tender, about 6 hours.

➤ Transfer pork to cutting board; cover and keep warm for about 15 minutes before cutting into chop-size slices. Discard bay leaves.

➤ Meanwhile, skim fat from liquid in slow cooker. In small bowl, whisk cornstarch with ½ cup (125 mL) water; whisk into liquid.

➤ Cover and cook on high until thickened, about 15 minutes. Stir in parsley. Serve with pork.

PER EACH OF 12 SERVINGS: about 272 cal, 20 g pro, 18 g total fat (6 g sat. fat), 8 g carb, 1 g fibre, 65 mg chol, 210 mg sodium. % RDI: 3% calcium, 11% iron, 2% vit A, 10% vit C, 5% folate.

TEST KITCHEN TIP
If you prefer more of a sauce than a thick gravy, reduce the cornstarch to 2 tbsp (30 mL).

Saucy Pulled Pork

Tender enough to be shredded with a fork, pulled pork has become a buffet party mainstay. The best cut is the good-value shoulder blade pork roast.

5- to 6-quart (5 to 6 L) slow cooker

Makes 8 servings

3½ lb	boneless pork shoulder blade roast	1.75 kg
¾ tsp	each salt and pepper	4 mL
2 tbsp	vegetable oil	30 mL
2	onions, diced	2
4	cloves garlic, minced	4
2 tbsp	chili powder	30 mL
2 tsp	ground coriander	10 mL

2	bay leaves	2
¼ cup	tomato paste	50 mL
1	can (14 oz/398 mL) tomato sauce	1
2 tbsp	each packed brown sugar and cider vinegar	30 mL
2 tbsp	Worcestershire sauce	30 mL
2	green onions, sliced	2

❧ Sprinkle pork with salt and pepper. In Dutch oven, heat oil over medium-high heat; brown pork all over. Transfer to slow cooker.

❧ Drain all but 1 tbsp (15 mL) fat from Dutch oven; reduce heat to medium. Fry onions, garlic, chili powder, coriander and bay leaves, stirring often, until onions are softened, about 5 minutes.

❧ Add tomato paste; cook, stirring, until darkened, 2 minutes. Add tomato sauce, sugar, vinegar and Worcestershire; bring to boil, scraping up brown bits. Scrape into slow cooker. Cover; cook on low until tender, 8 to 10 hours.

❧ Transfer pork to cutting board; cover and keep warm for about 10 minutes. With 2 forks, shred or "pull" pork.

❧ Meanwhile, skim fat from liquid. If liquid measures more than 3 cups (750 mL), bring to boil in large shallow saucepan over high heat; boil until reduced to 3 cups (750 mL), 15 minutes. Discard bay leaves. Add pork. (Make-ahead: Let cool for 30 minutes. Refrigerate, uncovered, in airtight containers until cold. Cover and refrigerate for up to 3 days or freeze for up to 1 month.)

❧ Reduce heat; simmer until hot, 4 minutes. Sprinkle with green onions.

PER SERVING: about 342 cal, 43 g pro, 12 g total fat (3 g sat. fat), 13 g carb, 2 g fibre, 118 mg chol, 735 mg sodium. % RDI: 7% calcium, 27% iron, 14% vit A, 22% vit C, 10% folate.

VARIATION

Saucy Pulled Beef: Replace pork with boneless beef blade or cross rib pot roast, and ground coriander with dried oregano. Increase tomato sauce to one 20-oz (680 mL) can. Stir in ½ tsp (2 mL) hot pepper sauce before serving.

TEST KITCHEN TIP
Beside the slow cooker, arrange buns for filling generously with the pork and barbecue sauce, and be sure to include a bowl of tangy coleslaw. It's delicious on the side or spooned into your sandwich.

Green Chili Pot Roast

5- to 6-quart (5 to 6 L) slow cooker

Makes 6 servings

Although mild, green chilies perk up a pork roast and bring home the taste of the Southwest.

4 cups	chopped carrots (4 large)	1 L	Half	can (4½ oz/127 mL can) peeled green chilies, drained, rinsed and chopped	Half
6	small onions, halved	6	2	cloves garlic, minced	2
3 tbsp	all-purpose flour	45 mL	1 tsp	each dried oregano, ground cumin and ground coriander	5 mL
3 lb	boneless pork shoulder blade roast	1.5 kg			
1 tbsp	vegetable oil	15 mL	½ tsp	each salt and pepper	2 mL
1 cup	chicken broth	250 mL			

❧ Arrange carrots and onions in slow cooker.

❧ Spread flour on plate. Pat pork dry; roll in flour to coat. Reserve any remaining flour.

❧ In Dutch oven, heat oil over medium-high heat; brown pork all over. Place on vegetables in slow cooker.

❧ Drain fat from Dutch oven. Add broth, chilies, garlic, oregano, cumin, coriander, salt and pepper; bring to boil, scraping up brown bits from bottom of pan. Scrape over pork.

❧ Cover and cook on low until pork is tender, about 5 to 6 hours.

❧ Transfer pork to cutting board; cover and keep warm for 15 minutes before slicing across the grain.

❧ Meanwhile, skim any fat from liquid in slow cooker. Move vegetables to 1 side. In small bowl, whisk remaining flour with ⅓ cup (75 mL) water; whisk into liquid. Stir to redistribute ingredients.

❧ Cover and cook on high until thickened, about 15 minutes. Serve with pork.

PER SERVING: about 574 cal, 40 g pro, 38 g total fat (13 g sat. fat), 18 g carb, 4 g fibre, 147 mg chol, 542 mg sodium. % RDI: 5% calcium, 24% iron, 130% vit A, 12% vit C, 19% folate.

Cider-Braised Pork Shoulder

You can braise less-expensive pork shoulder or use a more expensive centre-cut loin. We prefer the shoulder because it's well-marbled and stays moist despite long cooking.

5- to 6-quart (5 to 6 L)
slow cooker

Makes 8 servings

3 lb	boneless pork shoulder blade roast	1.5 kg	1 tbsp	crumbled dried sage	15 mL
1 tsp	each salt and pepper	5 mL	1 cup	apple cider	250 mL
1 tbsp	vegetable oil	15 mL	1 cup	sodium-reduced chicken broth	250 mL
4	onions, sliced	4	1 tbsp	cider vinegar	15 mL
2	cloves garlic, minced	2	4 tsp	all-purpose flour	20 mL

❧ Sprinkle pork with half each of the salt and pepper. In Dutch oven, heat oil over medium-high heat; brown pork all over. Transfer to slow cooker.

❧ Drain fat from Dutch oven. Fry onions, garlic, sage and remaining salt and pepper over medium heat, stirring occasionally, until onions are golden, about 10 to 12 minutes. Add cider, broth and vinegar; bring to boil, scraping up brown bits from bottom of pan. Scrape over pork.

❧ Cover and cook on low until pork is tender, about 6 to 8 hours.

❧ Transfer pork to cutting board; cover and keep warm for about 15 minutes before pulling meat apart in chunks.

❧ Meanwhile, skim fat from liquid in slow cooker. Move onions to 1 side. In small bowl, whisk flour with ¼ cup (50 mL) water; whisk into liquid. Stir to redistribute ingredients.

❧ Cover and cook on high until thickened, about 15 minutes. Serve with pork.

PER SERVING: about 420 cal, 30 g pro, 28 g total fat (10 g sat. fat), 12 g carb, 1 g fibre, 110 mg chol, 461 mg sodium. % RDI: 2% calcium, 16% iron, 1% vit A, 3% vit C, 9% folate.

What's a Dutch Oven?

A large, heavy-gauge pot with a lid and two handles, a Dutch oven is a flameproof covered casserole. It's designed for both stove top and oven cooking, making it indispensable for browning big items, such as pot roasts.

Five-Spice Braised Pork Loin

Look for a roast with the backbone (chine) removed or with the chops separated at the backbone.

5- to 6-quart (5 to 6 L)
slow cooker

Makes 8 servings

3 lb	pork loin centre roast, tied	1.5 kg		¾ tsp	five-spice powder	4 mL
½ tsp	pepper	2 mL		1 cup	sodium-reduced chicken broth	250 mL
1 tbsp	vegetable oil	15 mL		¼ cup	Chinese rice wine, sherry or water	50 mL
1	onion, chopped	1				
6	cloves garlic, minced	6		2 cups	pearl onions (one 10-oz/284 g pkg), peeled	500 mL
2 tbsp	finely grated gingerroot	30 mL				
				2 tbsp	cornstarch	30 mL

TEST KITCHEN TIP

In our photo, the rib bones have been frenched, meaning any meat or fat has been scraped off the bones that extend beyond the meaty part of the loin.

❧ Sprinkle pork with half of the pepper. In Dutch oven, heat oil over medium-high heat; brown pork all over. Transfer to slow cooker.

❧ Drain fat from Dutch oven. Fry chopped onion, garlic, ginger, five-spice powder and remaining pepper over medium heat, stirring often, until onion is softened, about 5 minutes. Add broth; bring to boil, scraping up brown bits from bottom of pan. Scrape over pork along with rice wine and pearl onions. Stir to combine.

❧ Cover and cook on low until pork is tender, about 5 to 6 hours.

❧ Transfer pork to cutting board; cover and keep warm for 15 minutes before cutting any strings and cutting across the grain into chop-size slices.

❧ Meanwhile, skim fat from liquid in slow cooker. Move onions to 1 side. In small bowl, whisk cornstarch with ¼ cup (50 mL) water; whisk into liquid. Stir to redistribute ingredients.

❧ Cover; cook on high until thickened, about 15 minutes. Serve with pork.

PER SERVING: about 282 cal, 25 g pro, 16 g total fat (5 g sat. fat), 8 g carb, 1 g fibre, 79 mg chol, 149 mg sodium. % RDI: 4% calcium, 9% iron, 5% vit C, 5% folate.

Shredded Pork Tacos

5- to 6-quart (5 to 6 L)
slow cooker

Makes 8 servings

Pineapple gives a sweet, tangy twist to long-cooked shredded pork. For a party, set the slow cooker on the buffet and surround it with taco shells, tortillas and taco fixings: pico de gallo or salsa, sour cream, shredded lettuce and Monterey Jack cheese, chopped avocados and pickled onions and jalapeños. Welcome, friends!

2 tbsp	packed brown sugar	30 mL	3	cloves garlic, minced	3
2 tsp	each chili powder, ground cumin and dried thyme	10 mL	1	can (5½ oz/156 mL) tomato paste	1
1 tsp	each salt and pepper	5 mL	3 tbsp	cider vinegar	45 mL
			½ tsp	hot pepper sauce	2 mL
3 lb	boneless pork shoulder blade roast	1.5 kg	1	can (14 oz/398 mL) crushed pineapple	1
2 tbsp	vegetable oil	30 mL	¼ cup	chopped fresh coriander	50 mL
2	onions, diced	2			

🍂 In large bowl, combine sugar, chili powder, cumin, thyme, salt and pepper; add pork to bowl and rub spice mixture all over. Cover and refrigerate for 4 hours, turning occasionally. Remove pork from bowl; pat dry.

🍂 In large Dutch oven, heat oil over medium-high heat; brown pork all over. Transfer to slow cooker.

🍂 Drain fat from Dutch oven. Fry onions and garlic over medium heat, stirring, until onions are softened, 4 minutes. Add tomato paste, vinegar and hot pepper sauce; cook, stirring, for 2 minutes. Add pineapple and juices; bring to boil, scraping up brown bits from bottom of pan. Scrape over pork.

🍂 Cover and cook on low until pork is tender, about 6 to 7 hours.

🍂 Transfer pork to cutting board; cover and keep warm for 10 minutes. With 2 forks, shred pork.

🍂 Meanwhile, skim fat from liquid in slow cooker. Pour liquid into large shallow saucepan; bring to boil over high heat. Boil vigorously until reduced to 3 cups (750 mL), about 8 minutes. Add pork. (Make-ahead: Let cool for 30 minutes. Refrigerate, uncovered, in airtight containers until cold. Cover and refrigerate for up to 3 days or freeze for up to 1 month.)

🍂 Heat until bubbling, about 4 minutes. Sprinkle with coriander.

PER SERVING: about 503 cal, 32 g pro, 33 g total fat (10 g sat. fat), 20 g carb, 2 g fibre, 97 mg chol, 427 mg sodium. % RDI: 7% calcium, 26% iron, 6% vit A, 17% vit C, 7% folate.

Pork Steaks with Dried Fruit

Pork steaks are trimmed boneless cuts of pork from the shoulder, loin or leg. The shoulder blade steak is the least expensive and is so good in braising dishes like this one. Grill pork loin steaks and make lean leg steaks into schnitzel.

4½- to 6-quart (4.5 to 6 L) slow cooker

Makes 6 servings

1 tbsp	vegetable oil	15 mL
6	pork shoulder blade steaks (about 2½ lb/ 1.25 kg), trimmed	6
2	onions, cut into wedges	2
2	cloves garlic, minced	2
1 cup	each dried apricots and pitted prunes	250 mL
½ cup	orange juice	125 mL
½ cup	chicken broth	125 mL
2 tsp	each ground cumin and sweet paprika	10 mL
1 tsp	ground coriander	5 mL
½ tsp	each cinnamon and salt	2 mL
¼ tsp	pepper	1 mL

❧ In large skillet, heat oil over medium-high heat; brown pork, in batches if necessary. Transfer to slow cooker with onions, garlic, apricots and prunes.

❧ Drain fat from skillet; add orange juice, broth, cumin, paprika, coriander, cinnamon, salt and pepper. Bring to boil, scraping up brown bits from bottom of skillet. Scrape into slow cooker. Stir to combine.

❧ Cover and cook on low until pork is tender, about 4 to 5 hours.

❧ Transfer pork and fruit to serving platter; cover and keep warm. Skim fat from liquid in slow cooker.

❧ Cover and cook on high until sauce is slightly thickened, about 5 minutes. Spoon over pork.

PER SERVING: about 394 cal, 27 g pro, 17 g total fat (5 g sat. fat), 35 g carb, 6 g fibre, 92 mg chol, 321 mg sodium. % RDI: 6% calcium, 29% iron, 21% vit A, 23% vit C, 7% folate.

Slow Cooker Ham

A 3- to 4-lb (1.5 to 2 kg) boneless ham stays beautifully moist in the slow cooker. There's no point trying to gussy it up with coatings of mustard and spices – the flavours won't penetrate. Instead, serve with a fruity fresh salsa or sauce. Or mustard!

❧ Place ham in slow cooker; add ¼ cup (50 mL) water. Cover and cook on low until thermometer inserted in centre registers 140°F (60°C), about 2 to 3 hours. Transfer to cutting board; let stand for 10 to 20 minutes before slicing. **Makes 10 to 12 servings.**

Fall-off-the-Bone Ribs in Barbecue Sauce

You'll need plenty of napkins for these saucy ribs. Because this sauce – and the two in the variations – is sticky, a wise cook will line the slow cooker insert with foil before adding the ribs. Cleanup is then a breeze.

5- to 6-quart (5 to 6 L) slow cooker

Makes 4 to 6 servings

3 lb	pork back ribs (2 racks)	1.5 kg
4 tsp	mesquite or Cajun seasoning	20 mL
½ tsp	each salt and pepper	2 mL

BARBECUE SAUCE:

2 cups	ketchup	500 mL
½ cup	wine vinegar	125 mL
2 tbsp	granulated sugar	30 mL
2 tbsp	Worcestershire sauce	30 mL

❧ Trim any fat from ribs. If necessary, remove membrane from underside. Cut into 2-rib portions.

❧ In small bowl, stir together mesquite seasoning, salt and pepper; rub all over ribs. Arrange on broiler pan; broil until browned, about 5 minutes per side. Transfer to slow cooker.

❧ **BARBECUE SAUCE:** In bowl, whisk together ketchup, vinegar, sugar and Worcestershire sauce; scrape over ribs, stirring to coat all over.

❧ Cover and cook on low until tender, about 6 hours.

PER EACH OF 6 SERVINGS: about 533 cal, 33 g pro, 32 g total fat (12 g sat. fat), 31 g carb, 2 g fibre, 88 mg chol, 1,452 mg sodium. % RDI: 4% calcium, 16% iron, 14% vit A, 25% vit C, 7% folate.

VARIATIONS

Honey Mustard Ribs: Omit mesquite seasoning; reserve salt and pepper for sauce. Instead of Barbecue Sauce, combine ¼ cup (50 mL) each Dijon and grainy mustards; 2 tbsp (30 mL) liquid honey; 2 tbsp (30 mL) cider vinegar; and 2 cloves garlic, minced, along with the salt and pepper. Cook as directed.

Black Bean Ribs: Omit mesquite seasoning, salt and pepper. Instead of Barbecue Sauce, combine ⅓ cup (75 mL) black bean and garlic sauce; ¼ cup (50 mL) hoisin sauce; 2 tbsp (30 mL) each liquid honey and ketchup; 1 tbsp (15 mL) each sodium-reduced soy sauce, sesame oil, rice vinegar and Dijon mustard; and 2 cloves garlic, minced. Cook as directed.

Jerk Barbecue Pork Steaks

4½- to 5½-quart (4.5 to 5.5 L) slow cooker

Makes 4 servings

Mixing up the spices for real Jamaican jerk pork steaks takes time. Prepared jerk seasoning, like Indian or Thai curry paste, rescues the cook and still delivers delicious food – with less fuss.

3	thick pork shoulder blade steaks (about 2 lb/1 kg), trimmed	3
¼ tsp	each salt and pepper	1 mL
1 tbsp	vegetable oil	15 mL
1 cup	ketchup	250 mL
¼ cup	wine vinegar	50 mL
1 tbsp	packed brown sugar	15 mL
1 tbsp	Worcestershire sauce	15 mL
1 tbsp	jerk seasoning	15 mL

➤ Sprinkle pork steaks with salt and pepper. In large skillet, heat oil over medium-high heat; brown steaks on both sides. Transfer to slow cooker. Drain fat from skillet.

➤ Add ¼ cup (50 mL) water to skillet; bring to boil, scraping up brown bits from bottom of skillet. Stir in ketchup, vinegar, brown sugar, Worcestershire sauce and jerk seasoning; scrape over steaks.

➤ Cover and cook until tender, about 3 hours.

PER SERVING: about 482 cal, 36 g pro, 28 g total fat (9 g sat. fat), 24 g carb, 1 g fibre, 134 mg chol, 1,383 mg sodium. % RDI: 6% calcium, 22% iron, 7% vit A, 20% vit C, 5% folate.

Pork Cuts for the Slow Cooker

> **ROASTS:** Chewier, more-marbled shoulder roasts pack big taste in each bite and suit the long moist heat of slow cooking better than leaner leg and loin cuts. Budget-friendly bone-in or boneless shoulder blade (butt) or shoulder picnic roasts slice less neatly but are perfect for pulled or shredded pork recipes. Rib roasts, or the elegant rib roast rack, slice beautifully into single portions.

> **RIBS:** Back and side ribs work extremely well in the slow cooker.

> **CHOPS AND STEAKS:** Look for shoulder blade chops or steaks.

Simple Choucroute Garnie

This braised sauerkraut recipe, a specialty of the Alsace region of France, gets sweetness from apple and onion. Its smokiness, the essential of a good choucroute, comes from a thick piece of bacon. The only other meat in this pared-down version is lean kielbasa. Serve with boiled potatoes and a selection of mustards.

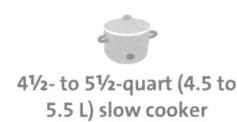

4½- to 5½-quart (4.5 to 5.5 L) slow cooker

Makes 6 servings

8 oz	double-smoked bacon	250 g	¼ tsp	caraway seeds	1 mL
12 oz	lean kielbasa	375 g	¼ tsp	coriander seeds	1 mL
1	jar or can (28 oz/ 810 g) sauerkraut	1	1	bay leaf	1
1	large onion, sliced	1	4	juniper berries (or 4 tsp/20 mL gin)	4
1	large apple, sliced	1	1½ cups	dry white wine or sodium-reduced chicken broth	375 mL
2	cloves garlic, minced	2			

❧ Slice bacon thickly; line bottom and partway up side of slow cooker with slices. Place kielbasa in centre.

❧ Drain and rinse sauerkraut. In large bowl, toss together sauerkraut, onion, apple, garlic, caraway and coriander seeds, bay leaf and juniper berries. Add to slow cooker. Drizzle wine over top.

❧ Cover and cook on low until onions are tender and juices are reduced to a shallow pool in bottom of slow cooker, about 3½ hours. Discard bay leaf.

❧ To serve, slice kielbasa and serve with sauerkraut mixture and bacon.

PER SERVING: about 348 cal, 15 g pro, 26 g total fat (13 g sat. fat), 14 g carb, 4 g fibre, 63 mg chol, 1,529 mg sodium. % RDI: 7% calcium, 21% iron, 30% vit C, 16% folate.

Italian Meat Loaf

The moistened crumbs add liquid to the meat loaf, keeping it juicy.

5- to 6-quart (5 to 6 L)
slow cooker

Makes 8 servings

1¼ cups	fresh bread crumbs	300 mL
½ cup	milk	125 mL
4 tsp	extra-virgin olive oil	20 mL
1½ cups	chopped onions	375 mL
2	cloves garlic, minced	2
1 tsp	dried oregano	5 mL
2	eggs	2
½ cup	chopped oil-packed sun-dried tomatoes	125 mL
½ cup	chopped fresh parsley	125 mL
½ cup	grated Parmesan cheese	125 mL
½ tsp	each salt and pepper	2 mL
1 lb	ground veal or beef	500 g
1 lb	ground pork	500 g

TOPPING:

¾ cup	shredded provolone cheese	175 mL
2 tbsp	chopped fresh parsley	30 mL
2 tbsp	chopped oil-packed sun-dried tomatoes	30 mL

TEST KITCHEN TIP

Leftover meat loaf – if you have any – makes a mean sandwich, especially with pickles or relish.

➥ Line bottom and side of slow cooker with heavy-duty or double thickness foil; set aside. In bowl, stir bread crumbs with milk; let stand for 10 minutes.

➥ Meanwhile, in skillet, heat oil over medium heat; fry onions, garlic and oregano, stirring occasionally, until golden, about 6 minutes.

➥ In large bowl, whisk eggs. Add sun-dried tomatoes, parsley, Parmesan cheese, salt, pepper, bread crumb mixture and onion mixture; combine with wooden spoon. Mix in veal and pork, using hands if necessary. Place in centre of prepared slow cooker; shape into loaf.

➥ Cover; cook on low until thermometer registers 170°F (75°C), 6 to 8 hours.

➥ TOPPING: Sprinkle loaf with cheese; sprinkle parsley and sun-dried tomatoes down centre. Cover; cook on high until cheese is melted, 5 minutes. Using foil as handles, lift out of slow cooker. Let stand on cutting board for 5 minutes, letting fat drain off onto foil. Transfer to cutting board and slice.

PER SERVING: about 344 cal, 30 g pro, 20 g total fat (8 g sat. fat), 10 g carb, 1 g fibre, 137 mg chol, 488 mg sodium. % RDI: 19% calcium, 15% iron, 11% vit A, 25% vit C, 15% folate.

VARIATION

Bacon-Topped Meat Loaf: Omit sun-dried tomatoes and Parmesan cheese. Replace dried oregano with dried sage, and ground veal and pork with 2 lb (500 g) lean ground beef. Add ½ cup (125 mL) ketchup and 2 tbsp (30 mL) Worcestershire sauce. Cook as directed. Omit topping; top with 4 slices bacon, cooked and crumbled.

5- to 6-quart (5 to 6 L)
slow cooker

Makes 8 servings

Braised Lamb Shoulder with Green Beans & Balsamic Jus

Nestled among beans, this quick-to-prep roast is fancy enough for company. When beans aren't in season, serve with brussels sprouts or broccoli florets.

2¾ lb	boneless lamb shoulder roast	1.375 kg
¼ tsp	each salt and pepper	1 mL
2 tbsp	vegetable oil	30 mL
4	slices bacon, chopped	4
1	onion, chopped	1
4	cloves garlic, sliced	4

⅓ cup	tomato paste	75 mL
2 cups	beef broth	500 mL
1½ lb	green beans, trimmed and halved crosswise	750 g
1 tbsp	cornstarch	15 mL
1 tbsp	balsamic vinegar	15 mL

➴ Sprinkle lamb with salt and pepper. In Dutch oven, heat oil over medium-high heat; brown lamb all over. Transfer to slow cooker.

➴ Drain any fat from Dutch oven. Fry bacon over medium heat, stirring occasionally, until crisp, about 5 minutes. Add to slow cooker.

➴ Drain fat from Dutch oven. Fry onion and garlic until softened, about 4 minutes. Add tomato paste; cook, stirring, until slightly darkened, about 2 minutes. Add broth; bring to boil, scraping up brown bits from bottom of pan. Scrape into slow cooker.

➴ Cover and cook on low until lamb is tender, about 5 to 6 hours.

➴ Transfer lamb to cutting board; cover and keep warm for 15 minutes before slicing.

➴ Meanwhile, in saucepan of boiling salted water, cover and cook green beans until tender-crisp, about 5 to 7 minutes; drain.

➴ Meanwhile, skim fat from liquid in slow cooker. Whisk cornstarch with 2 tbsp (30 mL) water; whisk into liquid. Cover and cook on high until sauce is glossy and thickened, about 10 minutes.

➴ Arrange lamb and beans on platter. Stir balsamic vinegar into sauce; drizzle over lamb and beans.

PER SERVING: about 382 cal, 29 g pro, 24 g total fat (9 g sat. fat), 11 g carb, 3 g fibre, 99 mg chol, 775 mg sodium. % RDI: 6% calcium, 24% iron, 6% vit A, 17% vit C, 20% folate.

Lamb Shanks with Gremolada

Gremolada, or gremolata, is a mixture of finely chopped fresh parsley, grated lemon rind and minced garlic. Sprinkled fresh and raw over cooked dishes like these braised shanks, it adds a bold herbal finish.

6-quart (6 L) slow cooker

Makes 6 servings

6	lamb shanks (about 4 lb/2 kg)	6	1 cup	dry red wine	250 mL
½ tsp	pepper	2 mL	1	can (28 oz/796 mL) diced tomatoes	1
2 tbsp	extra-virgin olive oil	30 mL	¼ cup	tomato paste	50 mL
2 tsp	fennel seeds	10 mL	¼ cup	all-purpose flour	50 mL
1	onion, diced	1	3 tbsp	butter, softened	45 mL
2	each carrots and stalks celery, diced	2	GREMOLADA:		
6	cloves garlic, minced	6	¼ cup	chopped fresh parsley	50 mL
¾ tsp	salt	4 mL	1	clove garlic, minced	1
			1 tsp	grated lemon rind	5 mL

↝ Sprinkle lamb with pepper. In Dutch oven, heat half of the oil over medium-high heat; brown lamb shanks all over, in batches if necessary. Transfer to slow cooker.

↝ Drain fat from Dutch oven; add remaining oil. Fry fennel seeds over medium heat until seeds start to pop, about 10 seconds. Add onion, carrots, celery, garlic and salt; fry, stirring often, until onion is softened, about 5 minutes. Scrape into slow cooker.

↝ Add wine to Dutch oven; bring to boil, scraping up brown bits from bottom of pan. Scrape into slow cooker along with tomatoes and tomato paste. Stir to combine.

↝ Cover and cook on low until lamb is tender and separates easily from bone, about 6 hours.

↝ Skim fat from liquid in slow cooker. Move lamb and vegetables to 1 side. In small bowl, stir flour with butter; stir into liquid. Stir gently to redistribute ingredients. Cover and cook on high until thickened, about 15 minutes.

↝ GREMOLADA: Meanwhile, in bowl, stir together parsley, garlic and lemon rind; sprinkle over each portion of lamb.

PER SERVING: about 505 cal, 49 g pro, 25 g total fat (10 g sat. fat), 19 g carb, 3 g fibre, 166 mg chol, 721 mg sodium. % RDI: 9% calcium, 44% iron, 78% vit A, 50% vit C, 24% folate.

Lamb Shanks with Fennel & White Beans

Lamb shanks may not be as glamorous as boneless butterflied leg of lamb but they braise beautifully in the slow cooker, rewarding everyone with their tenderness and wonderful flavour. White beans are a classic accompaniment in French cooking.

6-quart (6 L) slow cooker

Makes 6 servings

6	lamb shanks (about 4 lb/2 kg)	6
½ tsp	each salt and pepper	2 mL
2 tbsp	vegetable oil	30 mL
1	onion, finely diced	1
1½ cups	diced carrot	375 mL
1½ cups	diced fennel or celery	375 mL
2	cloves garlic, minced	2
1 tsp	each dried thyme and fennel seeds	5 mL
1 cup	dry white wine or sodium-reduced chicken broth	250 mL
1 cup	sodium-reduced chicken broth	250 mL
2	cans (each 19 oz/ 540 mL) navy beans, drained and rinsed (or 4 cups/ 1 L cooked beans; recipe, page 213)	2
½ cup	chopped drained oil-packed sun-dried tomatoes	125 mL
¼ cup	chopped fresh parsley	50 mL

❧ Sprinkle lamb with salt and pepper. In Dutch oven, heat half of the oil over medium-high heat; brown lamb, in batches. Transfer to slow cooker.

❧ Drain fat from Dutch oven; add remaining oil. Fry onion, carrot, fennel, garlic, thyme and fennel seeds over medium heat, stirring occasionally, until onion is softened, about 5 minutes.

❧ Add wine and broth to Dutch oven; bring to boil, scraping up brown bits from bottom of pan. Scrape into slow cooker along with beans and tomatoes. Stir to combine.

❧ Cover and cook on low until lamb is tender and separates easily from bone, about 6 hours. Transfer lamb to platter; cover and keep warm.

❧ Skim fat from liquid in slow cooker. Stir in parsley. Spoon bean mixture into shallow bowls; top with lamb.

PER SERVING: about 649 cal, 58 g pro, 28 g total fat (9 g sat. fat), 40 g carb, 5 g fibre, 150 mg chol, 1,030 mg sodium. % RDI: 11% calcium, 53% iron, 52% vit A, 28% vit C, 55% folate.

TEST KITCHEN TIP
Bulbous fresh fennel is no longer an exotic vegetable. You'll find it in major grocery chains, usually displayed by the salad fixings. Rinse, then trim stems down to bulb, saving any delicate fronds for garnish. Halve fennel lengthwise. Pare out the core and slice crosswise before dicing.

Lamb Shanks Braised in Balsamic Tomato Sauce

6-quart (6 L) slow cooker

Makes 6 servings

Slow cooking is the ideal way to turn shanks into a feast. And that's exactly what chef Dany Thibault does with this recipe in his restaurant, Parcours des Saveurs, in Quebec. He builds their robust flavour with herbes de Provence, a mix of herbs found in the south of France that contains rosemary, thyme, basil, sage, savory, fennel and sometimes lavender. You can replace the mix with dried thyme.

6	lamb shanks (about 4 lb/2 kg)	6	1	bay leaf	1
1 tsp	herbes de Provence	5 mL	½ tsp	dried oregano	2 mL
½ tsp	each salt and pepper	2 mL	¼ tsp	each salt and pepper	1 mL
1 tbsp	extra-virgin olive oil	15 mL	1	can (28 oz/796 mL) tomatoes	1
BALSAMIC TOMATO SAUCE:			¼ cup	tomato paste	50 mL
1 tbsp	extra-virgin olive oil	15 mL	2 tbsp	granulated sugar	30 mL
2	onions, diced	2	2 tbsp	balsamic vinegar	30 mL
3	cloves garlic, minced	3	1	sprig fresh basil (or ¼ tsp/1 mL dried)	1

❧ Rub lamb with herbes de Provence, salt and pepper. In Dutch oven, heat oil over medium-high heat; brown lamb, in batches. Transfer to slow cooker.

❧ **BALSAMIC TOMATO SAUCE:** Drain fat from Dutch oven; heat oil over medium heat. Fry onions, garlic, bay leaf, oregano, salt and pepper until onions are softened, about 5 minutes. Scrape into slow cooker.

❧ Add tomatoes, tomato paste, sugar and vinegar to Dutch oven; mash tomatoes with potato masher or fork until slightly chunky. Bring to boil, scraping up brown bits from bottom of pan. Scrape into slow cooker. Stir to combine.

❧ Cover and cook on low until lamb is tender and separates easily from bone, about 6 hours. Transfer lamb to platter; cover and keep warm. Skim off fat.

❧ Pour cooking liquid into wide saucepan; bring to boil over high heat. Boil until thickened and reduced to 4 cups (1 L), about 15 minutes. Shred basil and sprinkle into sauce. Serve with lamb.

PER SERVING: about 473 cal, 50 g pro, 22 g total fat (8 g sat. fat), 17 g carb, 2 g fibre, 156 mg chol, 616 mg sodium. % RDI: 7% calcium, 45% iron, 4% vit A, 35% vit C, 17% folate.

Salmon Fillets with Braised Leeks

Just a few ingredients makes this a quick dish to put together. For even cooking, choose all centre-cut salmon fillets – the thickest part of the fish.

5- to 6-quart (5 to 6 L) slow cooker

Makes 4 servings

3 tbsp	butter	45 mL	4	centre-cut salmon fillets (about 6 oz/ 175 g each)		4
6	leeks (white and light green parts only), sliced	6	¼ cup	dry white wine		50 mL
¼ tsp	each salt and pepper	1 mL				

In large skillet, melt butter over medium heat; spoon 1 tbsp (15 mL) into small bowl. Set aside.

Fry leeks and half each of the salt and pepper in remaining butter, stirring often, until softened, about 8 minutes. Scrape all but ½ cup (125 mL) of the leeks into slow cooker.

Place salmon on leeks in slow cooker; brush with reserved butter. Sprinkle with remaining salt and pepper and reserved leeks. Drizzle wine over salmon.

Cover and cook on low until salmon flakes easily when tested, about 1 to 1½ hours.

PER SERVING: about 418 cal, 32 g pro, 26 g total fat (9 g sat. fat), 14 g carb, 2 g fibre, 114 mg chol, 314 mg sodium. % RDI: 7% calcium, 19% iron, 10% vit A, 20% vit C, 36% folate.

Pasta Sauces, Meatballs & Casseroles

Bolognese Sauce

This nourishing Italian sauce makes an effortless weekend supper, with plenty of leftovers to freeze for busy nights that follow.

4- to 6-quart (4 to 6 L) slow cooker

Makes about 8 cups (2 L)

1 lb	lean ground beef, pork or turkey	500 g	1 cup	milk	250 mL
1 tsp	fennel seeds	5 mL	1	can (28 oz/796 mL) tomatoes	1
4	slices bacon or pancetta, chopped	4	1	can (28 oz/796 mL) crushed tomatoes	1
2	onions, chopped	2	1 cup	dry red wine	250 mL
3	cloves garlic, minced	3	2 tbsp	tomato paste	30 mL
2	carrots, diced	2	1	bay leaf	1
2	stalks celery, chopped	2	Pinch	granulated sugar	Pinch
1 tsp	each dried oregano, salt and pepper	5 mL	¼ cup	minced fresh parsley	50 mL

TEST KITCHEN TIP
Calculate 12 oz (375 g) pasta for four starter-course servings or 1 lb (500 g) for four main-course servings.

In large skillet, sauté beef over medium-high heat, breaking up with fork until crumbly and no longer pink, about 5 minutes. Drain any fat from skillet.

Meanwhile, in mortar using pestle or pressing with bottom of small saucepan, crush fennel seeds; add to skillet along with bacon, onions, garlic, carrots, celery, oregano, salt and pepper. Fry over medium heat, stirring occasionally, until vegetables are softened, about 8 minutes.

Stir in milk; simmer until almost no liquid remains, about 3 minutes. Scrape into slow cooker along with tomatoes, crushed tomatoes, red wine, tomato paste, bay leaf and sugar. Mash tomatoes with potato masher or fork until still slightly chunky. Stir to combine.

Cover and cook on low until vegetables are tender and sauce is thick enough to mound on spoon, about 5 hours. Discard bay leaf; stir in parsley. (Make-ahead: Let cool for 30 minutes. Refrigerate, uncovered, in airtight containers until cold. Cover and refrigerate for up to 3 days or freeze for up to 1 month.)

PER 1 CUP (250 mL): about 261 cal, 17 g pro, 13 g total fat (6 g sat. fat), 20 g carb, 4 g fibre, 41 mg chol, 614 mg sodium. % RDI: 12% calcium, 27% iron, 62% vit A, 48% vit C, 13% folate.

Herbed Spaghetti Sauce

Economical ground beef goes a long way in this tried-and-true sauce. Ground pork and turkey are other excellent options.

4- to 6-quart (4 to 6 L)
slow cooker

Makes 10 cups
(2.5 L)

1½ lb	lean ground beef	750 g	1	sweet red or yellow pepper, chopped	1	
2	cans (each 28 oz/ 796 mL) tomatoes	2	4	cloves garlic, minced	4	
1	can (5½ oz/156 mL) tomato paste	1	1 tbsp	each dried basil and oregano	15 mL	
1½ cups	sliced mushrooms	375 mL	1 tsp	each dried thyme and salt	5 mL	
2	carrots, chopped	2	½ tsp	pepper	2 mL	
2	stalks celery, chopped	2	¼ tsp	cayenne pepper	1 mL	
1	large onion, chopped	1	4 tsp	balsamic vinegar	20 mL	

TEST KITCHEN TIP
For a finer-looking sauce, dice vegetables all about the same size.

In large skillet, sauté beef over medium-high heat, breaking up with fork until crumbly and no longer pink, about 8 minutes.

Meanwhile, place tomatoes in slow cooker; mash with potato masher or fork until slightly chunky. Stir in tomato paste, mushrooms, carrots, celery, onion, red pepper, garlic, basil, oregano, thyme, salt, pepper and cayenne pepper. Using slotted spoon, transfer beef to slow cooker; mix well.

Cover and cook on low until vegetables are tender and sauce is thick enough to mound on spoon, about 8 to 10 hours. Stir in vinegar. (Make-ahead: Let cool for 30 minutes. Refrigerate, uncovered, in airtight containers until cold. Cover and refrigerate for up to 3 days or freeze for up to 1 month.)

PER 1¼ CUPS (300 mL): about 243 cal, 20 g pro, 10 g total fat (4 g sat. fat), 20 g carb, 4 g fibre, 44 mg chol, 706 mg sodium. % RDI: 9% calcium, 31% iron, 68% vit A, 93% vit C, 14% folate.

Which Pasta Shape Should I Use?

There are no hard-and-fast rules for matching pasta shapes with sauces, but here are some helpful guidelines.

> **CHUNKY VEGETABLE SAUCES:** Use pasta with crannies and crevices to catch and hold vegetables. Try fusilli, orecchiette and shells.

> **MEAT SAUCES:** Traditional favourites are macaroni, tagliatelle, pappardelle, fusilli, bucatini and, of course, spaghetti.

> **SMOOTH SAUCES:** Smooth sauces need pasta with lots of surface area. Try fusilli, farfalle, macaroni, penne or shells.

> **SOUPS:** Almost all small pasta, such as orzo, tubetti and stelline, do well in soup. Use broken pieces or leftover pasta in minestrone.

Sausage Eggplant Pasta Sauce

This robust sauce makes grand leftovers and freezes well for suppers on the fly. Rotini or any short pasta is an ideal match for the chunky sauce, but polenta or split baked russet potatoes are excellent for a change of base.

5½- to 6-quart (5.5 to 6 L) slow cooker

Makes 8 cups (2 L)

2	eggplants, cubed (about 2 lb/1 kg)	2	2	stalks celery, diced	2
1 tsp	salt	5 mL	4	cloves garlic, minced	4
1½ lb	hot or mild Italian sausages	750 g	2 tsp	dried oregano	10 mL
			½ tsp	pepper	2 mL
3 tbsp	extra-virgin olive oil	45 mL	¼ cup	tomato paste	50 mL
2	onions, diced	2	2	cans (each 28 oz/ 796 mL) tomatoes	2

↜ In colander, toss eggplant with ½ tsp (2 mL) of the salt; let stand for 30 minutes. Rinse; pat dry with towels and set aside.

↜ Meanwhile, remove casings from sausages. In large skillet, heat 1 tbsp (15 mL) of the oil over medium-high heat; sauté sausage meat, breaking up with fork until crumbly and no longer pink, about 8 minutes. Using slotted spoon, transfer to slow cooker.

↜ Drain fat from skillet; add remaining oil. Fry onions, celery, garlic, oregano, pepper, eggplant and remaining salt over medium heat, stirring occasionally, until eggplant is soft, about 10 minutes. Add tomato paste; cook, stirring often, for 5 minutes.

↜ Meanwhile, add tomatoes to slow cooker; mash with potato masher or fork into bite-size pieces. Scrape eggplant mixture into slow cooker. Stir to combine.

↜ Cover and cook on low until sauce is thickened around sausage and eggplant, about 5 to 6 hours. (Make-ahead: Let cool for 30 minutes. Refrigerate, uncovered, in airtight containers until cold. Cover and refrigerate for up to 3 days or freeze for up to 1 month.)

PER 1 CUP (250 ML): about 347 cal, 16 g pro, 23 g total fat (6 g sat. fat), 23 g carb, 5 g fibre, 43 mg chol, 1,058 mg sodium. % RDI: 10% calcium, 27% iron, 5% vit A, 53% vit C, 16% folate.

TEST KITCHEN TIPS

If you like a spicy hot sauce, choose hot sausages and add a generous pinch of hot pepper flakes.

After emptying cans of tomatoes, or tomato sauce or paste, swirl about ½ cup (125 mL) water in the cans to get every last drop of tomato residue. You can add this to the sauce or use it to deglaze the skillet after emptying the eggplant mixture into the slow cooker.

Braised Beef & Rosemary Pasta Sauce

5½- to 6-quart (5.5 to 6 L) slow cooker

Makes 6 servings

The splash of balsamic vinegar adds polish to a rich beef sauce. Look no further than your favourite short pasta to go with it.

1½ lb	stewing beef cubes	750 g		1	can (28 oz/796 mL) stewed tomatoes	1
1 tbsp	vegetable oil	15 mL		2 tbsp	balsamic or red wine vinegar	30 mL
1	small onion, chopped	1		¼ cup	grated Parmesan cheese	50 mL
1 tbsp	dried rosemary	15 mL				
½ tsp	each salt and pepper	2 mL				

TEST KITCHEN TIP

Plenty of water is the secret to keeping pasta from clumping. Use 4 cups (1 L) water for each 4 oz (125 g) dry pasta. Bring water to boil in a large covered saucepan. Add salt, then pasta, stirring often until water returns to boil. Start the timer when the boiling gets vigorous.

↝ Trim and cut beef into 1-inch (2.5 cm) cubes. In large skillet, heat oil over medium-high heat; brown beef, in batches. Using slotted spoon, transfer to slow cooker.

↝ Drain fat from skillet. Fry onion, rosemary, salt and pepper over medium-low heat, stirring occasionally, until softened, about 4 minutes. Add to slow cooker.

↝ Add ¼ cup (50 mL) water to skillet; bring to boil, scraping up brown bits from bottom of skillet. Scrape into slow cooker along with tomatoes and vinegar.

↝ Cover and cook on high until beef is tender, about 4 to 6 hours. (Make-ahead: Let cool for 30 minutes. Refrigerate, uncovered, in airtight containers until cold. Cover and refrigerate for up to 3 days or freeze for up to 1 month.)

↝ Serve sprinkled with Parmesan cheese.

PER SERVING: about 258 cal, 28 g pro, 12 g total fat (4 g sat. fat), 9 g carb, 2 g fibre, 59 mg chol, 557 mg sodium. % RDI: 10% calcium, 24% iron, 9% vit A, 22% vit C, 7% folate.

Chunky Tomato Pasta Sauce

Consider this a good mother sauce – handy for pasta, of course, but also fine as a topper for pizza, layered in casseroles or wherever you need a tasty tomato sauce. Purée if you prefer a smooth texture.

4½- to 6-quart (4.5 to 6 L) slow cooker

Makes about 6 cups (1.5 L)

2 tbsp	extra-virgin olive oil	30 mL	½ tsp	hot pepper flakes	2 mL
2	onions, diced	2	¼ cup	tomato paste	50 mL
4	cloves garlic, minced	4	2	cans (each 28 oz/ 796 mL) diced tomatoes	2
2	each carrots and stalks celery, diced	2	2 tbsp	balsamic vinegar	30 mL
1	sweet yellow or red pepper, diced	1	½ cup	grated Parmesan cheese	125 mL
2 tsp	dried Italian herb seasoning	10 mL	¼ cup	minced fresh parsley	50 mL
1 tsp	salt	5 mL			

~ In large skillet, heat oil over medium heat; fry onions, garlic, carrots, celery, yellow pepper, Italian herb seasoning, salt and hot pepper flakes until vegetables are softened, about 5 minutes. Stir in tomato paste; cook for 2 minutes. Scrape into slow cooker.

~ Add ½ cup (125 mL) water to skillet; bring to boil, scraping up brown bits from bottom of skillet. Scrape into slow cooker along with tomatoes and vinegar.

~ Cover and cook on low until sauce is thickened around vegetable chunks, about 5 to 6 hours. Stir in Parmesan cheese. (Make-ahead: Let cool for 30 minutes. Refrigerate, uncovered, in airtight containers until cold. Cover and refrigerate for up to 3 days or freeze for up to 1 month.) Stir in parsley.

PER ½ CUP (125 mL): about 86 cal, 4 g pro, 4 g total fat (1 g sat. fat), 11 g carb, 2 g fibre, 4 mg chol, 447 mg sodium. % RDI: 10% calcium, 14% iron, 26% vit A, 48% vit C, 8% folate.

VARIATION

Chunky Mushroom Tomato Pasta Sauce: Add 1 to 2 cups (250 to 500 mL) sliced white or cremini mushrooms along with the carrots.

TEST KITCHEN TIP

Don't rinse cooked pasta. The surface starch helps the sauce stick. Do drain it well, though, to avoid diluting the sauce.

Puttanesca Sauce

This piquant combination of tomatoes, garlic, olives and capers is a classic atop any long pasta. Another choice for the black olives is the oil-cured variety, which are glossy, slightly wrinkled and mellower than the Kalamatas. Avoid bland canned olives, because they do little more than provide contrasting colour in a sauce that requires some zip.

4½- to 6-quart (4.5 to 6 L) slow cooker

Makes 6 cups (1.5 L)

2 tbsp	extra-virgin olive oil	30 mL
8	cloves garlic, minced	8
½ tsp	dried oregano	2 mL
½ tsp	hot pepper flakes	2 mL
Pinch	pepper	Pinch
2	cans (each 19 oz/ 540 mL) tomatoes	2

1	can (5½ oz/156 mL) tomato paste	1
1 cup	sliced pitted Kalamata olives	250 mL
1 cup	pimiento-stuffed olives, sliced	250 mL
¼ cup	drained capers	50 mL
½ cup	minced fresh parsley	125 mL

❧ In skillet, heat oil over medium heat; fry garlic, oregano, hot pepper flakes and pepper until fragrant, about 1 minute. Scrape into slow cooker.

❧ Add tomatoes to slow cooker; mash with potato masher or fork until slightly chunky. Stir in tomato paste.

❧ Cover and cook on low until slightly thickened and spicy tasting, about 5 hours. (Make-ahead: Let cool for 30 minutes. Refrigerate, uncovered, in airtight containers until cold. Cover and refrigerate for up to 3 days or freeze for up to 1 month.)

❧ Stir in Kalamata and pimiento-stuffed olives, capers and half of the parsley. Cover and cook on low for 15 minutes. Stir in remaining parsley.

PER ¾ CUP (175 mL): about 165 cal, 3 g pro, 13 g total fat (2 g sat. fat), 13 g carb, 3 g fibre, 0 mg chol, 1,392 mg sodium. % RDI: 8% calcium, 17% iron, 16% vit A, 55% vit C, 8% folate.

Marinara Pasta Sauce

4½- to 6-quart (4.5 to 6 L)
slow cooker

Makes 6 cups (1.5 L)

When a plain tomato sauce is in order – for pasta, cutlets, chicken, fish, meatballs, chops or pizza – here's the one to choose. While "plain" in the sense of no meat or chunky vegetables, this sauce's vigorous tomato taste is definitely not plain.

2 tbsp	extra-virgin olive oil	30 mL		1 tbsp	balsamic vinegar	15 mL
4	large cloves garlic	4		Pinch	each salt and granulated sugar	Pinch
2 tsp	dried basil	10 mL				
1 tbsp	tomato paste	15 mL		Pinch	hot pepper flakes	Pinch
2	cans (each 28 oz/ 796 mL) tomatoes	2				

SUBSTITUTION

In season, replace dried basil with 10 luscious fresh basil leaves. Whenever you can, shred a few more fresh basil leaves and stir them into the finished Marinara Pasta Sauce.

In skillet, heat oil over medium-low heat; fry garlic and basil, stirring often, until garlic starts to soften but does not colour, about 5 minutes. Stir in tomato paste; cook, stirring, for 2 minutes. Pour in ½ cup (125 mL) water, stirring to loosen sauce. Scrape into slow cooker.

Add tomatoes to slow cooker; mash with potato masher or fork until slightly chunky. Stir in vinegar, salt, sugar and hot pepper flakes. Cover and cook on low until sauce is thick enough to coat spoon, about 5 hours.

Using immersion blender, or in blender, purée sauce until smooth. (Make-ahead: Let cool for 30 minutes. Refrigerate, uncovered, in airtight containers until cold. Cover and refrigerate for up to 3 days or freeze for up to 1 month.)

PER ¼ CUP (50 mL): about 23 cal, 1 g pro, 1 g total fat (trace sat. fat), 3 g carb, 1 g fibre, 0 mg chol, 87 mg sodium. % RDI: 2% calcium, 5% iron, 1% vit A, 15% vit C, 2% folate.

Pantry Treasure: Canned Tomatoes

> **Plain canned tomatoes** (inevitably plum tomatoes) and **diced tomatoes** are our first choice. Try salt-free varieties for less sodium. Unless otherwise noted, use both tomatoes and juice.

> **Ground or puréed tomatoes** bump up tomato flavour in a dish, while **stewed tomatoes,** old-fashioned or with Mexican or Italian seasonings, reduce the need for other flavourings.

> The pricier **San Marzano tomato,** a variety of plum tomato, has a special reputation for deliciousness.

> **Strained tomatoes,** or *passata*, are simply seeded skinned plum tomatoes that have been puréed, lightly salted and processed in the Italian tradition. Strained tomatoes are generally available in 24-oz (680 mL) bottles.

> **Tomato paste** is often preferable over tomato sauce because it is preserved without salt and adds rich, deep flavour.

Roasted Red Pepper Tomato Sauce

4½- to 6-quart (4.5 to 6 L) slow cooker

Makes 8 cups (2 L)

This sweet, chunky sauce is perfect tossed with large tube or twist pasta. Or for a supper far from the sauce's pasta-topping origin, use it as a base for poached eggs or over scrambled eggs. To go with this homey but delicious supper, grill or toast baguette slices, rub a bit of garlic on the crunchy surface and brush with butter or good olive oil.

1 tbsp	vegetable oil	15 mL		2	cans (each 28 oz/ 796 mL) tomatoes	2
2	onions, chopped	2		1	can (5½ oz/156 mL) tomato paste	1
4	cloves garlic, minced	4		1 cup	chopped roasted red peppers	250 mL
1	carrot, diced	1				
2 tsp	dried basil	10 mL				
¼ tsp	each salt and pepper	1 mL				

SUBSTITUTION
To replace dried pasta with fresh, use about 1½ times the quantity called for. Cooking it for just 1 to 3 minutes.

In large skillet, heat oil over medium heat; fry onions, garlic, carrot, basil, salt and pepper, stirring occasionally, until vegetables are softened, about 8 minutes.

Meanwhile, add tomatoes to slow cooker; mash with potato masher or fork until slightly chunky. Scrape in onion mixture along with tomato paste and roasted red peppers. Stir to combine.

Cover and cook on low until bubbly and thick enough to mound on spoon, about 4 hours. (Make-ahead: Let cool for 30 minutes. Refrigerate, uncovered, in airtight containers until cold. Cover and refrigerate for up to 3 days or freeze for up to 1 month.)

PER GENEROUS ¾ CUP (175 mL): about 76 cal, 3 g pro, 2 g total fat (trace sat. fat), 15 g carb, 3 g fibre, 0 mg chol, 356 mg sodium. % RDI: 6% calcium, 12% iron, 39% vit A, 103% vit C, 9% folate.

Tomato Lentil Pasta Sauce

4½- to 6-quart (4.5 to 6 L)
slow cooker

Makes 8 cups (2 L)

For vegetarians, this pasta sauce is an excellent addition to a repertoire of satisfying supper dishes. The pancetta or bacon is an option meat eaters can add, although the sauce is just fine without it. This recipe makes enough for 8 servings, leaving plenty to put aside in the freezer and give you a night off.

2 tbsp	extra-virgin olive oil	30 mL	1 tsp	dried thyme	5 mL
2	onions, diced	2	½ tsp	each salt and pepper	2 mL
2	carrots, diced	2	2	cans (each 28 oz/ 796 mL) tomatoes	2
2	stalks celery, diced	2			
6	cloves garlic, minced	6	1½ cups	green lentils	375 mL
½ cup	diced pancetta or bacon (optional)	125 mL	½ cup	red wine or water	125 mL
3	bay leaves	3	¼ cup	minced celery leaves and/or fresh parsley	50 mL

➤ In large skillet, heat oil over medium heat; fry onions, carrots, celery, garlic, pancetta (if using), bay leaves, thyme, salt and pepper, stirring occasionally, until vegetables are softened, about 8 minutes.

➤ Meanwhile, add tomatoes to slow cooker; mash with potato masher or fork until in bite-size pieces. Scrape in onion mixture along with lentils, wine and 1½ cups (375 mL) water. Stir to combine.

➤ Cover and cook on low until lentils are tender and sauce is thick enough to mound on spoon, about 4 to 5 hours. Discard bay leaves. (Make-ahead: Let cool for 30 minutes. Refrigerate, uncovered, in airtight containers until cold. Cover and refrigerate for up to 3 days or freeze for up to 1 month.)

➤ Stir in celery leaves.

PER ½ CUP (125 mL): about 105 cal, 6 g pro, 2 g total fat (trace sat. fat), 17 g carb, 4 g fibre, 0 mg chol, 213 mg sodium. % RDI: 5% calcium, 21% iron, 18% vit A, 27% vit C, 48% folate.

Glazed Ginger Meatballs

4½- to 6-quart (4.5 to 6 L)
slow cooker

Makes 8 servings

These glossy meatballs are full of the fresh flavours of ginger and coriander and have a nice crunch, thanks to the water chestnuts and sprouts. Enjoy over rice or Chinese noodles.

1	egg	1	2 cups	beef broth	500 mL
1	small onion, grated	1	2 tbsp	liquid honey	30 mL
½ cup	dry bread crumbs	125 mL	8	cloves garlic, minced	8
¼ cup	chopped fresh coriander or parsley	50 mL	1	can (14 oz/398 mL) sliced water chestnuts, drained	1
¼ cup	soy sauce	50 mL	2	carrots, halved lengthwise and thinly sliced	2
1 tbsp	minced gingerroot (or 1 tsp/5 mL ground ginger)	15 mL			
½ tsp	Asian chili paste or hot pepper sauce	2 mL	Pinch	each salt and pepper	Pinch
			3 tbsp	cornstarch	45 mL
1 lb	each lean ground beef and lean ground pork	500 g	1 cup	bean sprouts	250 mL

❧ In bowl, beat egg; stir in ¼ cup (50 mL) water, onion, bread crumbs, half each of the coriander and soy sauce, the ginger and chili paste; mix in beef and pork. Roll by rounded tablespoonfuls (15 mL) into 1-inch (2.5 cm) balls.

❧ Bake on greased rimmed baking sheets in 400°F (200°C) oven until firm, 10 to 15 minutes. Transfer to slow cooker.

❧ Combine broth and honey; add to meatballs along with garlic, water chestnuts, carrots, salt and pepper. Stir gently to distribute ingredients around meatballs. Cover and cook on low until carrots are tender, about 4 to 5 hours.

❧ Move solids to 1 side of slow cooker. In bowl, whisk cornstarch with remaining soy sauce; whisk into liquid in slow cooker. Stir to redistribute.

❧ Cover and cook on high until sauce is glossy and thickened, about 15 minutes. (Make-ahead: Let cool for 30 minutes. Refrigerate, uncovered, in airtight containers until cold. Cover and refrigerate for up to 3 days.)

❧ Serve sprinkled with bean sprouts and remaining coriander.

PER SERVING: about 328 cal, 25 g pro, 15 g total fat (6 g sat. fat), 24 g carb, 2 g fibre, 94 mg chol, 839 mg sodium. % RDI: 4% calcium, 21% iron, 47% vit A, 8% vit C, 13% folate.

Greek Market Meatballs with Cumin & Pepper

4½- to 6-quart (4.5 to 6 L)
slow cooker

Makes 6 servings

Here is a slow cooker version of a best-seller at Winnipeg's Greek Market. Serve over rice, polenta or noodles, or with Garlic Roasted Potatoes (recipe, page 231).

1 tbsp	extra-virgin olive oil	15 mL
1	onion, finely chopped	1
½ tsp	each salt, pepper and ground cumin	2 mL
1	can (28 oz/796 mL) crushed tomatoes	1
½ cup	dry red wine or beef broth	125 mL
1 tsp	granulated sugar	5 mL
¼ cup	minced fresh parsley	50 mL

MEATBALLS:

2 tbsp	extra-virgin olive oil	30 mL
6	cloves garlic, halved	6
1	small onion, quartered	1
4 tsp	ground cumin	20 mL
2 tsp	pepper	10 mL
1 tsp	salt	5 mL
2	eggs	2
1 cup	dry bread crumbs	250 mL
1 lb	lean ground beef	500 g
2 tbsp	minced fresh parsley	30 mL

TEST KITCHEN TIP

Don't toss that little bit of leftover wine. (Also nix on keeping it at room or refrigerator temperature, hoping to use it up.) Instead, freeze it in small airtight containers or ice cube trays for spur-of-the-moment cooking. Freeze as soon as possible, then thaw at will. Just give it a quick shake in case the wine has separated.

🍃 **MEATBALLS:** In food processor, pulse together oil, garlic, onion, cumin, pepper and salt until smooth. Add eggs; pulse just until mixed. Add bread crumbs, beef and parsley; pulse just until mixed.

🍃 Using about 2 tbsp (30 mL) of the beef mixture for each, shape into 2-inch (5 cm) long ovals. Bake on greased rimmed baking sheet in 400°F (200°C) oven until firm, 10 to 15 minutes. Transfer to slow cooker.

🍃 Meanwhile, in large skillet, heat oil over medium-high heat; sauté onion, salt, pepper and cumin until onion is golden, about 5 minutes. Stir in tomatoes, wine and sugar; scrape over meatballs.

🍃 Cover and cook on low until sauce is bubbly and thickened, about 4 hours. (Make-ahead: Let cool for 30 minutes. Refrigerate, uncovered, in airtight containers until cold. Cover and refrigerate for up to 3 days or freeze for up to 1 month.)

🍃 Stir in parsley.

PER SERVING: about 387 cal, 22 g pro, 21 g total fat (6 g sat. fat), 29 g carb, 4 g fibre, 107 mg chol, 983 mg sodium. % RDI: 12% calcium, 44% iron, 13% vit A, 27% vit C, 16% folate.

Creamy Mushroom Meatballs

This sauce is made with 2% evaporated milk, which ups the calcium and maintains the dish's creamy consistency without the need for higher-fat cream.

4½- to 6-quart (4.5 to 6 L) slow cooker

Makes 8 servings

1 tbsp	vegetable oil	15 mL
6 cups	sliced mushrooms (1 lb/500 g)	1.5 L
1 tsp	dried dillweed	5 mL
¼ tsp	each salt and pepper	1 mL
1 cup	beef broth	250 mL
1	can (385 mL) 2% evaporated milk	1
3 tbsp	all-purpose flour	45 mL
1 tbsp	lemon juice	15 mL

2 tbsp	minced fresh parsley	30 mL
MEATBALLS:		
1	egg	1
1	small onion, grated	1
½ cup	dry bread crumbs	125 mL
½ tsp	each salt and pepper	2 mL
½ tsp	ground allspice	2 mL
¼ tsp	grated nutmeg	1 mL
2 lb	lean ground pork or beef	1 kg

❧ **MEATBALLS:** In large bowl, beat egg; mix in ¼ cup (50 mL) water, onion, bread crumbs, salt, pepper, allspice and nutmeg; mix in pork. Roll by rounded tablespoonfuls (15 mL) into 1-inch (2.5 cm) balls. Bake on greased rimmed baking sheet in 400°F (200°C) oven until firm, 10 to 15 minutes. Transfer to slow cooker.

❧ Meanwhile, in large skillet, heat oil over medium-high heat; sauté mushrooms, dill, salt and pepper until no liquid remains, about 10 minutes. Scrape into slow cooker.

❧ Add broth to skillet; bring to boil, scraping up brown bits from bottom of skillet. Scrape into slow cooker along with evaporated milk; stir gently to combine ingredients around meatballs.

❧ Cover and cook on low until sauce is bubbly and coats meatballs and mushrooms nicely, about 4 hours.

❧ Move meatballs to 1 side of slow cooker. Whisk flour with ⅓ cup (75 mL) water; whisk into liquid in slow cooker. Stir to redistribute meatballs. Cover and cook on high until sauce is thickened, about 20 minutes. Stir in lemon juice. (Make-ahead: Let cool for 30 minutes. Refrigerate, uncovered, in airtight containers until cold. Cover and refrigerate for up to 3 days or freeze for up to 1 month.) Sprinkle with parsley.

PER SERVING: about 372 cal, 29 g pro, 21 g total fat (7 g sat. fat), 16 g carb, 1 g fibre, 94 mg chol, 494 mg sodium. % RDI: 16% calcium, 19% iron, 5% vit A, 15% vit C, 12% folate.

Spaghetti & Meatballs

Definitely not ordinary (although they don't take any more time than the ordinary kind), these homemade meatballs taste a whole lot better than store-bought.

4½- to 6-quart (4.5 to 6 L)
slow cooker

Makes 4 servings

1 tbsp	extra-virgin olive oil	15 mL	**MEATBALLS:**		
1	onion, diced	1	1	egg	1
2	cloves garlic, minced	2	½ cup	grated onion	125 mL
½ tsp	each dried oregano and hot pepper flakes	2 mL	1	large clove garlic, minced	1
¼ tsp	salt	1 mL	¼ cup	dry bread crumbs	50 mL
1	can (28 oz/796 mL) crushed tomatoes	1	¼ cup	grated Parmesan cheese	50 mL
¼ cup	minced fresh parsley	50 mL	½ tsp	each salt, pepper, dried basil and oregano	2 mL
1 lb	spaghetti, cooked	500 g			
			1 lb	lean ground beef	500 g

TEST KITCHEN TIP
While you're at it, make extra meatballs and freeze for another spaghetti dinner or to heat in homemade barbecue sauce (recipes, pages 216 and 217) to fill crusty rolls.

❧ **MEATBALLS:** In bowl, beat egg; mix in onion, garlic, bread crumbs, cheese, salt, pepper, basil and oregano; mix in beef. Shape into 16 balls.

❧ Bake on greased rimmed baking sheet in 400°F (200°C) oven until firm, about 10 to 15 minutes. Transfer to slow cooker.

❧ Meanwhile, in large skillet, heat oil over medium heat; fry onion, garlic, oregano, hot pepper flakes and salt, stirring occasionally, until onion is softened, about 5 minutes. Stir in tomatoes; scrape over meatballs.

❧ Cover and cook on low until sauce is slightly thickened, about 4 to 6 hours. (Make-ahead: Let cool for 30 minutes. Refrigerate, uncovered, in airtight containers until cold. Cover and refrigerate for up to 3 days or freeze for up to 1 month.)

❧ Stir in parsley. Spoon over spaghetti.

PER SERVING: about 849 cal, 46 g pro, 25 g total fat (9 g sat. fat), 111 g carb, 10 g fibre, 120 mg chol, 1,024 mg sodium. % RDI: 20% calcium, 72% iron, 21% vit A, 40% vit C, 128% folate.

Turkey Meatball Subs

Hearty subs are a satisfying supper or lunch. On their own, the saucy meatballs are also delicious over cooked pasta, rice or mashed potatoes. For variety, you can substitute lean ground beef, pork or chicken for the turkey.

4½- to 6-quart (4.5 to 6 L)
slow cooker

Makes 4 servings

1 tbsp	vegetable oil	15 mL		**MEATBALLS:**		
1	onion, chopped	1		1	egg	1
½ tsp	each dried basil and oregano	2 mL		½ cup	grated onion	125 mL
¼ tsp	each salt and pepper	1 mL		2	cloves garlic, minced	2
1	can (28 oz/796 mL) ground tomatoes	1		2 tbsp	dry bread crumbs	30 mL
				2 tbsp	grated Parmesan cheese	30 mL
2 tbsp	chopped fresh parsley	30 mL		½ tsp	each dried basil and oregano	2 mL
4	submarine buns	4				
1	sweet green pepper, finely diced	1		¼ tsp	each salt and pepper	1 mL
				1 lb	lean ground turkey	500 g
½ cup	grated Parmesan cheese	125 mL				

✦ **MEATBALLS:** In large bowl, beat egg; mix in onion, garlic, bread crumbs, cheese, basil, oregano, salt and pepper; mix in turkey. Shape into 16 balls.

✦ Bake on greased rimmed baking sheet in 400°F (200°C) oven until firm, 10 to 15 minutes. Transfer to slow cooker.

✦ Meanwhile, in skillet, heat oil over medium heat; fry onion, basil, oregano, salt and pepper until onion is softened, about 5 minutes. Scrape into slow cooker along with tomatoes. Stir gently to combine ingredients around meatballs.

✦ Cover and cook on low until bubbly, about 4 hours. (Make-ahead: Let cool for 30 minutes. Refrigerate, uncovered, in airtight containers until cold. Cover and refrigerate for up to 3 days or freeze for up to 1 month.)

✦ Stir in parsley. Divide meatballs among buns; spoon sauce over meatballs. Sprinkle with green pepper and cheese.

PER SERVING: about 684 cal, 41 g pro, 25 g total fat (6 g sat. fat), 75 g carb, 8 g fibre, 133 mg chol, 1,323 mg sodium. % RDI: 44% calcium, 59% iron, 21% vit A, 82% vit C, 65% folate.

Macaroni & Cheddar with Ham

5- to 6-quart (5 to 6 L) slow cooker

Makes 8 to 10 servings

Cottage cheese and light sour cream make this soothing baked pasta super creamy without having to dress the macaroni with a cooked cream sauce. You can leave the ham out if you like.

3 cups	macaroni	750 mL	1½ cups	2% cottage cheese	375 mL
2	eggs	2	1	sweet red pepper, diced	1
3 cups	shredded extra-old Cheddar cheese	750 mL	2 tbsp	dried parsley	30 mL
2 cups	light sour cream	500 mL	¼ tsp	pepper	1 mL
1½ cups	diced ham	375 mL			

➤ In large pot of boiling salted water, cook macaroni until tender but firm, about 8 minutes. Drain and add to slow cooker.

➤ In large bowl, beat eggs; mix in 2 cups (500 mL) of the Cheddar cheese, sour cream, ham, cottage cheese, red pepper, parsley and pepper. Stir into macaroni; smooth top.

➤ Cover and cook on low until bubbly and knife inserted in centre for 5 seconds comes out piping hot, about 4 hours.

➤ Sprinkle with remaining cheese; cover and cook on low until cheese is melted, about 5 minutes.

PER EACH OF 10 SERVINGS: about 390 cal, 27 g pro, 17 g total fat (10 g sat. fat), 32 g carb, 2 g fibre, 94 mg chol, 765 mg sodium. % RDI: 34% calcium, 11% iron, 18% vit A, 33% vit C, 28% folate.

Old-Fashioned Creamy Macaroni & Cheese

Searching for a quintessential Canadian dish? Mac and cheese is a contender. This is a family-pleaser that kids love.

4½- to 6-quart (4.5 to 6 L) slow cooker

Makes 4 to 6 servings

2 tbsp	butter	30 mL	2 tsp	Dijon mustard	10 mL
1	onion, diced	1	¾ tsp	salt	4 mL
⅓ cup	all-purpose flour	75 mL	½ tsp	pepper	2 mL
3 cups	milk	750 mL	2 cups	macaroni	500 mL
3 cups	shredded old Cheddar cheese	750 mL	¼ cup	chopped fresh parsley	50 mL

In large saucepan, melt butter over medium heat; fry onion, stirring occasionally, until softened, about 3 minutes.

Add flour; cook, whisking, for 1 minute. Whisk in milk; cook, whisking, until bubbly and thickened, about 8 minutes. Add Cheddar cheese, mustard, salt and pepper. Scrape into slow cooker.

Meanwhile, in large pot of boiling salted water, cook macaroni until tender but firm, 8 minutes. Drain and add to slow cooker; stir to combine.

Cover and cook on low until bubbly, about 3 hours. Sprinkle with parsley.

PER EACH OF 6 SERVINGS: about 487 cal, 24 g pro, 26 g total fat (16 g sat. fat), 40 g carb, 2 g fibre, 81 mg chol, 854 mg sodium. % RDI: 52% calcium, 13% iron, 26% vit A, 7% vit C, 35% folate.

Mushroom Spinach Lasagna

A slow cooker lasagna may not be as crisp as a baked one, and its noodles may be softer, but its gooey cheese topping makes the package pretty irresistible.

5½- to 6-quart (5.5 to 6 L)
slow cooker

Makes 8 servings

1	tub (500 g) 2% cottage cheese	1
¼ cup	grated Parmesan cheese	50 mL
1	egg, lightly beaten	1
¼ tsp	grated nutmeg	1 mL
¼ tsp	each salt and pepper	1 mL
1	pkg (10 oz/300 g) frozen spinach, thawed	1
12	no-cook lasagna noodles	12
1 cup	shredded provolone or mozzarella cheese	250 mL

TOMATO MUSHROOM SAUCE:

1 tbsp	vegetable oil	15 mL
1	onion, chopped	1
1	carrot, finely diced	1
3	cloves garlic, minced	3
4 cups	sliced cremini or white mushrooms (12 oz/375 g)	1 L
2 tsp	dried Italian herb seasoning	10 mL
¼ tsp	each salt and pepper	1 mL
Pinch	hot pepper flakes	Pinch
1	jar (700 mL) pasta sauce	1

TOMATO MUSHROOM SAUCE: In large saucepan, heat oil over medium-high heat; sauté onion, carrot, garlic, mushrooms, Italian herb seasoning, salt, pepper and hot pepper flakes until liquid is evaporated, about 8 minutes. Add pasta sauce and 1½ cups (375 mL) water; bring to boil. Keep warm.

Meanwhile, in bowl, combine cottage cheese, Parmesan cheese, egg, nutmeg, salt and pepper. In sieve, press excess moisture out of spinach; chop and add to cottage cheese mixture. Stir to combine.

Pour 1 cup (250 mL) of the tomato mushroom sauce into slow cooker. Arrange 3 of the noodles over sauce, breaking to fit if necessary. Top with half of the cheese mixture. Cover with 3 noodles and half of the remaining sauce. Repeat with noodles and remaining cheese mixture. Top with remaining noodles and remaining sauce. Sprinkle with provolone.

Cover and cook on low until bubbly and pasta is tender, about 3 hours.

PER SERVING: about 363 cal, 22 g pro, 11 g total fat (5 g sat. fat), 44 g carb, 5 g fibre, 41 mg chol, 999 mg sodium. % RDI: 25% calcium, 16% iron, 52% vit A, 18% vit C, 26% folate.

Gardener's Pie

This vegetarian version of shepherd's pie is chunky with lots of healthy vegetables. Veggie Ground Round is one brand-name for precooked ground soy protein.

5½- to 6-quart (5.5 to 6 L) slow cooker

Makes 6 servings

1 tbsp	vegetable oil	15 mL
1	onion, chopped	1
3	cloves garlic, minced	3
2	carrots, diced	2
2	stalks celery, diced	2
1	sweet red pepper, diced	1
3 cups	button mushrooms, halved (8 oz/250 g)	750 mL
1 tsp	dried basil	5 mL
¼ tsp	each salt and pepper	1 mL
2 tbsp	all-purpose flour	30 mL

1	pkg (12 oz/340 g) precooked ground soy protein mixture	1
1 cup	vegetable broth	250 mL
2 tbsp	tomato paste	30 mL
1 tsp	paprika	5 mL
POTATO TOPPING:		
8	potatoes (3 lb/1.5 kg)	8
¼ cup	milk	50 mL
2 tbsp	butter	30 mL
½ tsp	each salt and pepper	2 mL

In skillet, heat oil over medium-high heat; sauté onion, garlic, carrots, celery, red pepper, mushrooms, basil, salt and pepper until no liquid remains, about 8 minutes. Sprinkle with flour; cook, stirring, for 1 minute. Scrape into slow cooker. Stir in soy protein mixture, broth, tomato paste and paprika.

Cover and cook on low until bubbly, about 3 hours.

POTATO TOPPING: Meanwhile, peel and cut potatoes into chunks. In saucepan of boiling salted water, cover and cook potatoes until tender, about 12 minutes. Drain and return to pot; mash with milk, butter, salt and pepper.

Spread potato topping over vegetable mixture. Cover and cook on high until bubbly, about 20 minutes.

PER SERVING: about 325 cal, 16 g pro, 7 g total fat (3 g sat. fat), 51 g carb, 8 g fibre, 13 mg chol, 1,169 mg sodium. % RDI: 9% calcium, 33% iron, 76% vit A, 87% vit C, 17% folate.

VARIATION

Shepherd's Pie: Replace precooked ground soy protein mixture with 1 lb (500 g) lean ground beef or lamb. Before sautéing vegetables in skillet, sauté beef over medium-high heat in 1 tbsp (15 mL) vegetable oil, breaking up with fork until crumbly and no longer pink, 8 minutes. With slotted spoon, transfer to slow cooker. Drain off fat; continue with recipe.

TEST KITCHEN TIP
Check potatoes carefully, especially ones sold in plastic bags, before buying and avoid any tinged with green. Light causes chlorophylls to rise to the surface and form solanine, which makes potatoes greenish and bitter.

Store potatoes in a heavy paper bag. They'll keep for several weeks in a dry, dark, well-ventilated place that's 45 to 50°F (7 to 10°C). Buy just what you need — save those huge bargain bags for big-crowd holidays.

Never refrigerate potatoes. Cold makes them unappetizingly sweet, and the flesh will darken when cooked.

Cabbage Rolls

Serve with baked or boiled potatoes and sour cream for happiness around the table.

5½- to 6-quart (5.5 to 6 L)
slow cooker

Makes 6 to
9 servings

1	cabbage (3½ lb/1.75 kg)	1
3 cups	tomato juice	750 mL
2 tbsp	tomato paste	30 mL
1 tbsp	packed brown sugar	15 mL
2 cups	sauerkraut, rinsed and squeezed dry	500 mL
FILLING:		
6	slices bacon, diced	6
2	onions, diced	2
2	cloves garlic, minced	2
⅓ cup	diced sweet red pepper	75 mL

1 tsp	dried oregano	5 mL
½ tsp	salt	2 mL
¼ tsp	caraway seeds (optional), crushed	1 mL
¼ tsp	each pepper and dried thyme	1 mL
⅓ cup	parboiled rice	75 mL
1 cup	chicken broth	250 mL
1	egg	1
⅓ cup	minced fresh parsley	75 mL
2 tbsp	chopped fresh dill	30 mL
1 lb	lean ground pork	500 g

❧ Cut core from cabbage. In large pot of boiling salted water, cover and heat cabbage until leaves are easy to remove, 8 minutes. Chill in cold water. Without tearing, remove 18 leaves, submerging cabbage for 2 to 3 minutes if leaves become difficult to remove. Drain. Pare off coarse veins; set aside.

❧ FILLING: In saucepan over medium heat, fry bacon until crisp. With slotted spoon, transfer to large bowl. Drain off fat from skillet; fry onions, garlic, red pepper, oregano, salt, caraway seeds (if using), pepper and thyme until vegetables are softened, about 5 minutes.

❧ Stir in rice; cook for 1 minute. Add broth; bring to boil. Cover, reduce heat and simmer until rice is tender and liquid is absorbed, 20 minutes. Add to bacon. Let cool; mix in egg, parsley and dill. Stir in pork. Spoon rounded ¼ cup (50 mL) rice mixture onto each leaf just above stem. Fold bottom, then sides over filling; roll up.

❧ Whisk tomato juice, paste and sugar. Spread one-third of the sauerkraut in slow cooker. Arrange half of the cabbage rolls on top, seam side down; top with half of the remaining sauerkraut. Pour half of the tomato mixture over top. Cover with remaining cabbage rolls, sauerkraut and tomato mixture. Place foil directly on surface. Cover; cook on low until cabbage is tender, 6 to 7 hours. (Make-ahead: Let cool for 30 minutes. Refrigerate, uncovered, in airtight containers until cold. Cover and refrigerate for up to 3 days.)

PER EACH OF 9 SERVINGS: about 245 cal, 15 g pro, 12 g total fat (4 g sat. fat), 21 g carb, 4 g fibre, 56 mg chol, 963 mg sodium. % RDI: 7% calcium, 17% iron, 11% vit A, 73% vit C, 25% folate.

Barley Tomato Cabbage Rolls

This old favourite goes vegetarian with barley, a grain that cooks successfully in the slow cooker. Sauerkraut gives a memorable taste to cabbage rolls, so make sure to pick the best quality possible – the type in jars is often superior.

5½- to 6-quart (5.5 to 6 L)
slow cooker

Makes 6 servings

1	cabbage (3½ lb/ 1.75 kg)	1	1 cup	pot or pearl barley	250 mL
1 tbsp	vegetable oil	15 mL	2 cups	vegetable broth	500 mL
1	onion, diced	1	1	each carrot and zucchini, diced	1
1	clove garlic, minced	1	1	egg, beaten	1
1 tsp	dried oregano	5 mL	2½ cups	tomato juice	625 mL
½ tsp	dried thyme	2 mL	¼ cup	tomato paste	50 mL
½ tsp	each salt and pepper	2 mL	1 tsp	granulated sugar	5 mL
¼ tsp	caraway seeds (optional), crushed	1 mL	3 cups	sauerkraut	750 mL

❧ Cut core from cabbage. In large pot of boiling salted water, cover and heat cabbage until leaves are easy to remove, 8 minutes. Chill in cold water. Without tearing, remove 12 leaves, submerging cabbage for 2 to 3 minutes if leaves become difficult to remove. Drain. Pare off coarse veins; set aside.

❧ In saucepan, heat oil over medium heat; fry onion, garlic, oregano, thyme, salt, pepper, and caraway seeds (if using), stirring often, until onion is softened, about 5 minutes.

❧ Stir in barley. Add broth and bring to boil; reduce heat, cover and simmer until barley is tender and liquid is absorbed, 40 minutes. Stir in carrot and zucchini. Let cool. Stir in egg. Spoon rounded ⅓ cup (75 mL) barley mixture onto each leaf just above stem. Fold bottom, then sides over filling; roll up.

❧ Whisk together tomato juice, tomato paste and sugar. Spread one-third of the sauerkraut in slow cooker. Arrange half of the cabbage rolls on top, seam side down. Arrange half of the remaining sauerkraut over rolls. Pour half of the tomato mixture over top. Cover with remaining cabbage rolls, sauerkraut and tomato mixture. Place foil directly on surface.

❧ Cover and cook on low until cabbage is tender, about 6 to 7 hours. (Make-ahead: Let cool for 30 minutes. Refrigerate, uncovered, in airtight containers until cold. Cover and refrigerate for up to 3 days.)

PER SERVING: about 251 cal, 7 g pro, 5 g total fat (1 g sat. fat), 49 g carb, 10 g fibre, 31 mg chol, 1,817 mg sodium. % RDI: 10% calcium, 32% iron, 42% vit A, 90% vit C, 42% folate.

Baked Beans with Apples

4½- to 6-quart (4.5 to 6 L)
slow cooker

Makes 8 servings

This no-added-fat quick version of baked beans uses only a bit of molasses and the natural sweetness of apples, so the recipe scores only about half the fat and calories of traditional baked beans.

6 cups	cooked pinto or navy beans (recipe, page 213) or 3 cans (each 19 oz/ 540 mL) pinto or navy beans, drained and rinsed	1.5 L
2 cups	chopped dried apples	500 mL
1	can (28 oz/796 mL) crushed tomatoes	1
1	large onion, diced	1
2	cloves garlic, minced	2
1 cup	apple cider	250 mL
3 tbsp	fancy molasses	45 mL
2 tbsp	cider vinegar	30 mL
1 tbsp	dry mustard	15 mL
1 tsp	salt	5 mL
¼ tsp	pepper	1 mL
1	apple, peeled, cored and diced	1

In slow cooker, combine beans, dried apples, tomatoes, onion, garlic, apple cider, molasses, cider vinegar, mustard, salt and pepper.

Cover and cook on low until bubbly and thickened enough to scoop, about 6 to 8 hours. (Make-ahead: Let cool for 30 minutes. Refrigerate, uncovered, in airtight containers until cold. Cover and refrigerate for up to 3 days.) Stir in diced apple.

PER SERVING: about 328 cal, 14 g pro, 2 g total fat (trace sat. fat), 70 g carb, 16 g fibre, 0 mg chol, 341 mg sodium. % RDI: 11% calcium, 36% iron, 7% vit A, 20% vit C, 106% folate.

Out of Gas

Sadly, dried legumes can create uncomfortable gas. This is caused when their starches pass through the stomach undigested and move on to the intestine, where friendly bacteria ferment them, making you feel bloated.

Happily, you can eliminate much of the problem with the soaking and cooking methods described on page 213.

Another silver lining: the more beans you eat, the better you'll feel. When beans are regularly included in the diet, the stomach increases its ability to digest their starches.

Spanish Baked Beans

You can adjust from vegetarian to meaty by adding up to 8 oz (250 g) dry chorizo sausage or a piece of lean smoky bacon or smoked turkey thigh. While you're at it making your own baked beans, we recommend going all the way and soaking and simmering dried beans. The sodium count is lower than that of canned beans, even if they're drained and rinsed.

4½- to 6-quart (4.5 to 6 L) slow cooker

Makes 6 to 8 servings

⅓ cup	extra-virgin olive oil	75 mL	6 cups	cooked navy beans (recipe, page 213) or 3 cans (each 19 oz/ 540 mL) navy beans, drained and rinsed	1.5 L
4 cups	sliced Spanish onion (1 large)	1 L	1	can (28 oz/796 mL) diced tomatoes	1
4	cloves garlic, sliced	4	1½ tsp	salt	7 mL
2½ tsp	smoked or regular sweet paprika	12 mL	1	bay leaf	1
			1 tsp	dried rosemary	5 mL

⌣ In large skillet, heat oil over medium heat; fry onion, garlic and paprika, stirring often, until onions are softened, about 10 minutes. Scrape into slow cooker along with beans, tomatoes, salt, bay leaf and rosemary. Stir to combine.

⌣ Cover and cook on low until bubbly and thickened enough to scoop, about 6 hours. (Make-ahead: Let cool for 30 minutes. Refrigerate, uncovered, in airtight containers until cold. Cover and refrigerate for up to 3 days.)

PER EACH OF 8 SERVINGS: about 319 cal, 13 g pro, 10 g total fat (2 g sat. fat), 47 g carb, 11 g fibre, 0 mg chol, 563 mg sodium. % RDI: 13% calcium, 34% iron, 5% vit A, 27% vit C, 94% folate.

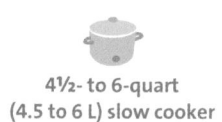

4½- to 6-quart
(4.5 to 6 L) slow cooker

Makes 6 to
8 servings

Comfy Baked Beans

The marriage of tart tomatoes, salty smoked bacon and sweet molasses is what makes the sauce for this classic so mellow and enticing.

1	can (28 oz/796 mL) tomatoes	1	2 cups	chopped onions	500 mL
			1 cup	ketchup	250 mL
6 cups	cooked navy beans (recipe, page 213) or 3 cans (each 19 oz/ 540 mL) navy beans, drained and rinsed	1.5 L	½ cup	fancy molasses	125 mL
			⅓ cup	packed brown sugar	75 mL
			1 tbsp	dry mustard	15 mL
4 oz	slab bacon or salt pork, diced	125 g	½ tsp	salt	2 mL
			¼ tsp	pepper	1 mL

❧ In slow cooker, mash tomatoes with potato masher or fork until slightly chunky. Stir in beans, bacon, onions, ketchup, molasses, brown sugar, mustard, salt and pepper.

❧ Cover and cook on low until bubbly and thickened enough to scoop, about 6 hours. (Make-ahead: Let cool for 30 minutes. Refrigerate, uncovered, in airtight containers until cold. Cover and refrigerate for up to 3 days or freeze for up to 1 month.)

PER EACH OF 8 SERVINGS: about 550 cal, 22 g pro, 10 g total fat (5 g sat. fat), 99 g carb, 15 g fibre, 13 mg chol, 1,072 mg sodium. % RDI: 26% calcium, 68% iron, 12% vit A, 45% vit C, 75% folate.

VARIATION

Saucy Vegetarian Beans: Omit bacon; add a tad of cayenne to spice beans up.

Cooked Dried Beans

Dried beans – whether they're chickpeas, black-eyed peas, lentils or kidney beans – are legumes, one of the most inexpensive and healthful foods. They have been around forever, but it seems as if they were created for slow cooking. Dried legumes, except for lentils, require a two-step soaking-then-cooking process before they're recipe-ready. Here are the guidelines.

Step 1: *Soak*

Long Soak: Rinse beans; place in large bowl with 3 times their volume of water. Let soak for 6 hours or for up to 24 hours. Drain, discarding soaking water, and rinse.

Quick Soak: Rinse beans; place in saucepan with 3 times their volume of water. Bring to boil; reduce heat, cover and simmer for 2 minutes. Remove from heat; let soak for 1 hour. Drain, discarding soaking water, and rinse.

Step 2: *Cook*

Stove Top: In saucepan, cover beans with 3 times their new volume of water; bring to boil. Start timer; reduce heat, cover and simmer until beans are tender, about 30 to 80 minutes, depending on variety and age (see Stove Top Cooking Times, below). Drain, discarding cooking water.

Slow Cooker: In slow cooker, cover beans with 3 times their new volume of water. Cover and cook on low until tender, about 10 hours for chickpeas or 12 hours for beans. Drain, discarding cooking water.

Stove Top Cooking Times

- Black beans: 30 minutes
- Black-eyed peas: 35 minutes
- Chickpeas: 45 minutes
- Kidney beans (white or red): 50 minutes
- Large lima beans: 55 minutes
- Navy beans: 40 minutes
- Romano beans: 45 minutes

Tips

> Count on 5 to 10 minutes less cooking time if using the Quick Soak method.

> Start checking beans, regardless of soaking method, 10 minutes before the end of the suggested cooking time, then every 5 minutes thereafter until done. Taste the beans; a well-cooked one is tender and easy to squash.

Yield

> Generally, 1 cup (250 mL) dried beans turns into about 2 cups (500 mL) cooked beans. Some varieties yield up to ½ cup (125 mL) more.

Storing Cooked Beans

> Let cool to room temperature. Refrigerate in airtight containers for up to 3 days or freeze for up to 1 month.

VARIATION

Seasoned Cooked Beans: Soak 3 cups (750 mL) dried beans. To the 6 cups (1.5 L) soaked beans they yield, add 18 cups (4.5 L) water. In 6-inch (15 cm) square cheesecloth, tie 1 small onion, quartered; 3 cloves garlic, smashed; 2 bay leaves; 6 sprigs fresh parsley; and 10 black peppercorns. Add to beans along with 1 each carrot and stalk celery, quartered. Cover and cook, using either method above. Drain; discard spice bag and vegetables. Use in salads or side dishes.

4½- to 6-quart (4.5 to 6 L)
slow cooker

Makes 6 to
8 servings

Black Beans & Sausage

Black beans and salsa give an up-to-date twist to a winter-warming classic. The cooking method for dried beans in this recipe is slightly different from our chart (page 213) – they're cooked in broth to maximize flavour.

3 cups	dried black beans	750 mL	½ cup	fancy molasses	125 mL
4 cups	chicken or vegetable broth	1 L	¼ cup	packed brown sugar	50 mL
8 oz	smoked sausage, chopped	250 g	2 tsp	dry mustard	10 mL
			½ tsp	salt	2 mL
3 cups	chopped onions (about 4)	750 mL	¼ tsp	pepper	1 mL
2 cups	salsa	500 mL	2 tbsp	cornstarch	30 mL

Cover beans with 3 times their volume of water; let soak for 12 hours or overnight. Drain and place beans in slow cooker; add broth.

Cover and cook on high until tender, about 3 hours. Add sausage, onions, salsa, molasses, brown sugar, mustard, salt and pepper; cover and cook on high until sauce is no longer watery, about 3 hours.

Whisk cornstarch with 2 tbsp (30 mL) water; whisk into liquid in slow cooker. Cover and cook until thickened, about 15 to 20 minutes. (Make-ahead: Let cool for 30 minutes. Refrigerate, uncovered, in airtight containers until cold. Cover and refrigerate for up to 3 days.)

PER EACH OF 8 SERVINGS: about 452 cal, 23 g pro, 8 g total fat (3 g sat. fat), 75 g carb, 13 g fibre, 25 mg chol, 1,021 mg sodium. % RDI: 17% calcium, 54% iron, 4% vit A, 25% vit C, 77% folate.

Legumes: Nutritional Powerhouses

> Beans, chickpeas and lentils are loaded with vitamins and minerals, such as potassium and folate. They are also rich in antioxidants and high in fibre.
> As "good carbs," beans have a low glycemic index rating, which means they help slow digestion and balance blood sugar levels.
> High in protein, legumes are an ideal ingredient in vegetarian – and non-vegetarian – meals.

Chili Barbecue Sauce

1½- to 2-quart (1.5 to 2 L)
slow cooker

Makes 5 cups
(1.25 L)

In a world of zany new flavours, sometimes all you want is a reliably delicious sauce – one everyone will like. This is it. Try it on meatballs, brisket, short ribs, baby back ribs, chicken pieces, pork tenderloin and chops, or anywhere else you want to slather on a no-nonsense barbecue sauce.

2 tbsp	vegetable oil	30 mL	¼ cup	fancy molasses	50 mL
1	large onion, chopped	1	⅓ cup	packed brown sugar	75 mL
4	cloves garlic, minced	4	3 tbsp	chili powder	45 mL
2 cups	strained tomatoes	500 mL	2 tbsp	yellow mustard	30 mL
¼ cup	Worcestershire sauce	50 mL	2 tsp	pepper	10 mL

TEST KITCHEN TIP

Look for strained tomatoes in jars on supermarket shelves where tomato products are displayed. The big advantage is the lack of seeds — a feature to admire in a barbecue sauce.

❧ In large skillet, heat oil over medium heat; fry onion and garlic until softened, about 5 minutes. Scrape into slow cooker along with tomatoes, 1 cup (250 mL) water, Worcestershire sauce, molasses, brown sugar, chili powder, mustard and pepper.

❧ Cover and cook on low until thickened enough to coat spoon, about 5 to 7 hours. (Make-ahead: Let cool for 30 minutes. Refrigerate, uncovered, in airtight containers until cold. Cover and refrigerate for up to 1 week or freeze for up to 1 month.)

PER ½ CUP (125 mL): about 111 cal, 1 g pro, 3 g total fat (trace sat. fat), 21 g carb, 1 g fibre, 0 mg chol, 227 mg sodium. % RDI: 5% calcium, 16% iron, 7% vit A, 7% vit C, 2% folate.

Maple Barbecue Sauce

Make enough sauce for the summer grilling season and for year-round roasted ribs, chicken wings and burgers.

2 tbsp	vegetable oil	30 mL		2 tbsp	dry mustard	30 mL
1	large onion, chopped	1		2 tbsp	packed brown sugar	30 mL
4	cloves garlic, minced	4		2 tbsp	Worcestershire sauce	30 mL
1½ cups	chili sauce	375 mL		4 tsp	chili powder	20 mL
1 cup	amber or medium maple syrup	250 mL		2 tsp	celery seeds	10 mL
⅔ cup	orange juice	150 mL		1 tsp	cinnamon	5 mL
½ cup	cider vinegar	125 mL		½ tsp	salt	2 mL

1½- to 2-quart (1.5 to 2 L) slow cooker

Makes 5 cups (1.25 L)

❧ In large skillet, heat oil over medium heat; fry onion and garlic until softened, about 5 minutes. Scrape into slow cooker along with chili sauce, maple syrup, orange juice, cider vinegar, mustard, brown sugar, Worcestershire sauce, chili powder, celery seeds, cinnamon and salt. Stir to combine.

❧ Cover and cook on low until thickened enough to coat spoon, about 5 to 7 hours. (Make-ahead: Let cool for 30 minutes. Refrigerate, uncovered, in airtight containers until cold. Cover and refrigerate for up to 1 week or freeze for up to 1 month.)

PER ½ CUP (125 ML): about 191 cal, 2 g pro, 4 g total fat (trace sat. fat), 39 g carb, 3 g fibre, 0 mg chol, 710 mg sodium. % RDI: 5% calcium, 11% iron, 6% vit A, 22% vit C, 5% folate.

TEST KITCHEN TIP
Medium maple syrup is the most commonly available in supermarkets. For amber, the darkest maple syrup of all, a farmer's market or sugar shack is the best source.

Vegetables & Side Dishes

Orange-Glazed Beets

Slowly cooked beets are juicy, and these beauties have locked-in orange flavour and a glossy coating. Choose medium beets all about the same size.

4½- to 6-quart (4.5 to 6 L)
slow cooker

Makes 8 servings

12	beets (2 lb/1 kg)	12	2 tbsp	extra-virgin olive oil	30 mL
2	cloves garlic, sliced	2	½ tsp	each salt and pepper	2 mL
1 tsp	grated orange rind	5 mL	¼ tsp	ground coriander	1 mL
¼ cup	orange juice	50 mL	1	green onion, thinly sliced	1

❧ Peel and quarter beets; place in slow cooker. Add garlic, orange rind and juice, oil, salt, pepper and coriander; stir to combine.

❧ Cover and cook on low until tender, about 5 to 6 hours. Toss gently; sprinkle with green onion.

PER SERVING: about 77 cal, 2 g pro, 4 g total fat (1 g sat. fat), 11 g carb, 2 g fibre, 0 mg chol, 215 mg sodium. % RDI: 2% calcium, 6% iron, 1% vit A, 12% vit C, 35% folate.

VARIATION

Thyme-Roasted Beets: Omit orange rind, coriander and green onion. Increase garlic to 4 cloves. Replace orange juice with ¼ cup (50 mL) water. Add 1 tsp (5 mL) dried thyme. Cook as directed. Sprinkle with 1 tbsp (15 mL) minced fresh parsley.

Apple-icious Rutabaga

An apple sweetens up a bowl of mashed rutabaga, more familiarly known in Canada as turnip.

4½- to 5½-quart (4.5 to 5.5 L) slow cooker

Makes 8 servings

1	apple	1	2 tbsp	lemon juice	30 mL
8 cups	cubed peeled rutabaga (3 lb/1.5 kg)	2 L	½ tsp	salt	2 mL
2 cups	apple juice or cider	500 mL	2 tbsp	butter	30 mL
			¼ tsp	grated nutmeg	1 mL

❧ Peel, core and chop apple. In slow cooker, combine apple, rutabaga, apple and lemon juices, and salt.

❧ Cover and cook on high until rutabaga is tender and most of the juice is evaporated, about 4 to 6 hours.

❧ Purée with immersion blender or mash with potato masher. Mix in butter and nutmeg. (Make-ahead: Let cool. Refrigerate in airtight container for up to 3 days.)

PER SERVING: about 114 cal, 2 g pro, 3 g total fat (2 g sat. fat), 21 g carb, 3 g fibre, 8 mg chol, 193 mg sodium. % RDI: 6% calcium, 6% iron, 10% vit A, 73% vit C, 9% folate.

TEST KITCHEN TIP
A beautiful rutabaga, hard and round, can be difficult to hold steady, making it daunting to peel and cube. The secret? Cut it into slices first. Here's how: Cut thick slice off bottom. Set rutabaga on this stable base on cutting board. With large knife, and tapping knife with mallet if necessary, cut rutabaga in half. Set on cut sides. One half at a time, cut vertically into slices about ¾ inch (2 cm) thick. Peel slices, then cut crosswise into sticks. Cut sticks crosswise into cubes. Voilà – cubed rutabaga!

Glazed Maple-Mustard Carrots & Parsnips

When there's a big gathering and lots of activity in the kitchen, a vegetable side dish that frees up room on the stove is a lifesaver. Especially when the vegetables are as colourful and glossy as these.

5- to 6-quart (5 to 6 L) slow cooker

Makes 8 to 10 servings

16	carrots, peeled and thinly sliced (3 lb/1.5 kg)	16
10	parsnips, peeled and thinly sliced (2 lb/1 kg)	10
¼ cup	butter, cubed	50 mL
¼ cup	maple syrup	50 mL
2 tbsp	Dijon mustard	30 mL
½ tsp	each salt and pepper	2 mL
1 tbsp	cornstarch	15 mL
1 tbsp	chopped fresh parsley	15 mL

❧ In slow cooker, combine carrots, parsnips, 1 cup (250 mL) water, butter, maple syrup, mustard, salt and pepper.

❧ Cover and cook on low until vegetables are tender, about 5 hours.

❧ Move vegetables to 1 side of slow cooker. In small bowl, whisk cornstarch with 2 tbsp (30 mL) water; whisk into liquid along with chopped parsley. Stir to coat vegetables.

❧ Cover and cook on high until sauce is thickened and vegetables are glazed, about 15 minutes.

PER EACH OF 10 SERVINGS: about 196 cal, 3 g pro, 5 g total fat (3 g sat. fat), 37 g carb, 6 g fibre, 15 mg chol, 290 mg sodium. % RDI: 8% calcium, 11% iron, 295% vit A, 25% vit C, 32% folate.

TEST KITCHEN TIPS

For full maple flavour, choose medium grade. It is a deep amber syrup usually available in grocery chains.

If you can, gently stir vegetables halfway through cooking time.

Carrots with a Moroccan Twist

Think of carrots as the palette on which you can paint a whole spectrum of flavours. Here, it's cumin for a mild Moroccan twist, and in the variation, it's ginger and lemon for an East Asian accent. Both are nutritious, all-season, multipurpose sides that complement poultry, pork, lamb and vegetarian dishes.

4- to 5½-quart (4 to 5.5 L)
slow cooker

Makes 4 to
6 servings

12	small carrots (2 lb/1 kg)	12	½ tsp	salt	2 mL
1	onion	1	¼ tsp	ground cumin	1 mL
3	cloves garlic, sliced	3	Pinch	cayenne pepper (optional)	Pinch
⅓ cup	chicken or vegetable broth, or water	75 mL	1 tbsp	cornstarch	15 mL
2 tbsp	butter	30 mL	1 tbsp	minced fresh coriander or parsley	15 mL

❧ Peel and cut carrots into 2-inch (5 cm) long, pencil-thin sticks. Peel and halve onion; slice crosswise. Combine carrots, onion and garlic in slow cooker.

❧ Add broth, butter, salt, cumin, and cayenne (if using); stir to coat carrots.

❧ Cover and cook on low until carrots are tender, about 3 hours.

❧ Whisk cornstarch with 2 tbsp (30 mL) water; drizzle over carrots. Toss to combine. Cover and cook on high until sauce clears and glazes carrots, about 10 minutes.

❧ Sprinkle with coriander.

PER EACH OF 6 SERVINGS: about 93 cal, 1 g pro, 4 g total fat (3 g sat. fat), 14 g carb, 4 g fibre, 10 mg chol, 341 mg sodium. % RDI: 4% calcium, 4% iron, 212% vit A, 8% vit C, 9% folate.

TEST KITCHEN TIP
Fresh coriander is often sold under its Spanish name, cilantro.

VARIATION

Ginger Lemon Carrots: Replace cumin with 1 tbsp (15 mL) grated gingerroot or ½ tsp (2 mL) ground ginger. Add 2 tbsp (30 mL) lemon juice and 1 tbsp (15 mL) liquid honey. Cook as directed. Instead of fresh coriander, sprinkle with 1 green onion, thinly sliced.

4½- to 5½-quart (4.5 to 5.5 L) slow cooker

Makes 6 servings

Mellow-Spiced Squash Purée

While this sweet deep orange vegetable is fine plain, a touch of spice adds to its allure.

2 tbsp	vegetable oil	30 mL	½ tsp	ground ginger	2 mL
1	onion, diced	1	¼ tsp	salt	1 mL
2	cloves garlic, minced	2	1	butternut squash (2 lb/1 kg)	1
1 tsp	each ground cumin and sweet paprika	5 mL	2 tbsp	butter	30 mL

✎ In skillet, heat oil over medium heat; fry onion, garlic, cumin, paprika, ginger and salt, stirring often, until onion is softened, about 6 minutes. Scrape into slow cooker.

✎ Meanwhile, peel and cut squash into 1-inch (2.5 cm) cubes; place in slow cooker. Add ½ cup (125 mL) water. Stir to combine.

✎ Cover and cook on low until squash is tender, about 5 to 6 hours.

✎ Add butter. With immersion blender or in food processor, purée until smooth (or mash with potato masher). (Make-ahead: Let cool. Refrigerate in airtight container for up to 2 days.)

PER SERVING: about 136 cal, 2 g pro, 9 g total fat (3 g sat. fat), 16 g carb, 3 g fibre, 10 mg chol, 129 mg sodium. % RDI: 6% calcium, 8% iron, 144% vit A, 32% vit C, 12% folate.

VARIATION

Mellow-Spiced Sweet Potato Purée: Use 4 large sweet potatoes (3 lb/1.5 kg), peeled, instead of squash. Cook as directed. Stir 2 tbsp (30 mL) lemon juice into purée.

Braised Red Cabbage

This flavourful side dish pairs well with beef and game, roast pork, duck or goose. Juniper berries can be hard to locate. Gin, flavoured with juniper, is an excellent substitute and is widely available.

4- to 5-quart (4 to 5 L)
slow cooker

Makes 8 servings

6 cups	thinly sliced red cabbage	1.5 L		1	apple, peeled, cored and sliced	1
¾ cup	dry red wine	175 mL		1	bay leaf	1
1 tbsp	maple syrup or liquid honey	15 mL		¾ tsp	salt	4 mL
2 tsp	vegetable oil	10 mL		½ tsp	dried thyme	2 mL
1	small red onion, sliced	1		5	juniper berries, crushed (or 2 tbsp/ 30 mL gin)	5

In slow cooker, combine cabbage, wine, maple syrup, oil, onion, apple, bay leaf, salt and thyme. In 4-inch (10 cm) square cheesecloth, tie juniper berries to form bag; nestle into cabbage mixture.

Cover and cook on low until cabbage is no longer crisp but not completely wilted, about 4 hours.

Stir well. Cover and cook on high until cabbage is completely tender, about 15 minutes. Discard bay leaf and juniper berries.

PER SERVING: about 56 cal, 1 g pro, 1 g total fat (trace sat. fat), 10 g carb, 2 g fibre, 0 mg chol, 227 mg sodium. % RDI: 3% calcium, 4% iron, 1% vit A, 23% vit C, 7% folate.

Mashed Potatoes with Celery Root

4½- to 6-quart (4.5 to 6 L) slow cooker

Makes 8 to 10 servings

Potatoes like company, be it trendy celery root, old-fashioned cabbage or flavourful cauliflower. For purists who demand plain mashed potatoes, replace these vegetable additions with an extra 3 potatoes, peeled and cubed (4 cups/1 L). For roasted garlic mashed potatoes, mash one or two heads' worth of Roasted Garlic (recipe, page 236) and stir into plain mashed potatoes.

10	russet potatoes (3 lb/1.5 kg)	10
4 cups	cubed peeled celery root (about half)	1 L
3	cloves garlic	3
1½ tsp	salt	7 mL
½ tsp	pepper	2 mL
⅔ cup	milk	150 mL
¼ cup	butter, cubed	50 mL
2 tbsp	snipped fresh chives or sliced green onion	30 mL

❧ Peel and cube potatoes; place in slow cooker. Add celery root, garlic, half of the salt and the pepper. Add enough water to just cover vegetables.

❧ Cover and cook on low until vegetables are soft, about 6 hours. Drain and return to slow cooker.

❧ With potato masher, mash vegetables until no large chunks remain. Stir in milk, butter and remaining salt; mash to desired smoothness. Sprinkle with chives.

PER EACH OF 10 SERVINGS: about 163 cal, 4 g pro, 5 g total fat (3 g sat. fat), 27 g carb, 3 g fibre, 13 mg chol, 448 mg sodium. % RDI: 6% calcium, 10% iron, 5% vit A, 33% vit C, 8% folate.

VARIATIONS

Colcannon: This combination of mashed potatoes and cabbage is a traditional Irish dish. Replace celery root with chopped green cabbage and omit garlic, if desired.

Mashed Potatoes with Cauliflower: Replace celery root with coarsely chopped cauliflower.

TEST KITCHEN TIPS

So what do you do with the rest of the celery root? Try a traditional winter salad of coarsely shredded celery root dressed with mayonnaise. Or cube and add to soups or stews in place of potatoes, sweet potatoes or parsnips. Or cut into chunks, toss with olive oil and roast alongside meats or poultry.

Don't let leftover mashed potatoes go to waste. Use them to top Shepherd's Pie or Gardener's Pie (recipes, page 206) or form into potato cakes, coat with crumbs and fry to serve with poached eggs and salsa.

Scalloped Potatoes

Traditional and comforting, this side dish is always popular at holiday dinners and buffets.

5- to 6-quart (5 to 6 L) slow cooker

Makes 6 servings

¼ cup	butter	50 mL
1	small onion, diced	1
¼ cup	all-purpose flour	50 mL
1 tsp	salt	5 mL
½ tsp	pepper	2 mL
½ tsp	dried thyme or marjoram	2 mL
2½ cups	milk	625 mL
1 cup	shredded Gruyère or Swiss cheese	250 mL
1 tbsp	dried parsley (optional)	15 mL
6	Yukon Gold potatoes	6
½ cup	chopped smoked ham or turkey (optional)	125 mL

❧ In heavy saucepan, melt butter over medium heat; fry onion, stirring occasionally, until softened, about 5 minutes.

❧ Add flour, salt, pepper and thyme; cook, stirring, for 1 minute. Gradually stir in milk and bring to boil; cook, whisking or stirring, until thickened and smooth, about 5 to 8 minutes. Stir in half each of the cheese and parsley (if using).

❧ Meanwhile, peel and thinly slice potatoes. Add to sauce along with ham (if using); stir to coat. Scrape into slow cooker. Smooth top; sprinkle with remaining cheese and parsley.

❧ Cover and cook on low until potatoes are tender and sauce is bubbly, about 6 hours.

PER SERVING: about 360 cal, 13 g pro, 16 g total fat (10 g sat. fat), 42 g carb, 3 g fibre, 53 mg chol, 587 mg sodium. % RDI: 31% calcium, 15% iron, 18% vit A, 47% vit C, 15% folate.

Garlic Roasted Potatoes

This chunky garlic-potato combo is a year-round dish that pairs as well with steaks, chops and pork tenderloin as it does with grilled or roasted chicken or fish.

6	large russet potatoes (2½ lb/1.25 kg)	6
¾ cup	chicken broth or water	175 mL
1 tbsp	extra-virgin olive oil	15 mL

¼ tsp	each salt and pepper	1 mL
4	cloves garlic, minced	4
2 tbsp	minced fresh parsley	30 mL

4- to 5-quart (4 to 5 L) slow cooker

Make 6 to 8 servings

❧ Peel potatoes, if desired, and trim; cut into ¾-inch (2 cm) cubes. In slow cooker, toss together potatoes, broth, oil, salt and pepper. Cover and cook on high until potatoes are tender, about 2 to 2½ hours.

❧ Remove insert from slow cooker. Sprinkle potatoes with garlic; cover and let stand for 5 minutes. Toss; sprinkle with parsley.

PER EACH OF 8 SERVINGS: about 131 cal, 3 g pro, 2 g total fat (trace sat. fat), 26 g carb, 2 g fibre, 0 mg chol, 166 mg sodium. % RDI: 2% calcium, 9% iron, 1% vit A, 38% vit C, 9% folate.

Winter Root Vegetables

A medley of vegetables makes an excellent side dish for almost any roasted meat or poultry, even fish and meat loaf. It's particularly good with turkey.

2	Yukon Gold potatoes	2
2	each carrots and parsnips	2
1	onion	1
Half	acorn squash	Half

2 cups	vegetable broth	500 mL
1 tsp	dried sage	5 mL
½ tsp	each salt and pepper	2 mL
2 tbsp	butter	30 mL

4½- to 6-quart (4.5 to 6 L) slow cooker

Makes 6 servings

TEST KITCHEN TIP
The vegetable mix is something you can play around with, using other squashes or focusing on more of one type of vegetable, such as parsnips.

❧ Peel potatoes, carrots, parsnips, onion and squash. Cut potatoes and squash into 1-inch (2.5 cm) cubes; carrots and parsnips into ¼-inch (5 mm) thick slices; and onion into 6 wedges, keeping root end intact. Place vegetables in slow cooker; stir in broth, sage, salt and pepper.

❧ Cover and cook on low until vegetables are tender and some liquid remains, about 4 to 6 hours. Add butter and toss gently to coat.

PER SERVING: about 156 cal, 3 g pro, 4 g total fat (3 g sat. fat), 30 g carb, 4 g fibre, 12 mg chol, 496 mg sodium. % RDI: 5% calcium, 6% iron, 48% vit A, 25% vit C, 21% folate.

Sweet & Sour Pearls

Although it takes time to peel pearl onions, they're a delight to eat, especially when braised in this Mediterranean mix of sweet raisins and tangy vinegar. Choose any small pearl onions: the traditional white ones or the recently popular red or yellow varieties.

4- to 5-quart (4 to 5 L)
slow cooker

Makes 8 servings

8 cups	pearl onions (four 10-oz/284 g pkg)	2 L		1 tsp	grated orange rind	5 mL
				1	bay leaf	1
1 cup	dark or golden raisins	250 mL		½ tsp	salt	2 mL
				¼ tsp	pepper	1 mL
2 tbsp	olive oil	30 mL		1	clove garlic, slivered	1
2 tbsp	red wine vinegar	30 mL		1 tbsp	cornstarch	15 mL
1 tbsp	tomato paste	15 mL				

❧ Place onions in heatproof bowl; cover with boiling water. Let stand for 1 minute; drain and peel.

❧ In slow cooker, combine onions, 1 cup (250 mL) water, raisins, oil, vinegar, tomato paste, orange rind, bay leaf, salt, pepper and garlic.

❧ Cover and cook on low until onions are tender, about 4 to 6 hours. Discard bay leaf.

❧ Move onions to 1 side of slow cooker. In small bowl, whisk cornstarch with 2 tbsp (30 mL) water; whisk into liquid. Stir gently to redistribute.

❧ Cover and cook on high until sauce is glossy and onions are coated, about 10 minutes.

PER SERVING: about 140 cal, 2 g pro, 4 g total fat (1 g sat. fat), 27 g carb, 3 g fibre, 0 mg chol, 154 mg sodium. % RDI: 3% calcium, 6% iron, 1% vit A, 13% vit C, 7% folate.

Rice & "Peas"

A slow cooker makes a slightly more tender version of this popular Jamaican dish. There's plenty for a hungry crowd.

4- to 5-quart (4 to 5 L) slow cooker

Makes 8 to 10 servings

2 cups	parboiled rice	500 mL	1	onion, chopped	1
1	can (19 oz/540 mL) pigeon peas or red kidney beans, drained and rinsed (or 2 cups/ 500 mL cooked beans; recipe, page 213)	1	2	cloves garlic, minced	2
			½ tsp	dried thyme	2 mL
			½ tsp	salt	2 mL
			Pinch	cayenne pepper	Pinch
2¼ cups	vegetable broth	550 mL	Half	sweet green pepper, diced	Half
1	can (400 mL) coconut milk	1	4	green onions, sliced	4

❧ In slow cooker, combine rice, pigeon peas, broth, coconut milk, chopped onion, garlic, thyme, salt and cayenne pepper.

❧ Cover and cook on low until rice is just tender and liquid is absorbed, about 2 hours.

❧ With fork, stir in green pepper and green onions. Cover and cook on high until pepper is tender-crisp, about 15 minutes.

PER EACH OF 10 SERVINGS: about 263 cal, 3 g pro, 9 g total fat (7 g sat. fat), 40 g carb, 4 g fibre, 0 mg chol, 387 mg sodium. % RDI: 4% calcium, 16% iron, 1% vit A, 10% vit C, 16% folate.

VARIATION

Rice & Black Beans: *Moros y Cristianos* is a traditional dish in Latin American cooking. Replace pigeon peas, which bespeak a Jamaican origin, with drained rinsed black beans. Replace the coconut milk with chicken broth or water.

Caramelized Onions

Caramelizing tames the natural fierceness of raw onions. While they make a satisfying side dish for liver or a flavourful topping for steaks and burgers, there are a variety of reasons to keep a supply of caramelized onions handy in your fridge (see The Pleasures of Caramelized Onions, below). You won't know how you lived without them.

5- to 6-quart (5 to 6 L)
slow cooker

Makes 4 cups (1 L)

12 cups	thinly sliced Spanish onions (3 lb/1.5 kg, 4 large)	3 L	1 tbsp	packed brown sugar	15 mL
			1 tbsp	cider vinegar	15 mL
¼ cup	butter, cubed	50 mL	1 tsp	salt	5 mL

Place onions in slow cooker. Top with butter, sugar, vinegar and salt; toss to combine.

Cover and cook on high, stirring occasionally, until golden but still moist, about 6 to 7 hours. (Make-ahead: Let cool for 30 minutes. Refrigerate, uncovered, in airtight containers until cold. Cover and refrigerate for up to 3 days or freeze for up to 1 month.)

PER ½ CUP (125 mL): about 130 cal, 2 g pro, 6 g total fat (4 g sat. fat), 19 g carb, 2 g fibre, 15 mg chol, 333 mg sodium. % RDI: 4% calcium, 3% iron, 5% vit A, 2% vit C, 12% folate.

The Pleasures of Caramelized Onions

A container of these golden, sweet onions in the fridge is like money in the bank – just tastier. Dip into your stash to:
> Spread over a pizza base
> Fill a quesadilla
> Layer with tomatoes and cheese in a melt or panini
> Add to a grilled cheese sandwich (Cheddar is classic but try Oka, Havarti or Brie)
> Make a quick pasta sauce, with grated Parmesan or Asiago cheese and a splash of pasta cooking water
> Top burgers, steaks, chops and, yes, even liver
> Build a beautiful Onion Soup with Gruyère Croûtes (recipe, page 50)

Roasted Garlic

4- to 6-quart (4 to 6 L)
slow cooker

Makes 6 heads

Like Caramelized Onions (recipe, page 235), roasted garlic is a great flavour booster. Now you can make large quantities of it easily, thanks to the slow cooker. Roasted garlic freezes beautifully, so keep plenty on hand to mash and add to salad dressings, pasta sauces, pizzas, mashed potatoes and more. Or spread it like butter on toasted baguette and top with goat cheese, half a cherry tomato and shredded basil.

6	plump heads garlic	6	1 tsp	dried thyme	5 mL
1 tbsp	extra-virgin olive oil	15 mL			

SUBSTITUTION

Other dried herbs, such as sage, oregano or marjoram, or herb blends, such as dried Italian herb seasoning, can stand in for the thyme.

➤ Rub loose papery skin off garlic. If desired, cut off top to just expose tips of cloves.

➤ Arrange garlic, root end down, in single layer on large sheet of foil. Drizzle with oil; sprinkle with thyme.

➤ Pull foil up and around garlic loosely; fold in edges to seal. Place in slow cooker.

➤ Cover and cook on low until fragrant and garlic cloves are tender and golden, about 2 hours. (Make-ahead: Let cool. Refrigerate in foil packet for up to 3 days. Or freeze packet in airtight container for up to 4 weeks.)

PER HEAD: about 76 cal, 2 g pro, 2 g total fat (trace sat. fat), 13 g carb, 1 g fibre, 0 mg chol, 7 mg sodium. % RDI: 6% calcium, 6% iron, 15% vit C.

Succotash

4- to 5½-quart (4 to 5.5 L)
slow cooker

Makes 8 servings

This delicious medley includes squash, corn and beans, slowly cooked together with tomatoes to bring out their natural flavours and sweetness. It's a dish that harks back to the Three Sisters – squash, corn and beans – cultivated by the First Nations long before the arrival of Europeans in Canada.

3	green onions	3	2	cloves garlic, minced	2
1	can (19 oz/540 mL) diced tomatoes	1	1 tsp	dried thyme	5 mL
			½ tsp	each salt and pepper	2 mL
3 cups	cubed peeled butternut squash (about half)	750 mL	2 cups	frozen lima beans	500 mL
			3 tbsp	tomato paste	45 mL
2 cups	frozen corn kernels	500 mL	2 tbsp	chopped fresh parsley	30 mL

TEST KITCHEN TIP
The juice drained from the can of tomatoes is a healthy addition to pasta sauces, soups or beverages. Store it in the fridge or freezer until you're ready to use it.

↪ Slice white parts of green onions; add to slow cooker. Thinly slice green parts; set aside. Drain tomatoes, reserving juice for another use.

↪ Add tomatoes, squash, corn, garlic, thyme, salt and pepper to slow cooker. Stir to combine.

↪ Cover and cook on low until squash is tender, about 2 hours.

↪ Gently stir in lima beans, tomato paste and reserved green parts of onions. Cover and cook on high until sauce is thickened around vegetables, about 20 minutes. Stir in parsley.

PER SERVING: about 120 cal, 5 g pro, 1 g total fat (0 g sat. fat), 27 g carb, 4 g fibre, 0 mg chol, 233 mg sodium. % RDI: 5% calcium, 15% iron, 47% vit A, 38% vit C, 17% folate.

Mushroom Barley Pilaf

The rich flavours of fresh and dried wild mushrooms and barley make a warm, comforting side dish or vegetarian main. Barley is a natural in the slow cooker; it stays firm and whole in spite of long cooking.

5- to 6-quart (5 to 6 L) slow cooker

Makes 8 to 10 servings

1	pkg (14 g) mixed dried mushrooms	1
2 tbsp	vegetable oil	30 mL
1	large onion, chopped	1
2 cups	sliced button mushrooms	500 mL
2 cups	sliced shiitake mushroom caps	500 mL
4	cloves garlic, minced	4
½ tsp	dried thyme	2 mL
½ tsp	each salt and pepper	2 mL
3½ cups	vegetable broth	875 mL
2 cups	pot or pearl barley	500 mL
2	small carrots, diced	2
2 tbsp	tomato paste	30 mL
2 tbsp	minced fresh parsley	30 mL

⌁ In bowl, soak dried mushrooms in 1½ cups (375 mL) warm water until softened, about 30 minutes. Reserving soaking liquid, drain and chop finely.

⌁ In large skillet, heat oil over medium-high heat; sauté soaked dried mushrooms, onion, button mushrooms, shiitake mushrooms, garlic, thyme, salt and pepper until liquid is evaporated and onion is golden, about 8 minutes. Scrape into slow cooker.

⌁ Add reserved soaking liquid to skillet; bring to boil, scraping up brown bits from bottom of skillet. Scrape into slow cooker along with broth, barley, carrots and tomato paste.

⌁ Cover and cook on low until barley is tender and liquid is absorbed, about 6 hours. Stir in parsley.

PER EACH OF 10 SERVINGS: about 198 cal, 4 g pro, 4 g total fat (trace sat. fat), 39 g carb, 4 g fibre, 0 mg chol, 356 mg sodium. % RDI: 3% calcium, 16% iron, 38% vit A, 7% vit C, 14% folate.

VARIATION

Mushroom Barley Risotto: Omit carrots and tomato paste. After cooking, stir in ¾ cup (175 mL) 18% cream and ½ cup (125 mL) grated Parmesan or Romano cheese along with the parsley. Serve with grated Parmesan or Romano cheese.

Warm Black-Eyed Pea & Fennel Salad

The secret to getting reconstituted beans or peas to absorb a dressing is to add it while the legumes are warm. To make sure they're moist at serving time, drizzle with a little additional oil and vinegar just before serving. A little water can also help moisten the salad without affecting the flavour or fat content.

4- to 6-quart (4 to 6 L)
slow cooker

Makes 6 to
8 servings

¼ cup	extra-virgin olive oil (approx)	50 mL	3 cups	cooked black-eyed peas (recipe, page 213)	750 mL
1 cup	thinly sliced cored fennel (half bulb)	250 mL	¼ cup	chopped fresh parsley	50 mL
½ cup	thinly sliced celery	125 mL	4 tsp	white wine vinegar (approx)	20 mL
3	cloves garlic, minced	3			
½ tsp	each dried thyme and salt	2 mL			

TEST KITCHEN TIP
You can make this delightful salad with other legumes, such as cooked green or brown lentils, chickpeas or beans (recipe, page 213).

❧ In large skillet, heat 3 tbsp (45 mL) of the oil over medium heat; fry fennel, celery, garlic, thyme and salt, stirring occasionally, until fennel is softened and beginning to colour, about 8 minutes.

❧ Stir in peas, parsley and 1 tbsp (15 mL) of the vinegar; cook, stirring, until peas are warm, about 2 minutes. Transfer to serving bowl; toss with remaining oil and vinegar, adding more, if desired. Serve warm.

PER EACH OF 8 SERVINGS: about 142 cal, 5 g pro, 7 g total fat (1 g sat. fat), 15 g carb, 5 g fibre, 0 mg chol, 159 mg sodium. % RDI: 3% calcium, 14% iron, 2% vit A, 7% vit C, 64% folate.

Wild Rice

2- to 4½-quart (2 to 4.5 L)
slow cooker

Makes 6 servings

Wild rice takes a fairly long time to cook, making this true-north Canadian product more of a special-occasion side dish. The slow cooker version takes a long time, too, but it's a no-tend kind of time. By making a fairly big batch, there will be enough leftovers to reheat in the microwave and/or incorporate into salads, soups, muffins and stuffings. Cooked wild rice freezes well, too.

3 cups	sodium-reduced chicken broth or water	750 mL		1	strip lemon peel	1
				1	bay leaf	1
1½ cups	wild rice	375 mL		2 tbsp	butter	30 mL
				2 tbsp	lemon juice	30 mL

❧ In slow cooker, stir together broth, rice, lemon peel and bay leaf.

❧ Cover and cook on high until rice is tender and split, and liquid is absorbed, about 1½ hours.

❧ Discard bay leaf. Toss together rice, butter and lemon juice. (Make-ahead: Let cool. Refrigerate in airtight container for up to 1 day or freeze for up to 1 month.)

PER SERVING: about 185 cal, 7 g pro, 4 g total fat (3 g sat. fat), 31 g carb, 3 g fibre, 10 mg chol, 327 mg sodium. % RDI: 1% calcium, 6% iron, 3% vit A, 3% vit C, 17% folate.

VARIATIONS

Herbed Wild Rice: Stir ¼ cup (50 mL) minced fresh parsley and 2 tbsp (30 mL) snipped fresh chives into cooked wild rice.

Mushroom Wild Rice: In large skillet, heat 2 tbsp (30 mL) butter over medium-high heat; sauté 3 cups (750 mL) sliced mushrooms until no liquid remains. Add ½ cup (125 mL) dry white wine and ½ tsp (2 mL) dried thyme; simmer until wine is absorbed. Toss with cooked wild rice, adding ¼ cup (50 mL) each minced fresh parsley and toasted slivered almonds, if desired.

Nutty Wild Rice: Stir ⅓ cup (75 mL) toasted slivered almonds or chopped walnut halves into cooked wild rice. Add ¼ cup (50 mL) minced fresh parsley, if desired.

Wild Rice Salad: Make Wild Rice as directed, omitting butter. While still hot, stir in ¾ cup (175 mL) chopped currants, or dried cherries, cranberries or apricots; ½ cup (125 mL) Italian salad dressing; and ¼ cup (50 mL) snipped chives.

Sausage & Mushroom Stuffing

If you like to roast turkey unstuffed but still yearn to serve stuffing, or you just love the stuff on its own, this recipe is for you. It produces a moist, frankly herbacious stuffing that's crunchy with toasted walnut halves.

5- to 6-quart (5 to 6 L)
slow cooker

Makes 12 servings

¼ cup	butter	50 mL		4	farmer's or Italian sausages (1 lb/500 g)	4
3 cups	sliced mushrooms (8 oz/250 g)	750 mL		¾ cup	sodium-reduced chicken broth	175 mL
2	onions, diced	2		12 cups	cubed day-old Italian, French or sourdough bread	3 L
2	stalks celery, finely chopped	2				
1 tbsp	dried sage	15 mL		1 cup	chopped walnut halves, toasted	250 mL
2 tsp	dried thyme	10 mL				
½ tsp	each salt and pepper	2 mL		¼ cup	chopped fresh parsley	50 mL

❧ In large skillet, melt butter over medium-high heat; sauté mushrooms, onions, celery, sage, thyme, salt and pepper until onions are golden and no liquid remains, about 10 minutes. Scrape into slow cooker.

❧ Remove casings from sausages. In same skillet, sauté sausages over medium-high heat, breaking up with fork until crumbly and no longer pink, about 5 minutes. With slotted spoon, transfer to slow cooker.

❧ Drain fat from skillet; add broth. Bring to boil, scraping up brown bits from bottom of skillet. Scrape into slow cooker along with bread. Toss to combine. Cover and cook on high for 1 hour.

❧ Stir in walnuts. Reduce heat to low; cook until fragrant and steaming hot, about 1 hour. Stir in parsley.

PER SERVING: about 276 cal, 11 g pro, 17 g total fat (5 g sat. fat), 22 g carb, 2 g fibre, 27 mg chol, 609 mg sodium. % RDI: 5% calcium, 16% iron, 5% vit A, 5% vit C, 30% folate.

Cranberry Sauce – Without the Can

Beat the holiday rush – make your own cranberry sauce the slow-and-easy way. Bonus: No telltale ridges from the can!

❧ In 4- to 4½-quart (4 to 4.5 L) slow cooker, stir together 6 cups (1.5 L) fresh or frozen cranberries; 2 cups (500 mL) granulated sugar; 1 strip orange rind; and ¼ cup (50 mL) orange juice.

❧ Cover and cook on high until cranberries are soft but not mushy, about 2 hours.

❧ Discard rind. Let cool. *(Make-ahead: Refrigerate in airtight container for up to 1 week.)* **Makes 3 cups (750 mL).**

Desserts

Baked Apples with Cider Butter Sauce

4- to 5-quart (4 to 5 L) slow cooker

Makes 6 servings

Baked apples are the kind of simple cold-weather dessert that never goes out of style, especially when served with some lovely vanilla frozen yogurt or ice cream. Baked apples, served with yogurt, are also a terrific snack or breakfast.

6	apples	6	½ tsp	cinnamon	2 mL
½ cup	packed brown sugar	125 mL	¼ tsp	grated nutmeg	1 mL
½ cup	chopped dried cherries, apricots, cranberries or raisins	125 mL	½ cup	apple cider or juice	125 mL
			2 tbsp	butter, melted	30 mL
			2 tsp	cornstarch	10 mL

TEST KITCHEN TIP

Choose Northern Spy, Spartan or Golden Delicious apples – they're reliable for their firm shapeliness, even when cooked.

❧ Core apples almost to bottom, leaving base intact. Slice off ¾-inch (2 cm) wide strip of peel around hole at top; trim base to level, if necessary.

❧ In bowl, combine brown sugar, dried cherries, cinnamon and nutmeg; pack into apples. Place in slow cooker. Whisk together apple cider and butter; pour over apples.

❧ Cover and cook on low, basting several times, until wrinkly and very tender, about 3 to 4 hours. Transfer apples to shallow serving dish and keep warm.

❧ Whisk cornstarch with 1 tbsp (15 mL) cold water; whisk into liquid in slow cooker. Cover and cook on high until sauce is thickened, about 15 minutes. (Make-ahead: Let apples and sauce cool separately. Store at room temperature for up to 8 hours or refrigerate in airtight containers for up to 3 days. Rewarm to serve.)

❧ Drizzle sauce over apples.

PER SERVING: about 229 cal, 1 g pro, 4 g total fat (3 g sat. fat), 50 g carb, 3 g fibre, 10 mg chol, 40 mg sodium. % RDI: 5% calcium, 6% iron, 6% vit A, 8% vit C, 2% folate.

Applesauce

4- to 5-quart (4 to 5 L)
slow cooker

Makes 4 cups (1 L)

Good apples for sauce are McIntosh, Royal Gala or Empire, which break down while cooking. An immersion blender is handy for puréeing the sauce right in the slow cooker, but you can use a potato masher or even a fork for a slightly chunky version. Or just leave it as is for more of a compote look.

8 cups	sliced peeled apples	2 L	2 tbsp	lemon juice	30 mL
½ cup	packed brown sugar	125 mL	Pinch	each cinnamon and grated nutmeg (optional)	Pinch
¼ cup	apple cider or juice	50 mL			
1	strip lemon rind	1			

In slow cooker, gently toss together apples, brown sugar, cider, and lemon rind and juice. Toss gently to mix.

Cover and cook on low until apples are tender and break down, about 6 to 8 hours. Discard lemon rind.

Using immersion blender or potato masher, purée or mash to desired texture. Stir in cinnamon and nutmeg (if using). (Make-ahead: Let cool. Refrigerate in airtight containers for up to 3 days or freeze for up to 1 month.)

TEST KITCHEN TIP
Calculate 1 medium apple for each 1 cup (250 mL) sliced.

PER ½ CUP (125 mL): about 109 cal, trace pro, trace total fat (0 g sat. fat), 29 g carb, 1 g fibre, 0 mg chol, 6 mg sodium. % RDI: 2% calcium, 3% iron, 8% vit C.

Five-Spice Poached Pears

Whole spices give the pears a pleasant zing. Bosc pears are best, because they keep their lovely shape. Serve over ice cream or frozen yogurt.

4½- to 6-quart (4.5 to 6 L)
slow cooker

Makes 4 to
6 servings

4	firm ripe pears (2 lb/1 kg)	4	4	each whole cloves, green cardamom pods and black peppercorns	4
2 tbsp	lemon juice	30 mL	2	slices fresh gingerroot	2
1 cup	white wine	250 mL	1	strip lemon rind	1
½ cup	granulated sugar	125 mL	1	whole star anise	1

❧ Peel pears; cut into quarters and core. Place in slow cooker. Sprinkle with lemon juice.

❧ In small saucepan or microwaveable bowl, heat together 1 cup (250 mL) water, wine, sugar, cloves, cardamom, peppercorns, gingerroot, lemon rind and star anise until sugar is dissolved; pour over pears.

❧ Cover and cook on low until pears are tender, about 3 to 4 hours.

❧ Using slotted spoon, transfer pears to serving dish. Discard whole spices and lemon rind. Pour cooking liquid into small saucepan; bring to boil. Boil until reduced to ¾ cup (175 mL), 8 to 10 minutes. Pour over pears. (Make-ahead: Let cool. Cover and refrigerate for up to 4 days.)

PER EACH OF 6 SERVINGS: about 136 cal, 1 g pro, trace total fat (0 g sat. fat), 36 g carb, 4 g fibre, 0 mg chol, 4 mg sodium. % RDI: 1% calcium, 2% iron, 12% vit C, 4% folate.

TEST KITCHEN TIP
If convenient, halfway through cooking, gently move bottom layer of pears to top.

4- to 5-quart (4 to 5 L)
slow cooker

Makes 4 cups (1 L)

Rhubarb Compote

If you're bothered by the stringy look of cooked rhubarb when it's simmered in a saucepan, this is the recipe for you. The slow cooker, no-stirring method keeps rhubarb pieces intact, creating a beautiful compote. Serve on its own or spoon over ice cream, frozen yogurt or angel food cake. For a morning treat, layer in a breakfast parfait with yogurt and granola.

1	cinnamon stick	1	½ cup	white grape or apple juice	125 mL
6 cups	chopped rhubarb (1-inch/2.5 cm pieces)	1.5 L	2	strips orange rind	2
1 cup	granulated sugar	250 mL			

❧ Break cinnamon stick into 2 pieces. Place in slow cooker along with rhubarb, sugar, grape juice and orange rind. Stir gently to coat rhubarb.

❧ Cover and cook on low until tender, about 2 hours.

❧ Remove insert from slow cooker; let cool. Discard cinnamon and orange rind. (Make-ahead: Refrigerate in airtight container for up to 4 days.)

PER ½ CUP (125 mL): about 125 cal, 1 g pro, trace total fat (0 g sat. fat), 31 g carb, 2 g fibre, 0 mg chol, 4 mg sodium. % RDI: 7% calcium, 1% iron, 1% vit A, 12% vit C, 3% folate.

VARIATION

Rhubarb Compote with Strawberries: After cooling, gently stir in 1½ cups (375 mL) sliced strawberries. The compote is equally delicious with the same amount of raspberries, blueberries, cubed fresh pineapple or sliced bananas.

Brandied Fruit Compote

Plump dried fruit in brandy is an elegant topping for ice cream or complement to cake. To start out, choose the moistest dried fruit available.

4- to 5-quart (4 to 5 L)
slow cooker

Makes 8 cups (2 L)

1½ cups	dried Calimyrna figs	375 mL
1½ cups	dried apricots	375 mL
1½ cups	pitted prunes	375 mL
1 cup	dried cherries or cranberries	250 mL
1 cup	dried apples	250 mL
3 cups	apple juice	750 mL
1 cup	boiling water	250 mL

1	strip each lemon and orange rind	1
¼ cup	liquid honey	50 mL
2 tbsp	lemon juice	30 mL
1	cinnamon stick	1
2	slices gingerroot	2
½ cup	brandy	125 mL

❧ Remove tough tips from figs. Place in slow cooker along with apricots, prunes, cherries and apples. Add apple juice, boiling water, lemon and orange rinds, honey, lemon juice, cinnamon and ginger. Stir to combine.

❧ Cover and cook on high, stirring twice, until fruit is tender and plump, about 2 to 3 hours.

❧ Add brandy; remove insert from slow cooker and let cool, covered. (Make-ahead: Refrigerate in airtight container for up to 4 days.)

PER ½ CUP (125 mL): about 187 cal, 2 g pro, 1 g total fat (trace sat. fat), 48 g carb, 5 g fibre, 0 mg chol, 13 mg sodium. % RDI: 5% calcium, 9% iron, 8% vit A, 27% vit C, 1% folate.

TEST KITCHEN TIP
Calimyrna figs are a lovely blond colour. You can use almost-black Mission figs for a darker compote.

Old-Fashioned Berry Cobbler

Because this comfy cobbler uses frozen berries – you can buy a mix or use your own – this dessert is in season any time of the year.

2- to 4½-quart (2 to 4.5 L)
slow cooker

Makes 8 servings

4 cups	frozen mixed berries	1 L		¼ cup	granulated sugar	50 mL
¼ cup	granulated sugar	50 mL		4 tsp	baking powder	20 mL
1 tbsp	all-purpose flour	15 mL		½ tsp	baking soda	2 mL
1 tbsp	lemon juice	15 mL		¼ tsp	salt	1 mL
BISCUIT TOPPING:				⅓ cup	cold butter, cubed	75 mL
1½ cups	all-purpose flour	375 mL		½ cup	buttermilk	125 mL

Butter bottom and side of slow cooker. Add berries, sugar, flour and lemon juice; toss gently to combine.

BISCUIT TOPPING: In large bowl, whisk together flour, sugar, baking powder, baking soda and salt; with pastry blender, cut in butter until crumbly. Add buttermilk all at once; stir with fork to make soft, slightly sticky dough. With floured hands, gather into ball.

On lightly floured surface, knead dough until surface is smooth, about 10 times. Pat into 8-inch (20 cm) circle or oval, depending on shape of insert. Cut into 8 wedges. Arrange in same order over fruit.

Cover and cook on high until biscuits are no longer doughy underneath, about 3 hours. Remove insert from slow cooker; let cool, uncovered, for 1 hour before serving.

PER SERVING: about 253 cal, 4 g pro, 9 g total fat (5 g sat. fat), 42 g carb, 3 g fibre, 22 mg chol, 371 mg sodium. % RDI: 10% calcium, 12% iron, 7% vit A, 15% vit C, 28% folate.

Apricot Almond Bread Pudding

5½- to 6-quart (5.5 to 6 L) slow cooker

Makes 8 servings

Bread puddings started out as a thrifty way to use up stale bread. Nowadays they tend to start with fresh bread, which is sliced and left to dry for 8 hours and get a bit stale. Serve with light cream or gussy it up with Crème Anglaise (recipe, below).

12 cups	cubed stale egg bread (1 loaf)	3 L		1 cup	milk	250 mL
1½ cups	coarsely chopped dried apricots	375 mL		¾ cup	granulated sugar	175 mL
6	eggs	6		1 tsp	vanilla	5 mL
2	cans (each 385 mL) evaporated milk	2		½ cup	sliced almonds, toasted	125 mL

TEST KITCHEN TIP
To keep a custard-based pudding from sticking to the slow cooker, you need to butter the insert generously. You'll need about 2 tbsp (30 mL) butter to do a thorough job.

❧ Generously butter bottom and side of slow cooker; add bread cubes and chopped apricots.

❧ In large bowl, whisk together eggs, evaporated milk, milk, sugar and vanilla; pour over bread mixture. Let stand for 30 minutes; stir gently to redistribute ingredients and ensure that all bread cubes are evenly soaked.

❧ Cover and cook on low until pudding is firm and knife inserted in centre comes out clean, about 3 to 4 hours. Sprinkle with almonds.

PER SERVING: about 565 cal, 20 g pro, 22 g total fat (9 g sat. fat), 75 g carb, 4 g fibre, 208 mg chol, 468 mg sodium. % RDI: 36% calcium, 23% iron, 24% vit A, 15% vit C, 34% folate.

Dress Up Humble Puddings with a Silky Sauce

Whether you call it fancy crème anglaise or plain-old pouring custard, this sauce dresses up bread puddings, like the one above, and poached pears (recipe, page 249). It's a snap to make on the stove top as dessert simmers in the slow cooker. Double for more-generous servings.

❧ In heatproof bowl, whisk 3 egg yolks, ¼ cup (50 mL) granulated sugar and ½ tsp (2 mL) cornstarch until smooth; whisk in 1¼ cups (300 mL) 10% or 18% cream. Set over saucepan of simmering water; cook, stirring, until thick enough to coat back of spoon, about 6 minutes.

❧ Remove from heat; stir in 1 tsp (5 mL) vanilla. Strain into pitcher. *(Make-ahead: Place plastic wrap directly on surface and refrigerate for up to 2 days. Serve cold or reheat in heatproof bowl over saucepan of simmering water.)* **Makes about 1½ cups (375 mL).**

Velvety Rice Pudding

Arborio rice, an Italian short-grain rice, gives this pudding a particularly creamy, flowing texture. For a touch of spice, grate a bit of cinnamon stick over top.

5 cups	homogenized milk	1.25 L	2 tsp	grated lemon rind	10 mL
1 cup	arborio rice	250 mL	1 tsp	vanilla	5 mL
⅔ cup	granulated sugar	150 mL	Pinch	each cinnamon and salt	Pinch

❧ In slow cooker, combine milk, rice, sugar, lemon rind, vanilla, cinnamon and salt.

❧ Cover and cook on low, stirring several times, until rice is tender and pudding is creamy, about 4 to 4½ hours.

❧ Remove insert from slow cooker; let cool, stirring often, for 20 minutes. Serve warm or refrigerate until cold. (Make-ahead: Let cool. Refrigerate in airtight container for up to 3 days. Add a little more milk, if necessary, to thin pudding.)

PER EACH OF 6 SERVINGS: about 331 cal, 9 g pro, 7 g total fat (4 g sat. fat), 58 g carb, trace fibre, 28 mg chol, 100 mg sodium. % RDI: 22% calcium, 2% iron, 5% vit A, 3% vit C, 5% folate.

4- to 4½-quart (4 to 4.5 L) slow cooker

Makes 4 to 6 servings

TEST KITCHEN TIP
While cinnamon is a nice touch, rice pudding welcomes a fresh fruit topping. Try blueberries, raspberries, blackberries or sliced strawberries. Skinned orange sections or pineapple chunks are equally delicious. You can go all Canadian with a modest pour of medium maple syrup over the top.

Blueberry Pudding Cake

When pudding cakes have just finished cooking, the hot juices appear thin, even a little runny. However, they thicken as the pudding cools. That's why we recommend letting any pudding cake (there are a bunch of superb ones in this chapter) sit for several minutes or for up to 1 hour before serving.

4- to 4½-quart (4 to 4.5 L) slow cooker

Makes 6 to 8 servings

4 cups	frozen wild blueberries	1 L		2	eggs	2
¾ cup	granulated sugar	175 mL		1 tsp	grated lemon rind	5 mL
4 tsp	cornstarch	20 mL		½ tsp	vanilla	2 mL
¼ cup	lemon juice	50 mL		1¼ cups	all-purpose flour	300 mL
CAKE TOPPING:				1½ tsp	baking powder	7 mL
½ cup	butter, softened	125 mL		Pinch	salt	Pinch
¾ cup	granulated sugar	175 mL		½ cup	milk	125 mL

❧ Butter bottom and side of slow cooker. Add blueberries, ½ cup (125 mL) of the sugar and cornstarch; toss to combine.

❧ **CAKE TOPPING:** In large bowl, beat butter with sugar until light. Beat in eggs, 1 at a time, beating well after each. Beat in lemon rind and vanilla.

❧ In separate bowl, whisk together flour, baking powder and salt. Add to butter mixture alternately with milk, making 3 additions of dry ingredients and 2 of milk. Scrape batter evenly over blueberries; smooth top.

❧ In small saucepan, bring ¾ cup (175 mL) water, lemon juice and remaining sugar to boil, stirring until sugar is dissolved. Pour over batter; do not stir.

❧ Cover and cook on high until cake tester inserted in centre comes out clean, about 3 hours. Remove insert from slow cooker; let cool, uncovered, for 1 hour before serving.

PER EACH OF 8 SERVINGS: about 392 cal, 5 g pro, 14 g total fat (8 g sat. fat), 65 g carb, 3 g fibre, 78 mg chol, 162 mg sodium. % RDI: 6% calcium, 9% iron, 13% vit A, 8% vit C, 23% folate.

Apple Spice Pudding Cake

What makes pudding cakes so lovable is their two layers: the bottom that's all fruit and butterscotchy juices, and the cakey top. Try this comfy dessert for a fall or winter brunch, using Northern Spy, Golden Delicious, Ambrosia or Idared apples.

4- to 4½-quart (4 to 4.5 L) slow cooker

Makes 8 servings

7 cups	thickly sliced peeled apples (2 lb/1 kg, about 7)	1.75 L
2 tbsp	lemon juice	30 mL
½ cup	packed brown sugar	125 mL
CAKE TOPPING:		
½ cup	butter, softened	125 mL
1¼ cups	packed brown sugar	300 mL
1	egg	1
1 tsp	vanilla	5 mL

1⅓ cups	all-purpose flour	325 mL
1½ tsp	baking powder	7 mL
1 tsp	cinnamon	5 mL
½ tsp	grated nutmeg	2 mL
¼ tsp	each salt and ground cloves	1 mL
¾ cup	milk	175 mL
1¼ cups	apple cider or juice	300 mL
4 tsp	cornstarch	20 mL

TEST KITCHEN TIP
When pouring hot liquid over top of pudding cake batter, hold a large spoon, bowl side down, over centre of batter. Let liquid flow over back of spoon. This disperses it evenly and prevents it from pitting the surface of the cake.

❧ Butter bottom and side of slow cooker; add apples. Sprinkle with lemon juice. Top with brown sugar; toss to coat apples. Gently press apples to level; set aside.

❧ CAKE TOPPING: In large bowl, beat butter with sugar until fluffy. Beat in egg and vanilla.

❧ In separate bowl, whisk together flour, baking powder, cinnamon, nutmeg, salt and cloves. Stir into butter mixture alternately with milk, making 3 additions of dry ingredients and 2 of milk. Scrape batter evenly over apples; smooth top.

❧ In small saucepan or large glass measuring cup, whisk cider with cornstarch; bring to boil on stove top or in microwave, whisking gently, to make slightly thickened sauce. Pour over batter; do not stir.

❧ Cover and cook on high until sauce is bubbling, apples are tender and cake tester inserted in centre comes out clean, about 2 to 3 hours.

❧ Remove insert from slow cooker; let cool for 20 minutes before serving.

PER SERVING: about 454 cal, 4 g pro, 13 g total fat (8 g sat. fat), 84 g carb, 2 g fibre, 56 mg chol, 249 mg sodium. % RDI: 10% calcium, 17% iron, 12% vit A, 7% vit C, 22% folate.

Date Pudding with Toffee Sauce

A little goes a long way when it comes to this heavenly moist cake sweetly sauced with a kick of rum. Homey looking, it's the antithesis of party fare, but try it on a buffet. No one will miss the fancy tarts, gâteaux or exotic crème brûlées.

4- to 4½-quart (4 to 4.5 L)
slow cooker

Makes 12 servings

2½ cups	chopped pitted dates	625 mL
1 tbsp	coarsely shredded orange rind	15 mL
1½ tsp	baking soda	7 mL
¾ cup	butter, softened	175 mL
¾ cup	packed brown sugar	175 mL
3	eggs	3
2 tsp	vanilla	10 mL
2½ cups	all-purpose flour	625 mL

2 tsp	baking powder	10 mL
½ tsp	salt	2 mL
TOFFEE SAUCE:		
¾ cup	butter	175 mL
1¼ cups	packed brown sugar	300 mL
1 cup	whipping cream	250 mL
¼ cup	dark rum or brandy (optional)	50 mL
2 tsp	vanilla	10 mL

❧ Butter bottom and side of slow cooker; set aside. In saucepan, bring dates, 1½ cups (375 mL) water and orange rind to boil; reduce heat and simmer until thick, no longer watery and dates are almost smooth, about 3 minutes. Stir in baking soda; let cool to room temperature.

❧ In large bowl, beat butter with sugar until fluffy. Beat in eggs, 1 at a time, beating well after each. Beat in vanilla.

❧ In separate bowl, whisk together flour, baking powder and salt. Sprinkle half over butter mixture; stir in gently. Stir in date mixture, then remaining dry ingredients. Scrape into slow cooker; smooth top.

❧ Cover and cook on low until top is firm to the touch and cake tester inserted in centre comes out clean, about 2 to 2½ hours.

❧ **TOFFEE SAUCE:** Meanwhile, in saucepan, melt butter over medium heat; add brown sugar, stirring until dissolved. Add cream; bring to simmer. Simmer, stirring occasionally, until thickened slightly, about 5 minutes. Stir in rum (if using) and vanilla. Keep warm.

❧ With skewer, poke about 25 holes over surface of pudding. Drizzle about ½ cup (125 mL) sauce over top to glaze pudding. Serve with remaining sauce.

PER SERVING: about 624 cal, 6 g pro, 32 g total fat (19 g sat. fat), 84 g carb, 4 g fibre, 133 mg chol, 506 mg sodium. % RDI: 9% calcium, 18% iron, 28% vit A, 2% vit C, 29% folate.

Chocolate Peanut Butter Pudding Cake

4- to 4½-quart (4 to 4.5 L) slow cooker

Makes 4 to 6 servings

This decadent dessert is utterly easy to make and utterly captivating. You can replace the peanut butter with other nut butters if you prefer.

¾ cup	all-purpose flour	175 mL		⅓ cup	milk	75 mL
⅓ cup	granulated sugar	75 mL		¾ cup	packed brown sugar	175 mL
1 tsp	baking powder	5 mL		¼ cup	cocoa powder	50 mL
1	egg	1		1 cup	boiling water	250 mL
3 tbsp	natural peanut butter	45 mL				

~ Butter bottom and side of slow cooker; set aside.

~ In large bowl, whisk flour, granulated sugar and baking powder. In separate bowl, whisk egg; whisk in peanut butter and milk until smooth. Scrape over flour mixture; stir to combine. Scrape into slow cooker; smooth top.

~ In heatproof bowl, whisk brown sugar with cocoa powder; whisk in boiling water until smooth. Pour over batter; do not stir.

~ Cover and cook on high until firm to the touch, about 2 hours. Remove insert from slow cooker; let cool for 10 minutes before serving.

PER EACH OF 6 SERVINGS: about 281 cal, 6 g pro, 6 g total fat (1 g sat. fat), 54 g carb, 2 g fibre, 32 mg chol, 81 mg sodium. % RDI: 7% calcium, 16% iron, 2% vit A, 17% folate.

The Perfect Measure

GRANULATED SUGAR AND ALL-PURPOSE, WHOLE WHEAT OR WHOLE GRAIN FLOURS
> Use dry measuring cups. They come in nesting metal or plastic sets.
> Spoon ingredient into measuring cup, filling to heaping. With flat back of knife, sweep excess back into canister or bag.
> For cake-and-pastry flour, sift flour before measuring as above.

> Use dry measuring cups for yogurt, sour cream, cottage cheese, jam and peanut butter, too.

LIQUID INGREDIENTS
> Use liquid measuring cups. They are usually glass with a convenient spout.
> Verify amounts by placing cup on counter and checking at eye level.

Devil's Food Pudding Cake

4- to 4½-quart (4 to 4.5 L)
slow cooker

Makes 8 servings

This dessert is fun to serve at family occasions, and it's equally pleasing to guests who think of themselves as sophisticated foodies. Do nestle a scoop of really good ice cream alongside each serving. Dulce de leche is a trendy change of pace, but good old vanilla is a faultless choice.

1¾ cups	packed brown sugar	425 mL	1	egg	1
1 cup	all-purpose flour	250 mL	⅔ cup	milk	150 mL
½ cup	cocoa powder	125 mL	¼ cup	butter, melted	50 mL
2 tsp	baking powder	10 mL	2 tsp	vanilla	10 mL
¼ tsp	salt	1 mL	2 tsp	cornstarch	10 mL

꙰ Butter bottom and side of slow cooker; set aside.

꙰ Into sieve placed over large mixing bowl, measure 1 cup (250 mL) of the brown sugar, flour, ¼ cup (50 mL) of the cocoa powder, baking powder and salt. With spatula, press ingredients through sieve into bowl. Whisk together if not completely blended.

꙰ In separate bowl, whisk together egg, milk, butter and vanilla. Pour over flour mixture; stir just until blended.

꙰ Scrape into slow cooker; smooth top.

꙰ In saucepan, whisk together 2 cups (500 mL) water, remaining brown sugar and cocoa, and cornstarch; bring to boil. Boil, stirring often, until slightly thickened, about 3 minutes. Pour over batter; do not stir.

꙰ Cover and cook on high until cake tester inserted in centre comes out clean and sauce is bubbling around edges, about 2 hours. Remove insert from slow cooker; let stand until sauce shrinks down and thickens slightly, about 30 minutes.

PER SERVING: about 325 cal, 4 g pro, 8 g total fat (5 g sat. fat), 64 g carb, 2 g fibre, 40 mg chol, 226 mg sodium. % RDI: 10% calcium, 19% iron, 7% vit A, 17% folate.

VARIATION

Mocha Pudding Cake: Replace water with coffee, either freshly brewed or made with instant espresso granules.

Chocolate Fondue

Fondue is the perfect interactive dessert to serve on a buffet or bring to the table for a cosy get-together. It's a delight with dippers like strawberries, or chunks of pineapple, kiwifruit, pear, apple or banana. Or spear up cubes of dense cake, such as banana loaf or pound cake, or mini cookies, such as soft macaroons or amaretti.

1½- to 2-quart (1.5 to 2 L) slow cooker

Makes 2½ cups (625 mL), or 12 servings

1 cup	whipping cream	250 mL		6 oz	milk chocolate, finely chopped	175 g
9 oz	bittersweet chocolate, finely chopped	275 g		2 tbsp	brandy, rum or liqueur such as amaretto	30 mL

❧ Combine whipping cream, bittersweet chocolate and milk chocolate in slow cooker.

❧ Cover and cook on low, whisking several times, until chocolate is melted and smooth, about 1 to 1½ hours. Stir in brandy.

❧ Reduce heat to warm; use up within 1 hour.

PER SERVING: about 259 cal, 3 g pro, 19 g total fat (12 g sat. fat), 20 g carb, 3 g fibre, 29 mg chol, 19 mg sodium. % RDI: 5% calcium, 8% iron, 7% vit A, 1% folate.

VARIATION

Milk Chocolate Nougat Fondue: Reduce bittersweet chocolate to 3 oz (90 g). Omit milk chocolate. Add 12 oz (375 g) milk chocolate nougat bar (such as Toblerone), finely chopped.

TEST KITCHEN TIP
Speed up the preparation by bringing the cream to a boil and pouring it over the chocolate in the slow cooker. Turn slow cooker to low and whisk until chocolate is melted. Keep warm for up to 1 hour.

Successful Substitutions

Nowhere are substitutions easier than in savoury slow-braised dishes. However, avoid using an alternative for a major ingredient.

Instead of	*Use*
Leeks or shallots	Regular onions
Pearl onions	Small regular onion, cut in 4 to 6 wedges, keeping root end intact to keep layers together
Chives	Green part of green onions
Sweet red, yellow or orange pepper	These colours are interchangeable as far as flavour is concerned. Save sweet green peppers for last-minute additions or garnishes. Try Cubanelle, shepherd or mild banana peppers for variety and enhanced flavour.
Frozen corn kernels	Canned corn kernels or fresh corn (increase cooking time by 10 minutes)
Fresh peas	Frozen peas
Beans, chickpeas, lentils	Almost all beans and chickpeas (dried and canned) are interchangeable. Ditto for brown and green lentils.
Pearl barley	Pot barley
Fresh herbs	Dried herbs (use one-third the amount)
Chicken or fish broth	Vegetable broth (sodium-reduced or homemade; see recipe, page 71)
Homemade chicken or beef broth	Ready-to-use, condensed, powdered or cubed commercial broth; sodium-reduced if possible. If using salty powders or cubes, reduce the salt in the recipe and season the dish to taste just before serving.
Cornstarch	Double the amount of all-purpose flour
Wine vinegar (red or white)	Apple cider vinegar or lemon juice (wine vinegars are usually interchangeable)
Wine	• *Up to ½ cup (125 mL) wine:* broth • *More than ½ cup (125 mL) wine:* pour 1 tbsp (15 mL) wine vinegar into liquid measuring cup; fill up with broth. Reduce the salt in the recipe and season the dish to taste just before serving.
Regular soy sauce	Sodium-reduced soy sauce
Beef or pork shoulder, boneless	Same weight of bone-in beef or pork shoulder or other shoulder cuts
Short pasta, long pasta	All short pastas are interchangeable in a pinch, as are long pastas with one another. Thicker, larger versions will require slightly longer cooking.
½ cup (125 mL) tomato sauce	¼ cup (50 mL) each tomato paste and water
1 cup (250 mL) granulated sugar	1 cup (250 mL) packed brown sugar (dark and light brown are interchangeable; the dark has a more pronounced molasses flavour)
1 tsp (5 mL) dry mustard	1 tbsp (15 mL) Dijon mustard

About Our Nutrition Information

To meet nutrient needs each day, moderately active women 25 to 49 need about 1,900 calories, 51 g protein, 261 g carbohydrate, 25 to 35 g fibre and not more than 63 g total fat (21 g saturated fat). Men and teenagers usually need more. Canadian sodium intake of approximately 3,500 to 4,500 mg daily should be reduced. Percentage of recommended daily intake (% RDI) is based on the highest recommended intakes (excluding those for pregnant and lactating women) for calcium, iron, vitamins A and C, and folate.

Figures are rounded off. They are based on the first ingredient listed when there is a choice and do not include optional ingredients or those with no specified amounts.

Abbreviations: cal = calories; **pro** = protein; **carb** = carbohydrate; **sat. fat** = saturated fat; **chol** = cholesterol

There's nothing slow about the folks who put together *The Canadian Living Slow Cooker Collection*. When it comes to acknowledging the people who contributed to this book, I have to go back to the cooks first – the members of The Canadian Living Test Kitchen. Food director Gabrielle Bright, food specialist Rheanna Kish and former food specialist Heather Howe developed many of the slow cooker recipes in this book, assisted by contributing editor Andrew Chase, special projects editor Alison Kent, and food specialists Adell Shneer, Soo Kim and Matthew Kimura. Sincere thanks also to senior editor Beverley Renahan, who gets first crack at editing the recipes, then sees them through to completion.

Since you eat with your eyes first, good recipes go hand-in-hand with inspiring photos. Many thanks to all the excellent photographers, food stylists and props stylists who made the images in this book positively lickable. You'll find all their names on page 272. Jodi Pudge, Claire Stubbs and Lynda Felton get special thanks for the beautiful new photos they shot specifically for this collection.

Next, to the backbone of this book, project editor Tina Anson Mine and designer Michael Erb. The creative director of *Canadian Living* Magazine, Michael gave it its enticing look and feel, while never forgetting that a cookbook is a tool that must be easy to open, read and use. Tina, the magazine's managing editor, has an incredible attention to detail; her mantra is "Let me check that one more time." Thanks to both, and to production coordinator Erin Poetschke and copy editor Miriam Osborne, who made sure both words and pictures were flawless.

Behind-the-scenes but very important to remember are Sharyn and Marc Joliat at InfoAccess for impeccable nutritional analysis, and Gillian Watts for creating an index that lets you find any recipe in a rush. Our ever-helpful administrative team of Teresa Sousa, Olga Goncalves Costa and Patrick Flynn lightened our load at every step. For testing recipes and photography, the slow cookers from the following companies were invaluable: All-Clad, Rival, Hamilton Beach, Cuisinart, KitchenAid and Breville.

Another hearty thanks goes to group publisher Lynn Chambers, who sets our cookbooks in motion. *Merci beaucoup* to Transcontinental Books publisher Jean Paré and coordinator Ann Nickner for their help at all stages of production. And, of course, to *Canadian Living* editor-in-chief Susan Antonacci, who is a big fan of slow cooking (her meatballs are legendary), sharing her table with friends and family, and supporting the publication of this book in a year when Canadians are, more than ever, looking for better and easier ways to feed their families wholesome homemade food.

Once the book leaves the printer, it heads to the distribution pros at Random House Canada – Frances Bedford, Janet Joy Wilson, Marlene Fraser and Duncan Shields – who make sure it gets to a bookstore near you. Our in-house promotions team of Avra Goldenblatt and Janis Davidson Pressick, and publicists such as Diane Hargrave, then help build awareness and get this book into the homes of Canadians.

We've never mentioned book sellers before, but we appreciate them all – from Costco to Chapters to the independents. Barbara-Jo McIntosh at Barbara-Jo's Books to Cooks in Vancouver and both Alison Fryer and Jennifer Grange at The Cookbook Store in Toronto have consistently welcomed me into their stores to meet-and-greet customers, sign books and sometimes do a spot of cooking, too!

Never has there been a greater need for Canadians to cook – and cook well – and to sit around the table together. To all of you, we who made this book dedicate our work.

Elizabeth Baird

Credits

RECIPES
All recipes were developed by
**The Canadian Living Test
Kitchen,** except the following.
Andrew Chase: page 211.
Heather Howe: page 154.
Tina Anson Mine: page 155.
Adell Shneer: page 33.

PHOTOGRAPHY
Michael Alberstat: pages 124
and 157.
Luis Albuquerque: page 25.
Yvonne Duivenvoorden: pages
28, 35, 53, 56, 64, 80, 87, 97, 105,
116, 121, 132, 139, 144, 162, 170,
178, 195, 198 and 221.
Kevin Hewitt: pages 38, 190, 205
and 232.

Edward Pond: pages 48, 69, 75,
92, 129, 149 and 229.
Jodi Pudge: pages 11, 17, 20, 61,
100, 113, 152, 167, 175, 208, 215,
224, 237, 247, 252, 257 and 260.
David Scott: pages 42, 108, 187
and 240.

FOOD STYLING
Julie Aldis: pages 64, 124 and 157.
Donna Bartolini: page 170.
Carol Dudar: page 25.
Lucie Richard: pages 28, 56, 75,
87, 105, 108, 116, 121, 187, 198,
221 and 240.
Claire Stancer: pages 35, 38, 53,
97, 132, 144, 162, 178 and 195.
Claire Stubbs: pages 17, 20, 42,
48, 69, 80, 92, 129, 139, 149, 152,

167, 175, 190, 205, 208, 215, 224,
229, 232, 237, 247, 252 and 257.
Nicole Young: pages 61, 100, 113
and 260.

PROPS STYLING
Catherine Doherty: pages 56
and 195.
Lynda Felton: pages 17, 20, 152,
167, 175, 208, 215, 224, 237, 247,
252 and 257.
Marc-Philippe Gagné: page 28.
Maggi Jones: page 25.
Oksana Slavutych: pages 35, 38,
42, 48, 53, 61, 64, 69, 75, 80, 87,
92, 97, 100, 105, 108, 113, 116,
121, 124, 129, 132, 139, 144, 149,
157, 162, 170, 178, 187, 190, 198,
205, 221, 229, 232, 240 and 260.